S0-AUI-345

ARCO

MASTER THE CORRECTIONS OFFICER EXAM

15th Edition

Gary D. Maynard, M.S.

THOMSON

PETERSON'S

Australia • Canada • Mexico • Singapore • Spain • United Kingdom • United States

An ARCO Book

ARCO is a registered trademark of Thomson Learning, Inc., and is used herein under license by Thomson Peterson's.

About Thomson Peterson's

Thomson Peterson's (www.petersons.com) is a leading provider of education information and advice, with books and online resources focusing on education search, test preparation, and financial aid. Its Web site offers searchable databases and interactive tools for contacting educational institutions, online practice tests and instruction, and planning tools for securing financial aid. Thomson Peterson's serves 110 million education consumers annually.

For more information, contact Thomson Peterson's, 2000 Lenox Drive, Lawrenceville, NJ 08648; 800-338-3282; or find us on the World Wide Web at www.petersons.com/about.

Editor: Joe Krasowski; Production Editor: Bernadette Webster; Manufacturing Manager: Ray Golaszewski; Composition Manager: Linda M. Williams

ISBN 0-7689-2259-3

Printed in the United States of America

10 9 8 7 6 5 4 3 2 1   08 07 06

Fifteenth Edition

Contents

Before You Begin

HOW THIS BOOK IS ORGANIZED

You want to pass this test. That's why you bought this book. Used correctly, this self-tutor will show you what to expect and will give the most effective review of the subjects you can expect to see on the actual exam. *ARCO Master the Corrections Officer Exam* will provide you with the necessary tools to make the most of the study time you have, including:

- **Top 10 Ways to Raise Your Score** gives you a preview of some of the test-taking strategies you'll learn in the book.

- **Part I** provides career information about Corrections Officers, along with information about the application and examination processes.

- **Part II** includes six full-length practice tests followed by detailed answer explanations.

- The **Appendixes** provide information about the training subjects that are necessary before a Corrections Officer begins to work in any facility, as well as a sample Physical Fitness Course.

SPECIAL STUDY FEATURES

ARCO Master the Corrections Officer Exam is designed to be as user-friendly as it is complete. To this end, it includes several features to make your preparation much more efficient.

Overview

Each chapter begins with a bulleted overview listing the topics to be covered in the chapter. This will allow you to quickly target the areas in which you are most interested.

Summing It Up

Each chapter ends with a point-by-point summary that captures the most important points contained in the chapter. They are a convenient way to review key points.

1

As you work your way through the book, keep your eye on the margins to find bonus information and advice. Information can be found in the following forms:

NOTE

Notes highlight critical information about a career as a Corrections Officer and the written exam.

TIP

Tips provide valuable advice for effectively handling the job-search process.

ALERT!

Alerts do just what they say—alert you to common pitfalls or misconceptions.

YOU'RE WELL ON YOUR WAY TO SUCCESS

You have made the decision to pursue a career as a Corrections Officer. *ARCO Master the Corrections Officer Exam* will prepare you for the steps you'll need to take to achieve your goal—from understanding the nuances of the job to scoring high on the exam. Good luck!

Top 10 Ways to Raise Your Score

1. **Get to the test center early.** Make sure you give yourself plenty of extra time to get there, park your car, if necessary, and even grab a cup of coffee before the test.

2. **Listen to the test monitors and follow their instructions carefully.**

3. **Read every word of the instructions. Read every word of every question.**

4. **Mark your answers by completely darkening the answer space of your choice.**

5. **Mark only ONE answer for each question, even if you think that more than one answer is correct.** You must choose only one. If you mark more than one answer, the scoring machine will record your answer as wrong.

6. **If you change your mind, erase completely.** Leave no doubt as to which answer you mean.

7. **Check often to be sure that the question number matches the answer space—that you have not skipped a space by mistake.**

8. **Stay alert.** Be careful not to mark a wrong answer just because you were not concentrating.

9. **Do not panic.** If you cannot finish any part before time is up, do not worry. If you are accurate, you can do well even without finishing. It is even possible to earn a scaled score of 100 without entirely finishing an exam part if you are very accurate. At any rate, do not let your performance on any one part affect your performance on any other part.

10. **Check and recheck, time permitting.** If you finish any part before time is up, use the remaining time to check that each question is answered in the right space and that there is only one answer for each question. Return to the difficult questions and rethink them.

PART I

ALL ABOUT A CAREER AS A CORRECTIONS OFFICER

Getting Started

chapter 1

OVERVIEW

- **Working conditions**
- **Salary**
- **Training and promotion**
- **Summing it up**

Corrections Officers are responsible for overseeing individuals who have been arrested and are awaiting trial or who have been convicted of a crime and sentenced to serve time in a jail, reformatory, or penitentiary. They maintain security and inmate accountability to prevent disturbances, assaults, or escapes. Officers have no law enforcement responsibilities outside the institution where they work.

Police and sheriffs' departments in county and municipal jails or precinct station houses employ many Corrections Officers, also known as *detention officers*. Most of the approximately 3,300 jails in the United States are operated by county governments, with about three-quarters of all jails under the jurisdiction of an elected sheriff. Individuals in the jail population change constantly as some are released, some are convicted and transferred to prison, and new offenders are arrested and enter the system. Corrections Officers in the U.S. jail system admit and process more than 11 million people a year, with about half a million offenders in jail at any given time. When individuals are first arrested, the jail staff may not know their true identity or criminal record, and violent detainees may be placed in the general population. This is the most dangerous phase of the incarceration process for Corrections Officers.

Most Corrections Officers are employed in large jails or state and federal prisons, watching over the approximately one million offenders who are incarcerated at any given time. In addition to jails and prisons, a relatively small number of Corrections Officers oversee individuals being held by the U.S. Immigration and Naturalization Service before they are released or deported, or they work for correctional institutions that are run by private for-profit organizations. While both jails and prisons can be dangerous places to work, prison populations are more stable than jail populations, and Corrections Officers in prisons know the security and custodial requirements of the prisoners with whom they are dealing.

Regardless of the setting, Corrections Officers maintain order within the institution, and enforce rules and regulations. To help ensure that inmates are orderly and obey rules, Corrections Officers monitor the activities and supervise the work assignments of inmates. Sometimes, it is necessary for officers to search inmates and their living quarters for contraband like weapons or drugs, settle disputes between inmates, and enforce discipline. Corrections Officers periodically inspect the facilities, checking cells and other areas of the institution for unsanitary conditions, contraband, fire hazards, and any evidence of infractions of rules. In addition, they routinely inspect locks, window bars, grilles, doors, and gates for signs of tampering. Finally, officers inspect mail and visitors for prohibited items.

Corrections Officers report orally and in writing on inmate conduct and on the quality and quantity of work done by inmates. Officers also report security breaches, disturbances, violations of rules, and any unusual occurrences. They usually keep a daily log or record of their activities. Corrections Officers cannot show favoritism and must report any inmate who violates the rules. Should the situation arise, they help the responsible law enforcement authorities investigate crimes committed within their institution or search for escaped inmates.

In jail and prison facilities with direct supervision cell blocks, officers work unarmed. They are equipped with communications devices so that they can summon help if necessary. These officers often work in a cell block alone, or with another officer, among the fifty to one hundred inmates who reside there. The officers enforce regulations primarily through their interpersonal communications skills and the use of progressive sanctions, such as loss of some privileges.

In the highest security facilities where the most dangerous inmates are housed, Corrections Officers often monitor the activities of prisoners from a centralized control center with the aid of closed-circuit television cameras and a computer tracking system. In such an environment, the inmates may not see anyone but officers for days or weeks at a time and only leave their cells for showers, solitary exercise time, or visitors. Depending on the offender's security classification within the institution, Corrections Officers may have to restrain inmates in handcuffs and leg irons to safely escort them to and from cells and other areas to see authorized visitors. Officers also escort prisoners between the institution and courtrooms, medical facilities, and other destinations outside the institution.

WORKING CONDITIONS

Prisons and jails operate seven days a week, 24 hours a day, 365 days per year. Since they operate around the clock, it is necessary that the staff work all hours. The senior personnel who have worked the longest at the facility will probably work the day shift, Monday through Friday.

Corrections Officers who are new to the prison or jail can expect to work the evening or midnight shift, as well as weekends and holidays for the first year. Even though there is not as much activity in the evenings and on weekends, there are still meals to serve, work for inmates to do, recreational activities, and visits. Most visits take place on the weekends, and they are generally supervised by Corrections Officers.

Uniforms and Equipment

When you begin your training you will probably receive a uniform to wear during the training or cadet period. This uniform may be similar to the Corrections Officer's uniform worn in the prison or jail, or it may be different and used only during the training period. It will be issued to you and you will not have to pay for it.

When you graduate from the Corrections Officer training academy or class, you will be issued new Corrections Officer uniforms. You will probably receive a minimum of three sets so you can rotate them in laundering and always have a clean uniform for duty.

Most prisons and jails will issue a hat or cap to wear during work. Most use a baseball-type hat with a cloth badge or logo sewn on front. Sometimes the hat is optional, depending on whether you are working indoors or outside.

You will probably be responsible for purchasing your own shoes or boots to wear at work. Most prisons and jails require black shoes or boots and will expect you to keep them clean, polished, and in good condition. You should find out what kind of shoes are authorized, and what the prison or jail recommends to buy. Because you will spend a lot of time on your feet, it's important to buy a comfortable, well-fitting shoe for work. You'll be glad you did.

Since you will be working in all weather conditions, the prison or jail where you work may issue cold-weather clothing and rain gear for inclement weather. You'll be responsible for taking care of the rain gear while you are using it, and turning it in clean and in serviceable condition.

There are no rifles, pistols, or shotguns routinely carried inside prisons or jails due to the danger of inmates getting the weapons and using them against the staff. Therefore, if you are working inside an institution, you will not be issued a weapon unless you are working in a tower or protected area. However, you will probably be issued a set of handcuffs, since you will use them for transporting or moving inmates from one jail or prison to another, or between units at the prison. It is advisable to check out handcuffs daily and return them each day at

NOTE

Most Corrections Officers will work 160 hours during a four-week period. Any time worked over the 160 hours will be overtime in most systems, and most systems pay time-and-a-half for overtime. Although most prisons and jails try to avoid overtime due to the expense, In emergencies and heavy workload periods, overtime is available.

TIP

You should make a habit of carrying a small notebook and pen or pencil with you at all times. This will be helpful for taking notes during shift briefings, as well as recording activities or incidents that may occur with the inmate population each day.

the end of the shift. Even though there will be days you won't use the handcuffs, you will have them, if necessary.

Some prisons and jails issue some form of spray or gas canisters that clip on your belt to be used to subdue an inmate who is out of control. Not all prisons and jails issue the gas canisters to the Corrections Officers. If you are issued spray or gas to use as necessary, you will be required to have training on its use and effects.

Security

As a Corrections Officer, your role will be centered around security. There are many aspects of security, including inspections; making counts; taking disciplinary action; and supervising inmates in work, school, or recreation programs. You will also be responsible for ensuring the safety of other staff, as well as the inmates.

Security is the most important part of working in a prison or jail. In the past, the Corrections Officer's job was to provide counseling and rehabilitation programs for inmates. But today, public safety and security is the primary role of the Corrections Officer.

Prisons and jails are critically judged by the number of escapes that occur. When an inmate escapes from a prison or jail, the public is alarmed and demands better security. There typically is no excuse that can be given that will make the public feel any better or any safer. The prison or jail needs to protect the public first. Therefore, the first priority is to prevent escapes.

ALERT!

You must protect the public first, but you must also protect each other. The inmates will, from time to time, take out their frustration on the correctional staff. The prevention of assaults on staff is crucial. All officers must work together, follow the institutional policy, and control inmate behavior.

The third aspect of security is to protect the inmates. They must be protected from each other as well as themselves. Inmates are sometimes self-destructive and will injure themselves, or do things that will cause them to be hurt by other inmates. You will be able to help the inmates learn better behaviors by your good example. Possibly even more important than the physical protection you will provide is the counseling and understanding you will give that may teach them new skills, improve their self-esteem, and help prevent them from returning to prison. It is up to Corrections Officers to protect themselves, and their fellow officers, while at the same time protecting the inmates and looking out for their safety and well-being.

MINIMUM SECURITY

Three security levels are normally used in prisons. In most systems, minimum security means that the prisons are not fenced, and inmates can travel outside the boundaries of the prison for work or activities when escorted by a Corrections Officer. Since the inmates are better behaved at minimum security prisons, there is less time spent by staff in security procedures. There are fewer counts, and inmates attend meals and assignments without an Officer's escort. Inmates generally sign out of their dorm, and sign in at their job assignment or program. The housing units are usually open dormitories where each room may hold twenty or more inmates. Inmates usually have a locker with a key that they can use to secure their valuables. Corrections Officers will also have a key to each inmate's locker so that it may be inspected at any time.

MEDIUM SECURITY

Medium security prisons usually have a double chain-link fence and armed perimeter security. Most have one or more towers that are manned by a Corrections Officer armed with a rifle and a shotgun. Inmates in medium security are a risk to the public, and are considered to be escape risks. They are escorted from their housing units to their assignments daily.

MAXIMUM SECURITY

The most dangerous inmates are kept in maximum security. In states that have capital punishment, death-row inmates would be housed at the maximum security institution. High-escape-risk inmates, who pose a serious threat to public safety, would be in maximum security. The working conditions are probably the most difficult at this security level, but some Corrections Officers find maximum security to be the most challenging and the most rewarding.

Some inmates are housed in protective custody. Due to the nature of their crime, or because of bad relationships with other inmates, they are in fear for their lives. It may be because of gambling debts, or a word that was given and broken. Inmates who have informed on other inmates sometimes find it necessary to seek protection in order to survive. As a Corrections Officer, you may be assigned to this security level.

Death Row

Most state correctional systems have inmates who are sentenced to death. These inmates are housed on death row, usually at the state's maximum security penitentiary. Jails do not have death row, even though they may temporarily hold inmates sentenced to death. As a Corrections Officer in a prison, you may be assigned to work this high-security job. You would probably not be assigned to work on death row until you had considerable experience. The requirements of the job on death row are similar to those for other assignments, but the consequences of making an error in judgment are far greater. These inmates have little to lose, and as a result are more manipulative and desperate.

Inmates on death row will have to be fed, normally in their cells; will have visits in the secure visiting area; and must be exercised under strict supervision at least one hour a day, five days per week. They are normally escorted in handcuffs or restraints to each activity or program. They will have access to the Law Library, and will either be escorted to the library or check out books that will be brought to their cells. The U.S. Constitution requires that they have exercise, access to the courts, attorney visits, and a nutritious and balanced diet. They receive these constitutional guarantees just like other inmates; however, the security and conditions will be much more strict.

TIP

Most prison systems put a premium on work experience in maximum security, and therefore Corrections Officers who get their experience in the highest security level will find it a great benefit in future promotion opportunities.

Corrections Officers assigned to death row must be willing to work in an environment that is more regimented and controlled than the other assignments in the prisons. Some Corrections Officers find this environment to be stressful and personally undesirable. Other Corrections Officers prefer the controlled and regimented job, and as a result, make special requests to work on death row. It depends on the individual Officer and the experience and temperament of that particular person.

Many Corrections Officers who work many years in prisons have no desire to work on death row. Again, other officers realize that it is part of their job, and deal with the relationship and eventual execution without a great deal of stress. As a Corrections Officer, you must consider the possibility of working on death row and decide in your own mind if you would be comfortable working there.

Inspections

As a Corrections Officer, you'll be required to make inspections of many areas in a prison or jail. Inmates must be periodically searched for contraband in their possession. Their rooms and cells must be randomly and routinely inspected and searched for weapons or drugs. During the day, you will be escorting inmates from their cells to different activities in the facility. As you're working around the inmates' cells, you'll have the opportunity to look for contraband and observe the inmates' behavior. You may be assigned to supervise a work crew, during which you would have the opportunity to notice any unusual behavior. You'll learn to perform inspections as you observe inmates in the yard, in the dining hall, or in other areas of the prison or jail. These are informal inspections. Formal inspections are generally scheduled and would include a specific list of items to be inspected.

Discipline

Some inmates will continually test and violate the rules of the prison or jail. The Corrections Officer is primarily charged with the enforcement of these rules. If an inmate is observed violating the rules, or there is evidence that an inmate has violated the rules, it's up to you to file a misconduct report and hold the inmate accountable. After you file a report, the incident will be investigated and the inmate brought to institutional court. The court will be held in one of the institution's conference rooms and you may be called to testify. Taking firm and fair disciplinary action is an important aspect of the Corrections Officer's job.

Counts

All prisons and jails have a system of counting inmates to ensure that all inmates are accounted for or are present in the proper place. The number, frequency, and time of counts may vary from one prison to another, but in any case, you'll be responsible for taking accurate and efficient counts. Every inmate must either be in his or her cell during a count or accounted for in writing if on a job, at a visit, in the infirmary, or in any other authorized location.

NOTE

Corrections Officers who work on death row must also be willing to develop the proper working relationship with the inmates, and eventually must be prepared to assist in the execution of the inmate.

Incident Reports

Report writing is very important to the operation of prisons and jails. Reports may be used in court at a later time. They also become records of history for the facility. Decisions made regarding the future of the facility may depend on these records. It may be difficult for the administration to remember what occurred in the past, but a good record in the Incident Report will help reconstruct the history. During a normal workday you will write one or more reports. A report may be of a serious incident or simply a written account of something that you felt was unusual.

Counseling

As a Corrections Officer, you will not be required to counsel inmates, but the nature of the job makes it quite possible that counseling will come naturally. You will spend a lot of time with the inmate population. As you become more familiar with certain inmates, you will develop an acquaintance. There will be occasions where you will talk at length with inmates and come to know them well. This relationship that you develop sets up the opportunity to counsel them.

Since a good counseling relationship is built on trust, you will become a significant person to the inmates you counsel. You will have control over the inmates, but will also have a degree of concern for them. The combination of control and concern will make you a significant force in their lives.

Supervising

Inmates in most of the prisons across the country will be involved in some type of work, education, or recreation program. Inmates in jail and prison will be given visitation rights. In most cases, there will be another staff employee who will supervise the specific job or activity, but you will be responsible for supervising the overall safety and security of the program. If you are assigned to supervise visitation, you must be alert for unauthorized activity, as well as contraband that may be smuggled into the visiting room. Some prisons and jails have secure visiting facilities where the inmate and the visitor cannot come into contact; however, at lower security levels, contact visiting is allowed.

Danger

The majority of inmates in the prisons and jails in this country have been proven to have violated one or more federal, state, or local laws. They are being held against their will, and in close quarters. Some of the inmates are violent in their behavior. Being a Corrections Officer could be a dangerous job if it were not for the training and teamwork of the staff. Some of the dangers common to prisons and jails will be discussed, followed by the actions that you and your fellow officers can take to minimize the risks and make the prison or jail a safe and rewarding place to work.

ALERT!

As a Corrections Officer, you may be assigned to supervise any or all activities. You must be very alert to ensure the security and the safety of the inmates involved.

RIOTS

Riots in prisons or jails are situations where inmates momentarily gain some degree of control over part or all of the institution. Riots are usually not well planned by the inmates, and it is normally just a matter of time before the institution regains control. Corrections Officers are trained in emergency procedures to deal with riots. Every prison and jail will have a Policy and Procedure Manual that explains what you should do in case of a riot.

ESCAPES

When an inmate escapes from a secure facility, it is a sign that the security system broke down. Escapes put the public in jeopardy, since an inmate who escapes is probably desperate to get out and every escapee is considered to be dangerous. Frequent inspection of the cells and the inmates will reduce the risk of escape. Perimeter fences and cell bars must continually be inspected to determine if one or more inmates are planning to escape. Inmates have many hours to plan escapes, but you'll have only 8 hours a day to prevent them. You must be smarter, and more alert, to prevent escapes. Every prison and jail will have procedures to take to prevent escapes, as well as procedures to follow in the event of an escape.

HOSTAGE SITUATIONS

Everyone who works in a prison or jail is vulnerable to being taken hostage by inmates. Sometimes, inmates see taking a hostage as the only way to escape or have their grievances heard. There is generally no intent on the part of the inmates to harm the hostage, and if the hostage is well trained, most likely no harm will come. Most prisons and jails today have procedures to deal with hostage situations, and some institutions have training programs for employees in the event they are taken hostage.

DRILLS AND PROCEDURES TO REDUCE DANGER

TIP

Always maintain good communication with the inmate population and be aware of and report any changes in the mood of the inmates.

The best solution for a disturbance or a hostage situation is prevention. Prevention is best accomplished by good training. Every institution will have a Policy and Procedure Manual that will contain the emergency procedures. You will receive instruction on these topics during your entry training, and will probably receive more training once you are assigned to a facility. Take the information seriously, ask questions during the training, and insure you understand what you should do in the event of an emergency situation.

The best prevention for riots or disturbances in a prison or jail is good communication between the Corrections Officers and good communication with the administration.

SALARY

Median annual earnings of correctional officers and jailers were $32,670 in 2002. The middle 50 percent earned between $25,950 and $42,620. The lowest 10 percent earned less than $22,010, and the highest 10 percent earned more than $52,370. Median annual earnings in the public sector were $40,900 in the federal government; $33,260 in state government, and $31,380 in local government. In the management and public relations industry, where the relatively small number of officers employed by privately operated prisons are classified, median annual earnings were $21,390. According to the Federal Bureau of Prisons, the starting salary for federal correctional officers was about $23,000 a year in 2003. Starting federal salaries were slightly higher in selected areas where prevailing local pay levels were higher.

Median annual earnings of first-line supervisors/managers of correctional officers were $44,940 in 2002. The middle 50 percent earned between $33,730 and $59,160. The lowest 10 percent earned less than $29,220, and the highest 10 percent earned more than $69,370. Median annual earnings were $43,240 in state government and $49,120 in local government.

Median annual earnings of bailiffs were $32,710 in 2002. The middle 50 percent earned between $22,960 and $44,280. The lowest 10 percent earned less than $16,870, and the highest 10 percent earned more than $55,270. Median annual earnings were $27,470 in local government.

In addition to typical benefits, Corrections Officers employed in the public sector usually are provided with uniforms or a clothing allowance to purchase their own uniforms. Civil service systems or merit boards cover officers employed by the federal government and most state governments. Their retirement coverage entitles them to retire at age 50 after 20 years of service or at any age with 25 years of service.

TRAINING AND PROMOTION

Most institutions require Corrections Officers to be at least 18 to 21 years of age and a U.S. citizen; have a high school education or its equivalent; demonstrate job stability, usually by accumulating two years of work experience; and have no felony convictions. Promotion prospects may be enhanced through obtaining a postsecondary education.

Corrections Officers must be in good health. Candidates for employment are generally required to meet formal standards of physical fitness, eyesight, and hearing. In addition, many jurisdictions use standard tests to determine applicant suitability to work in a correctional environment. Good judgment and the ability to think and act quickly are indispensable. Applicants are typically screened for drug abuse, subject to background checks, and required to pass a written examination.

Federal, state, and some local departments of corrections provide training for Corrections Officers based on guidelines established by the American Correctional Association and the

American Jail Association. Some states have regional training academies that are available to local agencies. All states and local correctional agencies provide on-the-job training at the conclusion of formal instruction, including legal restrictions and interpersonal relations. Many systems require firearms proficiency and self-defense skills. Officer trainees typically receive several weeks or months of training in an actual job setting under the supervision of an experienced officer. However, specific entry requirements and on-the-job training vary widely from agency to agency.

Academy trainees generally receive instruction on a number of subjects, including institutional policies, regulations, and operations, as well as custody and security procedures. As a condition of employment, new federal Corrections Officers must undergo 200 hours of formal training within the first year of employment. They also must complete 120 hours of specialized training at the U.S. Federal Bureau of Prisons residential training center at Glynco, Georgia, within the first sixty days after appointment. Experienced officers receive annual in-service training to keep abreast of new developments and procedures.

Some Corrections Officers are members of prison tactical response teams, which are trained to respond to disturbances, riots, hostage situations, forced cell moves, and other potentially dangerous confrontations. Team members receive training and practice with weapons, chemical agents, forced-entry methods, crisis management, and other tactics.

With education, experience, and training, qualified officers may advance to correctional sergeant. Correctional sergeants supervise Corrections Officers and usually are responsible for maintaining security and directing the activities of other officers during an assigned shift or in an assigned area. Ambitious and qualified Corrections Officers can be promoted to supervisory or administrative positions all the way up to warden. Officers sometimes transfer to related areas, such as probation officer, parole officer, or correctional treatment specialist.

SUMMING IT UP

- As a Corrections Officer, your role will be centered around protecting the public, fellow Corrections Officers, and inmates.

- Salary increases for Corrections Officers are based on the civil service merit system.

- Training requirements for Corrections Officers are extensive and consist of courses in institutional policies, regulations, and operations, as well as custody and security procedures.

Where the Jobs Are

OVERVIEW

- The prison system
- Where to start looking
- Application process
- Summing it up

THE PRISON SYSTEM

The work of the Corrections Officer is similar in federal, state, and municipal corrections. The main differences are the qualification, the pay, and the requirement to relocate.

Federal Prisons

The Federal Bureau of Prisons consists of more than 106 institutions and 28 community corrections facilities. Since there isn't a federal prison in every state, you may be required to relocate if you choose to work in the federal prison system. The salaries will be better in the federal system, but the requirements for employment will be greater. If you are going to work in the federal system, you must be employed before your thirty-fifth birthday. If you make corrections your career, and choose to move up to the administrative positions, you would no doubt be required to relocate to some other state in order to gain experience at a number of prisons.

State Prisons

In state prison systems, the pay varies from state to state. Relocation may be required for promotions as you rise in rank in a state system, but your move would be within that state.

chapter 2

Private Prisons and Jails

Private prisons and jails have become a significant employer of Corrections Officers within the last ten years. The working conditions are very similar to those of the federal and state jobs. The most significant difference is the flexibility that the corporations have to develop pay plans and personnel policies. A private prison or jail doesn't have oversight of its personnel policies by the state or federal government. Under government employment, there are certain policies governing leave and disciplinary procedures. The rules in the private prisons and jails are the policies of the private corporation.

WHERE TO START LOOKING

Where you may be employed is an important question to ask yourself before you apply for a job as a Corrections Officer. Listed below are the addresses of the Federal Bureau of Prisons and all State Departments of Corrections.

Federal Bureau of Prisons Locations

The Federal Bureau of Prisons home page is www.bop.gov. There, you will find employment information and other helpful information about the Bureau of Prisons.

Correctional Facilities

The American Corrections Association operates a Web site at www.corrections.com/aca. There are job listings for Corrections Officers in State Departments of Corrections as well as listings for Detention Officers in city and county jails. Different jurisdictions are allowed to post job vacancies, so there is always a current listing of jobs nationwide.

ABBREVIATIONS

CCM—Community Corrections Management Office
CI—Correctional Institution
CO—Central Office
DC—Detention Center
FCC—Federal Correctional Complex
FCI—Federal Correctional Institution
FMC—Federal Medical Center
FPC—Federal Prison Camp
FTC—Federal Transfer Center
MCC—Metropolitan Correctional Center
MCFP—Medical Center for Federal Prisoners
MDC—Metropolitan Detention Center
RO—Regional Office
USP—U.S. Penitentiary

MID-ATLANTIC REGION

ALDERSON FPC
Glen Ray Road
Box A
Alderson, WV 24910
Phone: 304-445-2901
Fax: 304-445-7736

ASHLAND FCI
Route 716
Ashland, KY 41105
Phone: 606-928-6414
Fax: 606-928-3635

ANNAPOLIS JUNCTION CCM
10010 Junction Drive, Suite 100-N
Annapolis Junction, MD 20701
Phone: 301-317-3142
Fax: 301-317-3138

BECKLEY FCI
1600 Industrial Road
Beaver, WV 25813
Phone: 304-252-9758
Fax: 304-256-4956

BIG SANDY USP
1197 Airport Road
Inez, KY 41224
Phone: 606-433-2400
Fax: 606-433-2577

BUTNER FMC
Old Highway 75
Butner, NC 27509
Phone: 919-575-3900
Fax: 919-575-4801

BUTNER LOW FCI
Old Highway 75
Butner, NC 27509
Phone: 919-575-5700
Fax: 919-575-5023

BUTNER MEDIUM FCI
Old Highway 75
Butner, NC 27509
Phone: 919-575-4541
Fax: 919-575-6341

CUMBERLAND FCI
14601 Burbridge Road SE
Cumberland, MD 21502
Phone: 301-784-1000
Fax: 301-784-1008

GILMER FCI
201 FCI Lane
Glenville, WV 26351
Phone: 304-462-0395
Fax: 304-462-0396

HAZELTON USP
Skyview Drive
Bruceton Mills, WV 26525
Phone: 304-379-5000
Fax: 304-379-5039

LEE USP
Lee County Industrial Park
Hickory Flats Road
Pennington Gap, VA 24277
Phone: 276-546-0150
Fax: 276-546-9115

LEXINGTON FMC
3301 Leestown Road
Lexington, KY 40511
Phone: 859-255-6812
Fax: 859-253-8821

MANCHESTER FCI
805 Fox Hollow Road
Manchester, KY 40962
Phone: 606-598-1900
Fax: 606-599-4115

McCREARY USP
330 Federal Way
Pine Knot, KY 42635
Phone: 606-354-7000
Fax: 606-354-7190

MEMPHIS FCI
1101 John A. Denie Road
Memphis, TN 38134
Phone: 901-372-2269
Fax: 901-380-2462

MID-ATLANTIC RO
10010 Junction Park; Suite 100-N
Annapolis Junction, MD 20701
Phone: 301-317-3100
Fax: 301-317-3214

NASHVILLE CCM
801 Broadway Street, #599
Nashville, TN 37203
Phone: 615-736-5148
Fax: 615-736-5148

RIVERS CI
145 Parker's Fishery Road
Winton, NC 27986
Phone: 252-358-5200
Fax: 252-358-5202

SEYMOUR JOHNSON FPC
1055 Peterson Avenue
Goldsboro, NC 27533
Phone: 919-735-9711
Fax: 919-735-0169

WASHINGTON, DC CCM
10010 Junction Drive, Suite 100-N
Annapolis Junction, MD 20701
Phone: 301-317-3142
Fax: 301-317-3138

NORTH CENTRAL REGION

CHICAGO CCM
200 W. Adams Street, Room 2915
Chicago, IL 60606
Phone: 312-886-2114
Fax: 312-886-2118

CHICAGO MCC
71 W. Van Buren Street
Chicago, IL 60605
Phone: 312-322-0567
Fax: 312-322-1120

DENVER CCM
721 19th Street, Suite 412
Denver, CO 80202
Phone: 303-844-5178
Fax: 303-844-6189

DETROIT CCM
211 W. Fort Street, Suite 620
Detroit, MI 48226
Phone: 313-226-6186
Fax: 313-226-7327

DULUTH FPC
6902 Stebner Road
Duluth, MN 55814
Phone: 218-722-8634
Fax: 218-733-4701

ENGLEWOOD FCI
9595 W. Quincy Avenue
Littleton, CO 80123
Phone: 303-985-1566
Fax: 303-763-2553

FLORENCE ADMAX USP
5880 Highway 67 South
Florence, CO 81226
Phone: 719-784-9464
Fax: 719-784-5290

FLORENCE FCI
5880 Highway 67 South
Florence, CO 81226
Phone: 719-784-9100
Fax: 719-784-9504

FLORENCE HIGH USP
5880 Highway 67 South
Florence, CO 81226
Phone: 719-784-9454
Fax: 719-784-5157

GREENVILLE FCI
100 U.S. Highway 40
Greenville, IL 62248
Phone: 618-664-6200
Fax: 618-664-6372

KANSAS CITY CCM
400 State Avenue, Room 131
Kansas City, KS 66101
Phone: 913-551-1117
Fax: 913-551-1120

LEAVENWORTH USP
1300 Metropolitan
Leavenworth, KS 66048
Phone: 913-682-8700
Fax: 913-578-1010

MARION USP
4500 Prison Road
Marion, IL 62959
Phone: 618-964-1441
Fax: 618-964-2058

MILAN FCI
E. Arkona Road
Milan, MI 48160
Phone: 734-439-1511
Fax: 734-439-0949

MINNEAPOLIS CCM
300 S. 4th Street, Suite 1210
Minneapolis, MN 55415
Phone: 612-664-5560
Fax: 612-664-5569

NORTH CENTRAL RO
400 State Avenue, Suite 800
Kansas City, KS 66101
Phone: 913-621-3939

OXFORD FCI
County Road G & Elk Avenue
Grand Marsh, WI 53936
Phone: 608-584-5511
Fax: 608-584-6371

PEKIN FCI
2600 S. Second Street
Pekin, IL 61555
Phone: 309-346-8588
Fax: 309-477-4685

ROCHESTER FMC
2110 E. Center Street
Rochester, MN 55904
Phone: 507-287-0674
Fax: 507-287-9601

SANDSTONE FCI
2300 County Road 29
Sandstone, MN 55072
Phone: 320-245-2262
Fax: 320-245-0385

SPRINGFIELD MCFP
1900 W. Sunshine
Springfield, MO 65807
Phone: 417-862-7041
Fax: 417-837-1711

ST. LOUIS CCM
1222 Spruce Street, Suite 6-101
St. Louis, MO 63101
Phone: 314-539-2376
Fax: 314-539-2465

TERRE HAUTE FCI
4200 Bureau Road North
Terre Haute, IN 47808
Phone: 812-238-1531
Fax: 812-238-9873

TERRE HAUTE USP
4700 Bureau Road South
Terre Haute, IN 47802
Phone: 812-244-4400
Fax: 812-244-4789

WASECA FCI
1000 University Drive SW
Waseca, MN 56093
Phone: 507-835-8972
Fax: 507-837-4547

YANKTON FPC
1016 Douglas Avenue
Yankton, SD 57078
Phone: 605-665-3262
Fax: 605-668-1113

NORTHEAST REGION

ALLENWOOD FPC
Route 15
Montgomery, PA 17752
Phone: 570-547-1641
Fax: 570-547-1740

ALLENWOOD LOW FCI
P.O. Box 1500
White Deer, PA 17887
Phone: 570-547-1990
Fax: 570-547-1740

ALLENWOOD MEDIUM FCI
Route 15
White Deer, PA 17810
Phone: 570-547-7950
Fax: 570-547-7751

ALLENWOOD USP
Route 15
Allenwood, PA 17810
Phone: 570-547-0963
Fax: 570-547-9201

BOSTON CCM
JFK Federal Building, Suite 2200
Boston, MA 02203
Phone: 617-565-4293
Fax: 617-565-4297

BROOKLYN MDC
80 29th Street
Brooklyn, NY 11232
Phone: 718-840-4200
Fax: 718-840-5005

CANAAN USP
3057 Easton Turnpike
Waymart, PA 18472
Phone: 570-488-8000
Fax: 570-488-8130

CINCINNATI CCM
36 E. 7th Street, Suite 2107-A
Cincinnati, OH 45202
Phone: 513-684-2603
Fax: 513-684-2603

DANBURY FCI
Route 37
Danbury, CT 06811
Phone: 203-743-6471
Fax: 203-312-5110

DEVENS FMC
42 Patton Road
Ayer, MA 01432
Phone: 978-796-1000
Fax: 978-796-1118

ELKTON FCI
8730 Scroggs Road
Elkton, OH 44415
Phone: 330-424-7448
Fax: 330-424-7075

FAIRTON FCI
655 Fairton-Millville Road
Fairton, NJ 08320
Phone: 856-453-1177
Fax: 856-453-4015

FORT DIX FCI
5756 Hartford & Pointville Road
Fort Dix, NJ 08640
Phone: 609-723-1100
Fax: 609-723-6847

LEWISBURG USP
2400 Robert F. Miller Drive
Lewisburg, PA 17837
Phone: 570-523-1251
Fax: 570-522-7745

LORETTO FCI
Rural Route 276
Loretto, PA 15940
Phone: 814-472-4140
Fax: 814-472-6046

McKEAN FCI
Route 59 & Big Shanty Road
Lewis Run, PA 16738
Phone: 814-362-8900
Fax: 814-363-6821

NE OHIO CI
2240 Hubbard Road
Youngstown, OH 44501
Phone: 330-746-3777
Fax: 330-746-3318

NEW YORK CCM
100 29th Street
Brooklyn, NY 11232
Phone: 718-840-4219
Fax: 718-840-4207

NEW YORK MCC
150 Park Row
New York, NY 10007
Phone: 646-836-6300
Fax: 646-836-7751

NORTHEAST RO
2nd & Chestnut Street, 7th Floor
Philadelphia, PA 19106
Phone: 215-521-7301
Fax: 215-596-1871

OTISVILLE FCI
Two Mile Drive
Otisville, NY 10963
Phone: 845-386-6700
Fax: 845-386-6727

PHILADELPHIA CCM
2nd & Chestnut Street, 7th Floor
Philadelphia, PA 19106
Phone: 215-521-7300
Fax: 215-521-7486

PHILADELPHIA FDC
700 Arch Street
Philadelphia, PA 19106
Phone: 215-521-4000
Fax: 215-521-7220

PITTSBURGH CCM
1000 Liberty Avenue, Room 831
Pittsburgh, PA 15222
Phone: 412-395-4740
Fax: 412-395-4730

RAY BROOK FCI
128 Ray Brook Road
Ray Brook, NY 12977
Phone: 518-897-4000
Fax: 518-897-4216

SCHUYLKILL FCI
Interstate 81 & 901 West
Minersville, PA 17954
Phone: 570-544-7100
Fax: 570-544-7350

SOUTH CENTRAL REGION

BASTROP FCI
1341 Highway 95 North
Bastrop, TX 78602
Phone: 512-321-3903
Fax: 512-304-0117

BEAUMONT LOW FCI
5560 Knauth Road
Beaumont, TX 77705
Phone: 409-727-8172
Fax: 409-626-3500

BEAUMONT MEDIUM FCI
5830 Knauth Road
Beaumont, TX 77705
Phone: 409-727-0101
Fax: 409-720-5000

BEAUMONT USP
6200 Knauth Road
Beaumont, TX 77705
Phone: 409-727-8188
Fax: 409-626-3700

BIG SPRING CI
1701 Apron Drive
Big Spring, TX 79720
Phone: 432-264-0060
Fax: 432-267-6522

BIG SPRING FCI
1900 Simler Avenue
Big Spring, TX 79720
Phone: 432-263-6699
Fax: 432-268-6867

BRYAN FPC
1100 Ursuline Avenue
Bryan, TX 77803
Phone: 979-823-1879
Fax: 979-775-5681

CARSWELL FMC
J Street, Building 3000
Fort Worth, TX 76127
Phone: 817-782-4000
Fax: 817-782-4875

CIBOLA COUNTY CI
2000 Cibola Loop
Milan, NM 87021
Phone: 505-285-6991
Fax: 505-285-6886

DALBY CI
805 N. Avenue F
Post, TX 79356
Phone: 806-495-2175
Fax: 806-495-3157

DALLAS CCM
4211 Cedar Springs Road, Suite 100
Dallas, TX 75219
Phone: 214-224-3522
Fax: 214-224-3367

EDEN CI
702 E. Broadway
Eden, TX 76837
Phone: 325-869-2704
Fax: 325-869-5147

EL PASO CCM
4849 N. Mesa Street, Room 208
El Paso, TX 79912
Phone: 915-534-6326
Fax: 915-534-6432

EL RENO FCI
4205 Highway 66 West
El Reno, OK 73036
Phone: 405-262-4875
Fax: 405-262-6266

FORREST CITY LOW FCI
1400 Dale Bumpers Road
Forrest City, AR 72335
Phone: 870-630-6000
Fax: 870-494-4496

FORREST CITY MEDIUM FCI
1301 Dale Bumpers Road
Forrest City, AR 72335
Phone: 870-494-4200
Fax: 870-494-4496

FORT WORTH FMC
3150 Horton Road
Fort Worth, TX 76119
Phone: 817-534-8400
Fax: 817-413-3350

HOUSTON CCM
515 Rusk, Room 12102
Houston, TX 77002
Phone: 713-718-4781
Fax: 713-718-4780

HOUSTON FDC
1200 Texas Avenue
Houston, TX 77002
Phone: 713-221-5400
Fax: 713-229-4200

LA TUNA FCI
8500 Doniphan Road
Anthony, TX 79821
Phone: 915-886-6600
Fax: 915-886-6628

LA TUNA FCI
SSG Sims Road, Building 11636
El Paso, TX 79906

NEW ORLEANS CCM
501 Magazine Street, Suite 1211
Hale Boggs Building
New Orleans, LA 70113
Phone: 504-589-2371
Fax: 504-589-2378

OAKDALE FDC
2105 E. Whatley Road
Oakdale, LA 71463
Phone: 318-335-4466
Fax: 318-215-2185

OKLAHOMA CITY FTC
7410 S. MacArthur
Oklahoma City, OK 73169
Phone: 405-682-4075
Fax: 405-680-4041

POLLOCK USP
1000 Airbase Road
Pollack, LA 71467
Phone: 318-561-5300
Fax: 318-561-5391

REEVES CI
98 W. County Road 204
Pecos, TX 79772
Phone: 432-447-2926
Fax: 432-447-9224

SAN ANTONIO CCM
727 E. Durango Boulevard, Room B138
San Antonio, TX 78206
Phone: 210-472-6225
Fax: 210-472-6224

SEAGOVILLE FCI
2113 N. Highway 175
Seagoville, TX 75159
Phone: 972-287-2911
Fax: 972-287-5466

SOUTH CENTRAL RO
4211 Cedar Springs Road
Dallas, TX 75219
Phone: 214-224-3389
Fax: 214-224-3420

TEXARKANA FCI
4001 Leopard Drive
Texarkana, TX 75501
Phone: 903-838-4587
Fax: 903-223-4424

THREE RIVERS FCI
U.S. Highway 72 West
Three Rivers, TX 78071
Phone: 361-786-3576
Fax: 361-786-5051

SOUTHEAST REGION

ATLANTA CCM
715 McDonough Boulevard SE
Atlanta, GA 30315
Phone: 404-635-5673
Fax: 404-730-9785

ATLANTA USP
601 McDonough Boulevard SE
Atlanta, GA 30315
Phone: 404-635-5100
Fax: 404-331-2403

BENNETTSVILLE FCI
696 Muckerman Road
Bennettsville, SC 29512
Phone: 843-454-8200
Fax: 843-454-8219

COLEMAN I USP
846 NE 54th Terrace
Coleman, FL 33521
Phone: 352-689-6000
Fax: 352-689-6012

COLEMAN II USP
846 NE 54th Terrace
Coleman, FL 33521
Phone: 352-689-7000
Fax: 352-689-7012

COLEMAN LOW FCI
846 NE 54th Terrace
Coleman, FL 33521
Phone: 352-689-4000
Fax: 352-330-0259

COLEMAN MEDIUM FCI
846 NE 54th Terrace
Coleman, FL 33521
Phone: 352-689-5000
Fax: 352-330-0552

EDGEFIELD FCI
501 Gary Hill Road
Edgefield, SC 29824
Phone: 803-637-1500
Fax: 803-637-9840

EGLIN FPC
50501 Inverness Road
Eglin AFB, FL 32542
Phone: 850-882-8522
Fax: 850-729-8190

ESTILL FCI
100 Prison Road
Estill, SC 29918
Phone: 803-625-4607
Fax: 803-625-5635

JESUP FCI
2600 Highway 301 South
Jesup, GA 31599
Phone: 912-427-0870
Fax: 912-427-1125

JESUP FCI-FSL
2600 Highway 301 South
Jesup, GA 31599

MARIANNA FCI
3625 FCI Road
Marianna, FL 32446
Phone: 850-526-2313
Fax: 850-718-2014

McRAE CI
1000 Jim Hammock Drive
McRae, GA 31055
Phone: 229-868-7778
Fax: 229-868-7640

MIAMI CCM
401 N. Miami Avenue
Miami, FL 33128
Phone: 305-536-5710
Fax: 305-536-6505

MIAMI FCI
15801 SW 137th Avenue
Miami, FL 33177
Phone: 305-259-2100
Fax: 305-259-2160

MIAMI FDC
33 NE 4th Street
Miami, FL 33132
Phone: 305-577-0010
Fax: 305-536-7368

MONTGOMERY CCM
2350 Fairlane Drive, Suite 110
Montgomery, AL 36116
Phone: 334-223-7464
Fax: 334-223-7012

MONTGOMERY FPC
Maxwell AFB
Montgomery, AL 36112
Phone: 334-293-2100
Fax: 334-293-2326

ORLANDO CCM
3659 Maguire Boulevard, Suite 100
Orlando, FL 32803
Phone: 407-648-6055
Fax: 407-648-6058

PENSACOLA FPC
110 Raby Avenue
Pensacola, FL 32509
Phone: 850-457-1911
Fax: 850-458-7295

SOUTHEAST RO
3800 Camp Creek Park SW, Building 2000
Atlanta, GA 30331
Phone: 678-686-1200
Fax: 678-686-1379

TALLADEGA FCI
565 E. Renfroe Road
Talladega, AL 35160
Phone: 256-315-4100
Fax: 256-315-4495

TALLAHASSEE FCI
501 Capital Circle NE
Tallahassee, FL 32301
Phone: 850-878-2173
Fax: 850-671-6105

WILLIAMSBURG FCI
8301 Highway 521
Salters, SC 29590
Phone: 843-387-9400
Fax: 843-387-6961

YAZOO CITY LOW FCI
2225 Haley Barbour Parkway
Yazoo City, MS 39194
Phone: 662-751-4800
Fax: 662-751-4905

YAZOO CITY MEDIUM FCI
P.O. Box 47
Yazoo City, MS 39194

WESTERN REGION

ATWATER USP
1 Federal Way
Atwater, CA 95301
Phone: 209-386-0257
Fax: 209-386-4635

CALIFORNIA CITY CI
22844 Virginia Boulevard
California City, CA 93504
Phone: 760-373-1764
Fax: 760-373-3529

DUBLIN FCI
5701 8th Street—Camp Parks
Dublin, CA 94568
Phone: 925-833-7500
Fax: 925-833-7599

ELOY DC
1705 E. Hanna Road
Eloy, AZ 85231
Phone: 520-466-4141
Fax: 520-466-7750

HERLONG FCI
741-925 Access Road A-25
Herlong, CA 96113
Phone: 530-827-8000
Fax: 530-827-8024

HONOLULU FDC
351 Elliott Street
Honolulu, HI 96819
Phone: 808-838-4200
Fax: 808-838-4507

LOMPOC FCI
3600 Guard Road
Lompoc, CA 93436
Phone: 805-736-4154
Fax: 805-736-7163

LOMPOC USP
3901 Klein Boulevard
Lompoc, CA 93436
Phone: 805-735-2771
Fax: 805-737-0295

LONG BEACH CCM
501 W. Ocean Boulevard, Suite 3260
Long Beach, CA 90802
Phone: 562-980-3536
Fax: 562-980-3543

LOS ANGELES MDC
535 N. Alameda Street
Los Angeles, CA 90012
Phone: 213-485-0439
Fax: 213-253-9510

NELLIS FPC
8221 Seymour Johnson Avenue
Las Vegas, NV 89191
Phone: 702-644-5001
Fax: 702-643-2303

PHOENIX FCI
37900 N. 45th Avenue
Phoenix, AZ 85086
Phone: 623-465-9757
Fax: 623-465-5199

PHOENIX CCM
230 N. First Avenue
Phoenix, AZ 85003
Phone: 602-514-7075
Fax: 602-514-7076

SACRAMENTO CCM
501 I Street, Suite 9-400
Sacramento, CA 95814
Phone: 916-930-2010
Fax: 916-930-2008

SAFFORD FCI
1529 W. Highway 366
Safford, AZ 85546
Phone: 928-428-6600
Fax: 928-348-1331

SALT LAKE CITY CCM
324 S. State Street, Suite 228
Salt Lake City, UT 84111
Phone: 801-524-4212
Fax: 801-524-3112

SAN DIEGO MCC
808 Union Street
San Diego, CA 92101
Phone: 619-232-4311
Fax: 619-595-0390

SEATAC FDC
2425 S. 200th Street
Seattle, WA 98198
Phone: 206-870-5700
Fax: 206-870-5717

SEATTLE CCM
915 Second Avenue, Room 3160
Seattle, WA 98174
Phone: 206-220-6593
Fax: 206-220-6591

SHERIDAN FCI
27072 Ballston Road
Sheridan, OR 97378
Phone: 503-843-4442
Fax: 503-843-3408

TAFT CI
1500 Cadet Road
Taft, CA 93268
Phone: 661-763-2510
Fax: 661-765-3034

TERMINAL ISLAND FCI
1299 Seaside Avenue
Terminal Island, CA 90731
Phone: 310-831-8961
Fax: 310-732-5335

TUCSON FCI
8901 S. Wilmot Road
Tucson, AZ 85706
Phone: 520-574-7100
Fax: 520-574-7341

VICTORVILLE MEDIUM I FCI
13777 Air Expressway Boulevard
Victorville, CA 92394
Phone: 760-246-2400
Fax: 760-246-2621

VICTORVILLE MEDIUM II FCI
13777 Air Expressway Boulevard
Victorville, CA 92394
Phone: 760-530-5700
Fax: 760-530-5706

VICTORVILLE USP
13777 Air Expressway Boulevard
Victorville, CA 92394
Phone: 760-530-5000
Fax: 760-530-5103

WESTERN RO
7950 Dublin Boulevard, 3rd Floor
Dublin, CA 94568
Phone: 925-803-4700
Fax: 925-803-4802

STATE DEPARTMENTS OF CORRECTIONS

Alabama: www.doc.state.al.us/inmate_search.htm

Alaska: www.correct.state.ak.us

Arizona: www.adc.state.az.us/ISearch.htm

Arkansas: www.state.ar.us/doc/inmate_info

California: www.cdc.state.ca.us/CDC/Inmate_Locator.asp

Colorado: www.doc.state.co.us

Connecticut: www.ctinmateinfo.state.ct.us/searchop.asp

Delaware: www.state.de.us/correct/default.shtml

Florida: www.dc.state.fl.us/inmateinfo/inmateinfomenu.asp

Georgia: www.dcor.state.ga.us

Hawaii: www.hawaii.gov/portal

Idaho: www.corr.state.id.us

Illinois: www.idoc.state.il.us/subsections/search/default.shtml

Indiana: www.ai.org/indcorrection/ofsearch/ODSdisclaim.html

Iowa: www.doc.state.ia.us

Kansas: http://docnet.dc.state.ks.us/kasper2/kasperexpl.htm

Kentucky: www.corrections.ky.gov

Louisiana: www.corrections.state.la.us

Maine: www.state.me.us/corrections

Maryland: www.dpscs.state.md.us

Massachusetts: www.mass.gov

Michigan: www.michigan.gov/corrections

Minnesota: http://info.doc.state.mn.us/publicviewer/main.asp

Mississippi: www.mdoc.state.ms.us

Missouri: www.corrections.state.mo.us

Montana: http://app.mt.gov/conweb

Nebraska: www.corrections.state.ne.us

Nevada: www.doc.nv.gov/ncis/index.php

New Hampshire: www.state.nh.us

New Jersey: www.state.nj.us/corrections

New Mexico: http://corrections.state.nm.us

New York: http://nysdocslookup.docs.state.ny.us/kinqw00

North Carolina: www.doc.state.nc.us/offenders

North Dakota: www.nd.gov

Ohio: www.drc.state.oh.us/search2.htm

Oklahoma: www.doc.state.ok.us/DOCS/offender_info.htm

Oregon: www.doc.state.or.us/welcome.shtml

Pennsylvania: www.cor.state.pa.us/portal/cwp/view.asp?a=380&q=126864

Rhode Island: www.doc.state.ri.us

South Carolina: www.doc.sc.gov

South Dakota: www.state.sd.us/corrections/corrections.html

Tennessee: www.tennesseeanytime.org/foil/foil_index.jsp

Texas: www.tdcj.state.tx.us/offender_information.htm

Utah: www.cr.ex.state.ut.us

Vermont: www.doc.state.vt.us/offender

Virginia: www.vadoc.state.va.us

Washington: http://access.wa.gov

West Virginia: www.wvf.state.wv.us/wvdoc

Wisconsin: www.wi-doc.com

Wyoming: http://doc.state.wy.us/corrections.asp

APPLICATION PROCESS

Before you fill out an application, you should make a copy of it to use as a rough draft. Always type the final application or print it in ink. Your application is the first impression that the hiring authority will receive regarding your worthiness to work in the prison or jail.

Think about what you are doing. Make sure that you have the sufficient interest necessary to work in this field. Not everyone is suited to work in a prison or jail. It takes a special person.

Sample Announcements

There are a number of ways to locate job information. Each state has a Department of Corrections, and these departments are listed in the phone book, usually with the listings for other state government offices. The State Department of Corrections is usually located in the state's capital city. The listing in the phone book will give information about which office to contact for job information. It will usually be the personnel office or the human resources office. Call to receive more information about the application process.

Most medium to large cities operate a jail system. You can usually find information about the Corrections Officer or Jail Deputy jobs by contacting the City Hall of the city that interests you. Someone there will be able to give you information about how to apply.

In most counties, the sheriffs operate the jails. You can get information about Jail Deputy or Corrections Officer jobs by contacting the sheriff's office.

Federal jobs can be located by looking in the front of the phone book under the Federal Agency listings. There will usually be information or phone numbers to call about jobs in the federal government.

The following are examples of job announcements you may see.

SAMPLE CITY ANNOUNCEMENT

Notice of Examination for Corrections Officer

Salary: The rate is subject to negotiated change. In addition, there is an annual uniform allowance, holiday pay, and contributions by the City to Welfare and Annuity Fund and City-paid health insurance. After appointment, incumbents will receive salary increments for five years.

Job Description: Under supervision, maintains security within correctional facilities and is responsible for the custody, control, care, job training, and work performance of inmates of detention and sentenced correctional facilities, and performs related work.

Examples of Typical Tasks: Supervises inmate meals, visits, recreational programs, and other congregate activities; inspects assigned areas for conditions that threaten safety and security; conducts searches in order to detect contraband; completes forms and reports; maintains appropriate log books; communicates with other area Corrections Officers to exchange pertinent information; issues verbal orders, announcements, and explanations to inmates; observes inmates and makes recommendations concerning medical and/or psychiatric referrals; safeguards Departmental supplies and equipment; escorts inmates within and outside of the facility; responds to unusual incidents and disturbances; enforces security procedures in accordance with Department guidelines; requests medical assistance for inmates when necessary; counts and verifies the number of inmates present in assigned areas; verifies identification of inmates; supervises inmates of either sex.

Other Job Factors: Listed below are examples of physical activities that Corrections Officers perform and environmental conditions in which their activities are conducted. This is not a comprehensive listing, only an indication of some of the job factors.

Stands for up to eight-and-one-half hours continuously; walks up several flights of stairs; uses physical force to break up fights; when assigned a double tour, works 17 hours continuously; works outdoors in all kinds of weather; lifts heavy objects; moves heavy items; is exposed to fumes from disinfectants and sanitary supplies; wears bulletproof or radiation protective vest; is subject to close contact with inmates.

Corrections Officers are required to change tours or work overtime, and to work rotating tours and shifts, including nights, Saturdays, Sundays, and holidays.

QUALIFICATION REQUIREMENTS

Candidates must possess a four-year high school diploma or its educational equivalent.

License Requirement: On the date of appointment, possession of a valid unrestricted New York State driver's license is required. Employees must maintain such license during their employment.

English Requirement: Candidates must be able to understand and be understood in English (see General Examination Regulation E.9).

Proof of Identity: Under the Immigration Reform and Control Act of 1986, applicants must be able to prove your identity and your right to obtain employment in the United States prior to employment with the City of New York.

Citizenship Requirement: United States citizenship is required at the time of appointment. All qualification requirements mentioned above must be met by the date of appointment.

Character Background: Proof of good character and satisfactory background will be absolute prerequisites to appointment. The following are among the factors that would ordinarily be cause for disqualification: (a) conviction of an offense, the nature of which indicates lack of good moral character or disposition towards violence or disorder, or which is punishable by one or more years of imprisonment; (b) repeated convictions of an offense, where such convictions indicate a disrespect for the law; (c) discharge from employment, where such discharge indicates poor behavior or inability to adjust to discipline; (d) dishonorable discharge from the Armed Forces; and (e) persons who have been convicted of petty larceny.

Medical, Psychological, and Physical Qualifications: Eligibles must pass medical and psychological tests. Eligibles will be rejected for any medical condition that impairs their ability to perform the duties of the position in a reasonable manner, or which may reasonably be expected to render them unfit to continue to perform those duties in a reasonable manner. All employees must be medically, psychologically, and physically fit to perform the full duties of the position, and must continue to meet prescribed standards throughout their careers. Periodic testing may be required. Medical standards are available at the Application Section of the Department of Personnel, 18 Washington Street, New York, NY 10004.

Candidates may be required to pass a qualifying physical test.

At the time of appointment, candidates will be required to provide documentation of immunization for rubella, measles, whooping cough, diphtheria, and chicken pox.

Drug Testing: A drug-screening test will be conducted as part of a pre-employment screening process. Drug tests will also be administered to all Probationary Corrections Officers during Academy Training and again as part of the medical examination at the end of probation. All employees may be drug tested on a random basis after their probationary periods are completed. Any member of the NYC Department of Correction found in possession of, or using, illegal drugs will be terminated.

TEST INFORMATION

Test Description: Written, multiple-choice test, weight 100. The written test may include questions requiring any of the following abilities: written comprehension, written expression, memorization, problem sensitivity, number facility, deductive reasoning, inductive reasoning, information ordering, spatial orientation, and visualization.

The passing score will be determined after an analysis of the results.

Applicants may be summoned for the test prior to a review of their qualifications.

Test Date: The multiple-choice test is expected to be held on Saturday, June 15.

Admission Card: Applicants who do not receive an admission card at least 4 days prior to the tentative test date must appear at the Examining Service Division of the Department of Personnel during normal business hours on one of the 4 days preceding the test date to obtain an admission card.

APPLICATION INFORMATION

Application Period: From February 7 through March 26. Application forms may be obtained in person or by mail from the Application Section, New York City Department of Personnel. Properly completed **ORIGINAL** application forms **(NO COPIES)** must be submitted only by mail to the New York City Department of Personnel, Bowling Green Station, P.O. Box 996, New York, NY 10274-0996. Application must be postmarked no later than the last date of the application period.

Application Fee: Payable by money order ONLY. Money orders should be made payable to the New York City Department of Personnel. The social security number of the candidate and the number(s) of the examination(s) for which he or she is applying must be written on the money order. Cash and checks will not be accepted. The applications fee will be waived for a New York City resident receiving public assistance who submits a clear photocopy of a current Medicaid card along with the application. Applicants should retain their money order receipt as proof of filing until they receive notice of their test results.

APPOINTMENT INFORMATION

Investigation: Candidates are subject to investigation before appointment. At the time of investigation, candidates will be required to pay a fee for fingerprint screening.

At the time of investigation and at the time of appointment, candidates must present originals or certified copies of all required documents and proof, including, but not limited to, proof of date and place of birth by transcript or record of the Bureau of Vital Statistics or other satisfactory evidence, naturalization papers if necessary, proof of any military service, and proof of meeting educational requirements.

Any willful misstatement or failure to present any documents required for investigation will be cause for disqualification.

Probationary Period: The probationary period is 24 months.

As part of the probationary period, probationers will be required to successfully complete a prescribed training course. In accordance with City Personnel Director's Rules and Regulations, probationers who fail to complete successfully such training course, at the close of such training course, may be terminated by their agency head.

Firearms Qualification: Candidates must qualify and remain qualified for firearms' usage as a condition of employment for the duration of their tenure. A firearms qualification test will be administered annually to determine qualification.

Residency Requirement: The New York State Public Officers Law requires that any person employed as a Corrections Officer in the New York City Department of Correction must be a resident of the City of New York or of Nassau, Westchester, Suffolk, Orange, Rockland, or Putnam counties.

Promotion Opportunities: Employees in the title of Corrections Officer are accorded the opportunity to be promoted to the title of Captain (Correction) and from that title to Warden (Correction) at several levels.

SPECIAL ARRANGEMENTS

Accommodations are available for applicants who provide satisfactory proof of disability. Applications for accommodations must be submitted as early as possible and in no event later than 30 work days before the test or part of a test for which accommodation is requested. Consult General Examination Regulation E.10 for further requirements.

The Department of Personnel makes provisions for candidates claiming inability to participate in an examination when originally scheduled because of the candidate's religious beliefs. Such candidates should consult General Examination Regulation E.11.2 for applicable procedures in requesting a special examination. Such requests must be submitted no later than 15 days before the scheduled date of regular examination.

PHYSICAL FITNESS TEST FOR CITY DEPARTMENT OF PERSONNEL CORRECTIONS OFFICER

In order to become a Corrections Officer, candidates must pass a qualifying physical fitness test. Candidates will be called to take the physical fitness test as the needs of the service require and may be called at any time during the life of the list. Candidates will be called in order of final rating.

Medical evidence to allow participation in the physical fitness test may be required, and the Department of Personnel reserves the right to exclude from the physical test any eligibles who, upon examination of such evidence, are apparently medically unfit. Eligibles will take the physical test at their own risk of injury, although efforts will be made to safeguard them.

Candidates must complete the *entire* course consisting of six events in not more than *42 seconds* (men); *52 seconds* (women).

Candidates who do not complete successfully event 3 will be penalized 8 seconds (men); 9 seconds (women). This penalty will be added to the time required by the candidate to complete the course. Candidates who do not complete successfully event 3 should proceed immediately to the next event. Candidates must remember that they have only 42 seconds (men); 52 seconds (women) to complete the course.

Description of Events

1. Run up 33 steps.

2. Run approximately 43 yards following a designated path, including at least four 90° turns, to a wood box.

3. Push the box, weighing approximately 100 pounds, forward a distance of approximately 5 yards and then back to its original position.

4. Run approximately 10 yards to a dummy, weighing approximately 125 pounds (men), 120 pounds (women), which is hanging with its lowest point approximately 3 feet above the floor.

5. Raise the dummy so as to remove it from its hook, and carry it approximately two yards to a bench. Place the dummy onto the bench under control. *One must not drop or throw*

NOTE

Candidates who do not complete successfully event 5 will fail the test. In order to complete successfully event 5, candidates must meet all of the conditions described for this event.

it down. (Failure to meet all of the conditions for this event will result in failure in the test as a whole.)

6. Run approximately 10 yards to the finish line.

Candidates who fail the test on their first trial will be allowed a second trial on the same date.

SAMPLE COUNTY ANNOUNCEMENT

Personnel Office Announces Civil Service Examination/Corrections Officer

Written Examination Date: April 23

Last File Date: April 6

Completed applications must be postmarked no later than the last filing date, or if not mailed, applications must be delivered to the above address no later than 5:00 p.m. on the last filing date.

DUTIES

Under supervision of a higher-ranking officer, a Corrections Officer is responsible for the custody and security of inmates of the Department of Corrections on an assigned shift. Corrections Officers supervise the movement and activities of inmates; make periodic rounds of assigned areas; conduct searches for contraband; maintain order within the facility; and prepare reports as necessary. They advise inmates on rules and regulations governing the operation of the facility and assist them in resolving problems. Corrections Officers have a high degree of responsibility for their actions and decisions. Officers may be required to carry firearms in the performance of certain duties and to perform other related work as required. Corrections Officers may supervise inmates assigned to work details, and are expected to cooperate in facilitating the prisoner rehabilitation program. They may also participate in the training of other Corrections Officers.

MINIMUM QUALIFICATIONS

Education: By the date of examination, either: (A) Graduation from a standard high school; or (B) possession of a high school equivalency diploma.

Age: Candidates must be not less than 20 years 6 months of age on the date of the written examination. Applicants must be 21 years of age.

Driver's License: Possession of a valid driver's license at time of probationary and permanent appointment.

Residence: There are no residence requirements to participate in the examination, but preference in appointment may be granted to eligibles who have been residents of the County at least 30 days immediately prior to the effective date of probationary appointment.

Medical and Physical Qualifications: Visual acuity must be binocular vision of 20/40 with or without the use of corrective lenses and not less than 20/100 unaided. Candidates who are successful on the written portion of the examination are subject to a medical examination and physical agility examination at a later date. Details on the other medical and physical requirements and content of the agility examination as set by the County Personnel office will be made available to candidates at a later date.

Background Investigation: All applicants will be subject to a pre-employment background investigation and a criminal record search TO BE CONDUCTED BY THE APPOINTING AUTHORITY. Conviction of a felony will bar appointment. Conviction of a misdemeanor or other violation of law may bar examination and/or appointment. A person adjudicated a youthful offender may be disqualified from appointment. Because of the nature of this position, successful candidates will undergo a thorough investigative screening to determine suitability for appointment as a Corrections Officer. Persons who fail to meet the standards set for the investigative screening may be required to submit a fee determined by the State Division of Criminal Justice Services to conduct a criminal record search. The refusal of any candidate to submit the required fee shall, in itself, constitute a declination of a valid offer of appointment. Candidates will be instructed at the appropriate time when and how to submit payment.

As part of the background investigation process, the candidate may be required to participate in substance abuse testing designated by the Appointing Authority, and thereafter may be required to participate in such testing on a periodic basis during the twelve (12)-month probationary period after appointment. Evidence of substance abuse may lead to disqualification from appointment or termination from employment.

Psychological Screening: Candidates who achieve a passing score on the written test may be required by the Appointing Authority to participate in a psychological screening process. Failure to meet the standards set for this screening may contribute to disqualification.

Training Requirements: Successfully complete a 12-week pre-service training program at the county training Academy. Corrections Officers are granted peace officer status under provisions of Section 1.20 of the State Penal Law, subject to the mandatory training requirements under Article 2 of the State Criminal Procedure Law. These training requirements include, but are not limited to, the following: (1) Firearms qualification course; (2) Peace Officer certification course, which meets criteria established by the Municipal Police Training Council; (3) State Basic Corrections Officer Test, administered under the auspices of the State Commission of Correction. All appointees will be required to serve and satisfactorily complete a 52-week probationary period. During this time, job performance will be periodically reviewed and carefully evaluated. Failure to meet training and/or performance standards while on probation may result in termination of employment at any time.

SUBJECT OF EXAMINATION

The *WRITTEN TEST* is designed to test for knowledge, skills, and/or abilities in such areas as:

NOTE

In accordance with law, a Corrections Officer is a peace officer and must be qualified to hold such office. Candidates must be U.S. citizens at the time of probationary appointment.

1. *Memory for Facts and Information.* These questions are designed to test how well the candidates can recall information presented. The candidates will be presented with information describing or depicting prison scenes or other facts. They will have a short time to memorize the information before it is collected by the monitor. They will then be asked to recall specific details.

2. *Reasoning Clearly and Making Sound Decisions Related to Security and Control of Inmates and General Officer–Inmate Relations.* This subtest is a sampling of fundamental concepts and/or their application to situations in the Correction field.

    The subtest will deal with, but will not necessarily be restricted to, such areas as relations with inmates, other officers including superior officers, and the general public. This subtest will not require the candidate to have any prior knowledge of rules, regulations, or procedures of any correction facility.

3. *Understanding and Interpreting Written Material.* These questions are designed to test how well the candidates comprehend written material.

    The candidates are provided with brief selections and are asked questions relating to the selections. All the information required to answer the questions is presented in the selections; the candidates are not required to have any special knowledge relating to the content area covered in the selections.

NOTE

If one does not have original copies of the documents, begin to secure them now. You will not be processed unless you have them on the date of your physical exam.

4. *Preparing Written Material.* These questions are designed to test how well the candidates can express themselves in writing. Particular emphasis is placed upon two major aspects of written communication: how to clearly and accurately express given information, and how to present written material in the most logical and comprehensive manner.

Upon passing the written part of the exam, applicants will be scheduled to appear for a medical exam. At that time, you will be required to show proof of the following documents:

- High school diploma or GED

- Birth certificate

- Residency (one month prior to the date of the written exam and one month prior to the date of your physical exam)

- Driver's license (Parts I and II include convictions)

- Citizenship certificate (if you are a naturalized U.S. citizen)

INSURANCE BENEFITS

Health: Hospital/Major Medical.

Dental: Coverage plan through the Tri-County Federation of Police.

Prescription Drugs: Full coverage PCS Plan, $3 service charge.

Optical Plan: Full coverage to employees and their dependents.

Life Insurance: After 1 year of employment in the State Retirement System. Additional coverage at low-cost premiums through COBA + Special Line-of-Duty Death Benefits—County Government ($100,000) and Federal Government ($50,000).

LEAVE BENEFITS

12 days—Paid holidays

10 days—Annual leave

15 days—After 1 year of service

20 days—After 15 years of service

5 days—Personal leave per year

12 days—Sick leave

Occupational Injury Benefits

OTHER BENEFITS

Credit Union: Payroll deduction savings and loan program.

Consumer Buying Power: Discount purchasing plan.

Disability Insurance: Optional coverage through COBA.

Retirement Plan: State Retirement System (Tier 4).

Work Schedule: Shift assignments (7–3, 3–11, 11–7) are made at the discretion of the Division administrator. Correction Officers work a 3–2/3–3 work schedule, with three successive days off every other week. Attendance on the three "pay-back" days per year for in-service training and/or firearms requalification is mandatory.

PERSONNEL OFFICE—INVESTIGATION SECTION

When appearing for the investigative screening at the medical examination, applicants must submit satisfactory evidence of the following:

1. Date and place of birth (birth certificate, baptismal certificate showing date and place of birth, school record, naturalization certificate).

2. Proof of residence (utility bills, tax receipts, leases, copy of tax return, W-2 forms, mortgage payments, rent receipts) *one month prior to date of Written Test and at the present time.*

3. High school graduation or equivalency diploma as claimed on the application.

4. Discharge papers and DD-214, if you served in the Armed Forces.

5. A valid state driver's license—Part I and Record of Convictions.

6. Personal History Statement must be completed, signed and brought to the screening.

7. Passport-sized picture (color or black and white).

NOTE

Only original documents listed above are acceptable. Failure to surrender these documents and to submit the necessary evidence will disqualify candidate until they are submitted.

County Personnel Office Medical Standards for Corrections Officer

ACCEPTABLE WEIGHT IN POUNDS ACCORDING TO FRAME (MEN)

A	B	C	D
Height (in bare feet) Feet/Inches	Small Frame	Medium Frame	Large Frame
5' 2"	128-134	131-141	138-150
5' 3"	130-136	133-143	140-153
5' 4"	132-148	135-145	142-153
5' 5"	134-140	137-148	144-160
5' 6"	136-142	139-151	146-164
5' 7"	138-145	142-154	149-168
5' 8"	140-148	145-157	152-172
5' 9"	142-151	148-160	155-176
5' 10"	144-154	151-163	158-180
5' 11"	146-157	154-166	161-184
6' 0"	149-160	157-170	164-188
6' 1"	152-164	160-174	168-192
6' 2"	155-168	164-178	172-197
6' 3"	158-172	167-182	176-202
6' 4"	162-176	171-187	181-207

ACCEPTABLE WEIGHT IN POUNDS ACCORDING TO FRAME (WOMEN)

A	B	C	D
Height (in bare feet) Feet/Inches	Small Frame	Medium Frame	Large Frame
4' 10"	102-111	109-121	118-131
4' 11"	103-113	111-123	120-134
5' 0"	104-115	113-126	122-137
5' 1"	106-118	115-129	125-140
5' 2"	108-121	116-132	128-143
5' 3"	111-124	121-135	131-147
5' 4"	114-127	124-138	134-151
5' 5"	117-130	127-141	137-155
5' 6"	120-133	130-144	149-159
5' 7"	123-136	133-147	143-163
5' 8"	126-139	136-150	146-167
5' 9"	129-142	139-153	149-170
5' 10"	132-145	142-156	152-173
5' 11"	135-148	145-159	155-176
6' 0"	138-151	148-162	158-179

NOTE: Although the above tables commence at specified heights, no minimum height requirement has been prescribed. These tables of height and weight will be adhered to in all instances except where the Civil Service examining physician certifies that weight in excess of that shown in the table (up to a maximum of 20 pounds) is lean body mass and not fat. Decision as to frame size of a candidate shall be made by the examining physician.

The following tests will be part of the physical examination:

- Vision
- Hearing
- Serology
- Urinalysis
- Chest X-Ray to be taken at a later date
- Blood Pressure

A color perception test will not be part of the examination since color blindness is not a disqualifying condition.

Visual Acuity Standards: The minimum acceptable standard of visual acuity (uncorrected) shall be 20/100 binocular vision, total vision corrected to 20/40. Candidates for whom visual acuity is recorded at 20/100 will be required to be re-examined at the county Medical Center at a later date. Vision at the time of such exam must be between 20/20 and 20/100 for candidate to be qualified.

CORRECTIONS OFFICER PHYSICAL FITNESS TEST

In order to become a Corrections Officer, candidates must pass a qualifying physical fitness test.

Medical evidence to allow participation in the physical fitness test may be required, and the Department of Personnel reserves the right to exclude from the physical test any eligibles who, upon examination of such evidence, are apparently medically unfit. Eligibles will take the physical fitness test at their own risk of injury, although efforts will be made to safeguard them.

Candidates must complete the *entire* course consisting of seven events in not more than *65 seconds.*

Description of Events

1. Run up approximately 40 steps.

2. Run approximately 40 yards following a designated path, including at least four 90° turns, to a sandbag.

3. Push the sandbag, weighing approximately 100 pounds, forward a distance of approximately 5 yards and then back to its original position. (Failure to meet all of the conditions for this event will result in failure in the test as a whole.)

4. Run approximately 10 yards to a dummy, weighing approximately 110 pounds, which is hanging with its lowest point approximately 3 feet above the floor.

5. Raise the dummy so as to lift the attached ring off the metal pipe. Allow the dummy to slide onto the floor. *You must not drop it or throw it down.* (Failure to meet all of the conditions for this event will result in failure in the test as a whole.)

6. Step up approximately 18 inches and walk across a 12-foot beam by placing one foot in front of the other until you reach the other end. (You must be in control at all times and falling off the beam will result in failure of the test as a whole.)

7. Run approximately 10 yards to the finish line.
   Candidates who fail the test on their first trial will be allowed a second trial on the same date after a rest period.

Candidates who do not successfully complete all the events in their proper sequence will fail the test.

NOTE

In accordance with the requirements of the Americans with Disabilities Act, there are some differential standards for women and older candidates in terms of time and weight lifting. **Candidates who do not successfully complete events 3, 5, and 6 will fail the test.**

SAMPLE COUNTY ANNOUNCEMENT

We're looking for a few good people. Why not you?

Our County, voted one of the best places to live and work, is seeking successful candidates for an interesting, challenging, and flexible career as a . . .

Civilian Detention Officer

Successful candidates must meet the following qualifications:

- U.S. citizenship

- 21 years of age (minimum)

- High school graduate (minimum)

- Good credit and driving history with no criminal background

- Flexibility to work all shifts

- Successful completion of basic training within the first year of employment

Salary: $23,500 (Negotiable based on education and experience)

Why not experience what our County has to offer? Excellent benefits package—health, dental, 5% contribution to 401(k), training opportunities, and more.

To become part of our team, visit our office.

SAMPLE COUNTY ANNOUNCEMENT

Detention Officer I

County Sheriff's Office

Our detention center is expanding by 70 percent. Many new positions are available. We need individuals who can manage inmates in a direct-supervision facility through conflict resolution and proactive problem solving.

Duties are: conducting inmate surveillance; performing searches and facility foot patrol; processing legal documents/reports; operating computers; fingerprinting/photographing arrestees; performing crisis intervention; mediating disputes; and restraining inmates. Rotating shift work is required.

Applications are accepted on a continuous basis; testing usually is performed in March, June, and September.

Testing consists of a written exam, interviews, background investigation, and medical and psychological exams. Must be at least 21 years old and a high school graduate.

Salary is $2,625/month plus benefits.

SAMPLE STATE ANNOUNCEMENT

Corrections Officer Trainee (Spanish Speaking)

The Positions: Corrections Officer positions are located throughout the state in the various facilities of the State Department of Correctional Services. As a Corrections Officer, under the direct supervision of a high-ranking officer, you would be responsible for the custody and security, as well as the safety and well-being, of criminal offenders in State correctional facilities and correction camps. As a Corrections Officer (Spanish Speaking), you would be assigned to a facility with a heavy concentration of Spanish-speaking inmates.

As a Corrections Officer, you would also supervise the movement and activities of inmates; make periodic rounds of assigned areas; conduct searches for contraband; maintain order within the facility; and prepare reports as necessary. You would advise inmates on the rules and regulations governing the operation of the facility and assist them in resolving problems. You would have a high degree of responsibility for your actions and decisions. You may also be required to carry firearms in the performance of certain duties and to perform other related work as required.

THERE ARE NO REQUIREMENTS FOR ADMISSION TO THE EXAMINATION.

If you pass the written test, you will be contacted, in rank order, to complete a background investigation, a physical/medical examination, and psychological evaluation. You must successfully complete each of these in order to be eligible for appointment.

It will be necessary for you to come to the state capital on two separate days, at your own expense, in order to complete these activities.

Background Investigation: If you pass the written test, you will undergo a thorough background investigation to determine your suitability for appointment as Corrections Officer. Conviction of a felony will bar appointment. Conviction of misdemeanors or violations of law may bar appointment. A person adjudicated a youthful offender may be disqualified from appointment. Failure to meet the standards for the background investigation will result in disqualification.

Physical/Medical: If you pass the written test, you must meet the physical/medical standards for Corrections Officer. These include binocular visual acuity not less than 20/20 with or without correction (if correction is required, binocular visual acuity not less than 20/40 without correction) and satisfactory hearing. You will also be required to pay a medical laboratory fee.

Psychological Screening: If you pass the written test, you will also be required to participate in a psychological screening process. Failure to meet the standards set for this screening will result in disqualification.

Minimum Age: You must be at least 21 years old. (If you are less than 20 years of age at the time of the written test, you are unlikely to become appointable before the eligible lists are superseded by eligible lists resulting from the next examinations for these titles.)

Education: You must be a high school graduate or have a high school equivalency diploma (issued by an appropriate State education authority). Diplomas issued through a home-study course and not by an appropriate educational authority are not acceptable.

NOTE: Written Test to be held on April 23. Applications MUST be postmarked no later than March 7.

1. In accordance with State law, a Corrections Officer is a peace officer and must be qualified to hold such office and must be a U.S. citizen.

2. If you pass the written test for Corrections Officer (Spanish Speaking) and are considered for appointment, you will be required to demonstrate your proficiency in the Spanish language. Proficiency must be at a level that will assure your ability to perform the duties of the position properly.

3. If you apply for Corrections Officer Trainee (Spanish Speaking), we urge you to apply for both examinations.

4. All appointees will be employed as Trainees.

Selection: There will be a written test that you must pass in order to be considered for appointment. The written test will be designed to test for knowledge, skills, and/or abilities in such areas as: reasoning clearly and making sound decisions related to security and control of inmates and general officer-inmate relations; understanding and interpreting written material; preparing material; and memory for facts and information.

Traineeship: Please notify the Department of Civil Service if you change your mailing address after filing for the examination. You will be required to participate in, and satisfactorily complete, all requirements of a 12-month training program before you can advance to Corrections Officer. As part of the program, you will attend the Correctional Services Training Academy. Training at the Academy will include academic courses in such areas as emergency response procedures, interpersonal communications, legal rights and responsibilities, security procedures, and concepts and issues in correction. Successful completion of the weapons training course is mandatory for continued employment. Trainees will also receive rigorous physical training to develop fitness, strength, and stamina. Failure to maintain the required academic standing, to qualify with weapons, or to qualify in meeting the physical standards will result in termination of employment. Formal Academy training will last six weeks, followed by a six-week period of on-the-job training. At that point, you will be assigned to a correctional facility for full duty. A probationer who fails to meet the training standards while at the Academy may be terminated because of such failure.

Probation: All appointees will be required to serve and satisfactorily complete a 52-week probationary period. During probation, performance will be periodically reviewed and carefully evaluated. A probationer who fails to meet the performance standards may be terminated at any time.

State Residence Requirements: If you are appointed from a list, you may be required to furnish the appointing authority with acceptable documentation establishing your identity and eligibility for employment in the United States.

Fees: File one processing fee. The required fee must accompany your application. Send check or money order payable to the Department of Civil Service and write the examination number(s) and your social security number on your check or money order. Do not send cash. As no refunds will be made, you are urged to compare your qualifications carefully with the requirements for admission and file only for those examinations for which you are clearly qualified. You are responsible for payment of a clinical laboratory test fee if medical examination is required prior to appointment.

An exception to both the processing fee and the clinical laboratory test fee, when required, will be made only for persons receiving Supplemental Social Security payments or public assistance (Home Relief or Aid to Dependent Children), provided Foster Care, or certified Job Training Partnership Act eligible through a state or local social service agency, and for those who are unemployed and primarily responsible for the support of a household. Individuals wishing to claim this waiver of fee on the basis of Supplemental Social Security, Home Relief, or Aid to Dependent Children must certify on their applications that they are receiving public assistance, and must indicate the type of assistance they are receiving, the agency providing the assistance and their case numbers. Persons claiming this waiver through the Foster Care or Job Training Partnership Act Certification must specify the program and name of their contact agency. Such claims are subject to later verification and, if not supported by appropriate documentation, are grounds for barring appointment.

NOTE: Fingerprints are sometimes required at the time of appointment. When they are required, the fee involved must be paid by the appointee.

It is the policy of the Department of Civil Service to provide for and promote the equal opportunity for employment, compensation, and other terms and conditions of employment without discrimination because of age, race, creed, color, national origin, sex, sexual orientation, disability, or marital status.

SAMPLE FEDERAL ANNOUNCEMENT

U.S. Department of Justice

Federal Bureau of Prisons Correctional Officer Application Booklet

AGE NOTICE

Public Law 101-509 establishes the mandatory retirement age of fifty-seven for persons in Federal law enforcement positions. 5 U.S.C. §3307 specifies that the head of an agency may determine and fix the maximum age limit for an original appointment to a position as a law enforcement officer. Therefore, the Attorney General has determined that the initial appointment of employees into Federal Bureau of Prisons' law enforcement positions must be prior to their thirty-seventh birthday.

Exceptions

Physician Assistant	No age limit
Medical Officer	No age limit
Registered Nurse	Waiver can be requested prior to fortieth birthday
Psychologist	Waiver can be requested prior to fortieth birthday
Chaplains:	
Catholic	No age limit
Islamic	No age limit
Jewish	No age limit

The above exceptions to the maximum entry age requirement pertaining to law enforcement officer positions have been granted by the Attorney General based on a determination that a shortage exists in the Federal Bureau of Prisons for qualified applicants under the age of thirty-seven.

DEAR CORRECTIONAL OFFICER APPLICANT:

The Bureau of Prisons Examining Section uses an automated rating system to process applications for the Correctional Officer Register. This system requires applicants to record responses to multiple-choice questions on a computerized form (Qualifications & Availability Form [Form C]).

Form "C" is a self-reporting examining instrument. Qualifications and ratings are based on the responses you report; therefore, respond accurately and completely to each of the occupational questions. It is extremely important for applicants to follow directions carefully and provide only one response that most accurately reflects your education, and/or experience, to each question. Also, it is extremely important to thoroughly read the enclosed correctional officer announcement 431 and the "Important Notice" prior to completing Form C. The "Important Notice" provides instructions on how to properly evaluate your education/experience. These instructions must be followed in order to accurately report your qualifications on Form C. If the instructions are not followed, your notice of results will not reflect an accurate evaluation of your qualifications for the position. You must also submit an application or resume reflecting the information on the "required information" sheet.

REQUIRED INFORMATION

Job Information

- Announcement number, title, and grade of the job you are applying for.

- Full name, mailing address (include ZIP Code), and home and work telephone numbers (include area codes).

- Social security number and birth date.

- Citizenship. (Most federal jobs require United States citizenship.)

- Veteran's preference. (Form SF-15, Claim for 10-point Veteran's preference and supporting proof if you are claiming preference.)

Education

- High school name, city, and state (ZIP Code if known) of high school where you earned diploma or GED (give dates).

- College name, city, and state (ZIP Code if known), majors, type and year of any degrees; or if no degree, show courses and credit hours earned (indicate semester or quarter).

Work Experience

Give the following for each job-related paid or non-paid civilian or military work experience (Do not send job descriptions.):

- job title (and series and grade if federal job)

- duties and accomplishments

- employer's name and address

- supervisor's name and telephone number

- starting and ending dates

- hours worked per week

- salary

Indicate if we may contact your current supervisor.

SUMMING IT UP

- Corrections Officers may work in a variety of settings, including federal, state, and private prisons or jails.

- The Federal Bureau of Prisons and State Departments of Corrections are two good places to start your job search.

- Take some time to think about your likes and dislikes prior to applying for a position as a Corrections Officer. Make sure that you have the sufficient interest necessary to work in this field. Not everyone is suited to work in a prison or jail.

The Examination Process

chapter 3

OVERVIEW

- Written exam
- Promotion exam
- Interview
- Drug test
- Medical examination
- Physical fitness test
- Background investigation
- Psychological interview
- Summing it up

WRITTEN EXAM

As you have learned from reading the various announcements, each jurisdiction that administers a Corrections Officer Exam seems to have a somewhat different idea of what skills and abilities should be tested and of how to go about testing them. The exams cover far too many subjects for us to give you detailed instruction in all of them. Furthermore, many exam subjects do not lend themselves to instruction. Judgment and reasoning, for instance, tend to be natural strengths that may be enhanced by life's experiences but cannot be taught.

Other subjects lend themselves more readily to further discussion and to suggestions for tackling the questions. The following descriptions explore some of the types of questions that appear on the Corrections Officer Exam, one type at a time. Our approach to each type of question is different because the demands made by each type of question are different.

Observation and Memory

This section concentrates on improving your powers of observation. It points out what to look for and how to look for it. The exercises direct your attention to details and help you to focus your concentration as you must when taking an exam and when serving as a Corrections Officer.

Take your time with these exercises. Try to anticipate the questions that might be asked about each photo. If you train yourself to notice the details in these exercises, you should feel more confident when faced with memory and observation questions on your exam.

HOW TO ANSWER OBSERVATION AND MEMORY QUESTIONS

Memory is a very individualized skill. Some people remember details of what they see and hear; others remember only the most obvious facts. Some people memorize easily; others find memorizing very difficult. Some people remember forever; others forget in a short time. Some people can memorize in a systematic manner; others are haphazard in their methods or have no method at all.

Car Repair

Let us begin by looking together at the photograph "Car Repair." Start with the people:

1. How many people are in the photograph?

2. How many men? How many women?

3. What do the people appear to be doing?

4. What is the man holding in his hands?

5. Note the clothing: Both are wearing light-colored shirts; the man is wearing shorts. Are any shoes visible in the photograph? Is the woman wearing any jewelry?

6. Note hair. Does the woman have light or dark hair? How would you describe her hairstyle? Does the man have a mustache or beard?

7. Note the expressions. Is the woman looking at the man? What is she looking at? How would you describe her expression?

Observe the action:

8. What part of the car is visible?

9. What does the man have in his right hand? What is he probably doing? What is he holding in his left hand?

10. What might be the relationship of the man to the woman?

11. Are both people under the hood of the car, or just the man?

Note the background:

12. What time of day is it?

13. What season could it be?

14. Is there anything visible in the background?

A good question writer could easily develop ten questions based upon these observations. Would you have noticed everything and made note as well about what was *not* there?

In looking at a photograph, focus first on the people. Notice their clothing, physical features, and activities. Count, but also make note of which person or persons are wearing what, doing what, interacting with whom, and so on. Then notice the prominent objects. Next, turn your attention to the background floors, walls, etc. Finally, start at the left side of the photograph and move your eyes slowly to the right, noticing special details such as numbers, calibrations, dirt spots, unidentified objects, etc. If you work very hard at noticing, you are likely to remember what you noticed, at least for the duration of the exam.

Refreshments

Let us look at the photograph "Refreshments."

1. The people in the picture are . . . number, sex, age.

2. The people are wearing . . . notice the pattern of the man's shirt, and the woman's sweater. (Also notice that she is wearing layered clothing. What are the girls wearing?

3. Notice hair color, type (curly or straight), and length and style.

4. Note that no shoes are visible. Is anyone wearing glasses, a watch, or a hat? Is the woman wearing a necklace or ring?

5. What is the woman holding in her hands?

6. Who is standing? Who is sitting? On what?

7. What is the design of the tablecloth?

8. What else is on the table? Notice beverages, bread, condiments, and other items.

9. What is on the ground? Snow? Sand? Gravel? Grass? Rocks? Flowers?

10. The day is ... Cold? Warm? Rainy? Cloudy? Sunny? Where is the sun in the picture?

11. In the background are (is) . . . Mountains? Trees? Water? Boats? Tents? More grass? Other people? Animals?

12. Is the sky visible" What else is on the land?

13. What is the shape of the table?

14. Is the family likely sitting on chairs or on a bench?

15. How many beverage cans or bottles?

16. Is there any activity in the background?

17. Describe the food on the table. Is anyone eating? Who is interacting with whom?

How did you do with this photograph? Are you developing skill at noticing everything?

A Family Camping

Study the photograph titled A Family Camping. On a plain piece of paper, make as comprehensive a list as you can. Try to notice every detail on which you could possibly be quizzed. When you have completed your list, compare it with ours that follows. If you noticed everything that we did, you are becoming very observant. Perhaps you found details that we missed. If so, congratulate yourself and keep up the good work.

On the actual exam, you will not be permitted to write any notes. You will have to make observations and hold them as mental notes only. This exercise, however, will be more effective if you jot down everything you see.

Here is our list:

1. There are five people in the photograph, two adults and three children.

2. Two people are sitting in chairs—a woman and a child.

3. The man on the bike has his right foot on the pedal and his left on the ground.

4. The child on the chair has a bandaid on his knee.

5. The man on his bike has dark hair; the other four people have light-colored hair.

6. The child on the chair is wearing sandals; the others are wearing sneakers.

7. The little girl has her right hand on the wheel of the bike.

8. The seated woman and the seated child are wearing denim overalls.

9. In the foreground is a light-colored dome tent with a canopy over the entrance.

10. The tent faces the cliff.

11. The girl leaning on the chair is wearing a striped, sleeveless shirt.

12. There are three chairs in the picture.

13. All five people are wearing light-colored socks.

14. The man on the bike has his right hand on the handle bars and his left hand is not visible.

15. There is no grass in the background; the ground is dirt.

16. The little girl and the man on the bike are both wearing denim shorts and white shirts.

17. Not visible: sky, trees, other people, animals, cars.

By now you should be getting pretty good at this activity.

Classroom

Study the final photograph of the Classroom. Make this exercise an observation and memory exercise rather than just an observation exercise. Study the photograph for 5 minutes. Make mental notes of as many details as you can, but do not do any writing at this time. Close the book and write as many details as you can remember. When you have written all that you can remember, draw a line on your paper and reopen the book. Add to the list any details that you forgot or previously overlooked. Then compare your list with ours.

1. The scene is a classroom. The students are male and female; the instructor is a woman.

2. The students are all seated; the teacher is standing.

3. The teacher has short, dark hair. She wears a dress, a jacket, and dark shoes.

4. The teacher wears a watch on her left wrist. She has papers in her right hand.

5. The teacher is not wearing glasses. She is facing the class and her mouth is open as if she is speaking to the class.

6. Seven students are visible.

7. One student is wearing overalls. The student is a female with short, dark hair.

8. The students are seated on chairs with attached desks.

9. The students all appear to be attentive.

10. While some students are holding a pen or pencil, none appears to be writing.

11. The room lighting is not visible.

12. The floor is made of square tiles.

13. On the wall beside the teacher is a chalkboard. There is writing on the chalkboard and a box around some of the writing.

14. An eraser and a piece of chalk are on the ledge of the chalkboard.

15. In the background are open windows.

16. Outside the windows are a tree and a grassy area.

17. There is an empty chair in the far left corner of the room.

18. The floor tiles are in dark and light squares and in a grid-like pattern.

19. There is a shelf beneath each of the desks.

20. One student is wearing sandals.

This was a very difficult exercise. The classroom is cluttered and the photograph filled with details. Your own exam, which will ask only a few questions about each photograph, is unlikely to quiz you about truly unimportant details or about features of the photographs that did not reproduce clearly. After your experience with these exercises, however, you should know how to look at photographs and how to commit important details to memory.

Reading Comprehension

There is a system to use in approaching reading comprehension passages and questions. This section will teach it to you.

TIP
The key to success with reading questions is not speed but comprehension.

Civil service exams are not, as a rule, heavily speeded. There is ample time in which to complete the exam, provided that you do not spend excessive time struggling with one or two "impossible" questions. If you are reading with comprehension, your mind will not wander, and your speed will be adequate.

Between now and test day, you must work to improve your reading concentration and comprehension. Your daily newspaper provides excellent material to improve your reading with the first paragraph or two of articles. Read with a pencil in hand. Underscore details and ideas that seem to be crucial to the meaning of the article. Notice points of view, arguments, and supporting information. When you have finished the article, summarize it for yourself. Do you know the purpose of the article? The main idea presented? The attitude of the writer? The points over which there is controversy? Did you find certain information lacking? As you answer these questions, skim back over the parts you have underlined. Did you focus on important words and ideas? Did you read with comprehension?

As you repeat this process day after day, you will find that your reading will become more efficient. You will read with greater understanding, and will "get more" from your newspaper. One aspect of your daily reading that deserves special attention is vocabulary building. The most effective reader has a rich, extensive vocabulary. As you read, make a list of unfamiliar words. Include in your list words that you understand within the context of the article but that you cannot really define. In addition, mark words that you do not understand at all. When you put aside your newspaper, go to the dictionary and look up every new and unfamiliar word. Write the word and its definition in a special notebook. Writing the words and their definitions helps seal them in your memory far better than just reading them, and the notebook serves as a handy reference for your own use. A sensitivity to the meanings of words and an understanding of more words will make reading easier and more enjoyable even if none of the words you learn in this way crops up on your exam. Vocabulary building is a good lifetime habit to develop.

Success with reading questions depends on more than reading comprehension. You must also know how to draw the answers from the reading selection and be able to distinguish the best answer from a number of answers that all seem to be good ones, or from a number of answers that all seem to be wrong.

Strange as it may seem, it's a good idea to approach reading comprehension questions by reading the questions—not the answer choices, just the questions themselves—before you read the selection. The questions will alert you to look for certain details, ideas, and points of view. Use your pencil. Underscore key words in the question. These will help you direct your attention as you read.

Next, skim the selection very rapidly to get an idea of its subject matter and its organization. If key words or ideas pop out at you, underline them, but do not consciously search out details in the preliminary skimming.

Now read the selection carefully with comprehension as your main goal. Underscore the important words as you have been doing in your newspaper reading.

Finally, return to the questions. Read each question carefully. Be sure you know what it asks. Misreading of questions is a major cause of error on reading comprehension tests. Read all the answer choices. Eliminate the obviously incorrect answers. You may be left with only one possible answer. If you find yourself with more than one possible answer, reread the question. Then skim the passage once more, focusing on the underlined segments. By now you should be able to conclude which answer is best.

Reading comprehension questions may take a number of different forms. These include:

1. **Question of fact or detail.** You may have to mentally rephrase or rearrange, but you should find the answer stated in the body of the selection.

2. **Best title or main idea.** The answer may be obvious, but the incorrect choices to the "main idea" question are often half-truths that are ideas or supporting ideas quoted directly from the text. The correct answer is the one that covers the largest part of the selection.

3. **Interpretation.** This type of question asks you what the question means, not just what it says.

4. **Inference.** This is the most difficult type of reading comprehension question. It asks you to go beyond what the selection says, and to predict what might happen next. Your answer must be based upon the information in the selection and your own common sense, but not upon any other information you may have about that subject. A variation of the inference question might be stated as, "The author would expect that . . . ." To answer this question, you must understand the author's point of view, and then make an inference from that viewpoint based upon the information in the selection.

5. **Vocabulary.** Some civil service reading sections, directly or indirectly, ask the meaning of certain words used in the selection.

Before you begin the practice tests, review this list of hints for scoring high on reading comprehension tests:

1 Read the questions and underline key words.

2 Skim the selection to get a general idea of the subject matter, the point that is being made, and organization of the material.

3 Reread the selection giving attention to details and point of view. Underscore key words and phrases.

4 If the author has quoted material from another source, be sure that you understand the purpose of the quote. Does the author agree or disagree?

5 Carefully read each question or incomplete statement. Determine exactly what is being asked. Watch for negatives or all-inclusive words, such as *always, never, all, only, every, absolutely, completely, none, entirely,* and *no.*

6 Read all the answer choices. Eliminate those choices that are obviously incorrect. Reread the remaining choices and refer to the selection, if necessary, to determine the *best* answer.

7 Avoid inserting your own judgments into your answers. Even if you disagree with the author or spot a factual error in the selection, you must answer on the basis of what is stated or implied in the selection.

8 Do not allow yourself to spend too much time on any one question. If looking back at the selection does not help you to find or figure out the answer, choose from among the answers, mark the question in the test booklet, and go on. If you have time at the end of the exam, go back and check your answers in that section.

English Grammar and Usage

Questions testing your facility with English usage and grammar are often included in employment examinations in an effort to test your ability to recognize good, clear writing. If you can choose the most effective means of expressing a thought, then, by inference, it is concluded that you are able to express yourself well in writing. The following Grammar and Usage Review is meant to serve as a quick refresher course. It should "bring back" the rules, hints, and suggestions supplied by many teachers over the years.

PARTS OF SPEECH

- A **noun** is the name of a person, place, thing, or idea: *teacher, city, desk, democracy.*
- A **pronoun** substitutes for a noun: *he, they, ours, those.*
- An **adjective** describes a noun: *warm, quick, tall, blue.*
- A **verb** expresses action or state of being: *yell, interpret, fell, are.*

- An **adverb** modifies a verb, an adjective, or another adverb: *fast, slowly, friendly, well.*

- A **conjunction** joins words, sentences, and phrases: *and, but, or.*

- A **preposition** shows position in time or space: *in, during, after, behind.*

Nouns

There are different kinds of nouns:

- **Common nouns** are general: *house, girl, street, city.*

- **Proper nouns** are specific: *White House, Jane, Main Street, New York.*

- **Collective nouns** name groups: *team, crowd, organization, Congress.*

Nouns have cases:

- **Nominative**—the subject, noun of address, or predicate noun.

- **Objective**—the direct object, indirect object, or object of the preposition.

- **Possessive**—the form that shows possession.

Pronouns

A pronoun must agree with the noun to which it refers in gender, person, and number. There are several kinds of pronouns:

- Demonstrative pronouns: *this, that, these, those*

- Indefinite pronouns: *all, any, anybody*

- Interrogative pronouns: *who, which, what*

Personal Pronouns			
	Nominative	**Objective**	**Possessive**
Singular			
1st person	I	me	mine
2nd person	you	you	yours
3rd person	he, she, it	him, her, it	his, hers, its
Plural			
1st person	we	us	ours
2nd person	you	you	yours
3rd person	they	them	theirs

Adjectives

Adjectives answer the questions "Which one?" "What kind?" and "How many?" There are three uses of adjectives:

- A **noun modifier** is usually placed directly before the noun it describes: He is a *tall* man.

- A **predicate adjective** follows an inactive verb and modifies the subject: He is *happy*. I feel *terrible*.

- An **article** (or **noun marker**) is another name for these adjectives: *the, a, an*.

Verbs

Verbs are the most important part of speech. A verb may stand alone, as an imperative sentence such as "Stop!" Conversely, no group of words can function as a sentence without a verb.

Attributes of a Verb

Mood	*I laugh.* (indicative—factual)
	If I were laughing . . . (subjective—wishful)
	Laugh! (imperative—forceful)
Voice	*I moved the chair.* (active)
	The chair was moved by me. (passive)
Agreement of Persons and Number	*We don't know.* (1st person plural subject and verb)
	He doesn't know. (3rd person singular subject and verb)
Tense	*I laugh.* (present)
	We had laughed. (past perfect)
	She will be laughing. (future progressive)

Type of Verbs

Transitive	*We invited our friends.* (completed by a noun or pronoun)
Intransitive	*She fell. She fell down.* (completed in itself or by an adverb)
Copulative	*She is pretty. We felt bad. He appeared depressed.* (a form of *is* or a sensory/seeming verb)

Principal Parts of a Verb			
	Present	**Past**	**Present Perfect**
Regular	walk	walked	have walked
	bathe	bathed	have bathed
Irregular	ring	rang	have rung
	eat	ate	have eaten

Verb Tenses			
Simple Tenses	**Past**	**Present**	**Future**
Simple	I walked.	I walk.	I will walk.
Progressive	I was walking.	I am walking.	I will be walking.
Emphatic	I did walk.	I do walk.	

Perfect Tenses		
Past Perfect	**Present Perfect**	**Future Perfect**
I had walked.	I have walked.	I will have walked.
I had walked three miles by the time you met me.	I have walked three miles to get here.	I will have walked three miles by the time you catch up with me.
Activity begun and completed in the past before some other past action	Activity begun in the past, completed in the present	Activity begun at any time and completed in the future

Adverbs

Adverbs answer the questions "Why?" "How?" "Where?" "When?" and "To what degree?" Adverbs modify:

ALERT!

Adverbs should NOT be used to modify nouns.

- Verbs: The old man walked *slowly*.

- Adjectives: It was an *unusually hot summer*.

- Other adverbs: The days passed *too quickly*.

SELECTED RULES OF GRAMMAR

1 The subject of a verb is in the nominative case even if the verb is understood and not expressed. *Example*:

> They are as old as *we*. (. . . as *we are*)

2 The word *who* is in the nominative case. *Whom* is in the objective case. *Examples*:

> The trapeze artist *who* ran away with the clown broke the lion tamer's heart. (*Who* is the subject of the verb *ran*.)

> The trapeze artist *whom* he loved ran away with the circus clown. (*Whom* is the object of the verb *loved*.)

3 The word *whoever* is in the nominative case. *Whomever* is in the objective case. *Examples*:

> *Whoever* comes to the door is welcome to join the party. (*Whoever* is the subject of the verb *comes*.)
>
> Invite *whomever* you wish to accompany you. (*Whomever* is the object of the verb *invite*.)

4 Nouns or pronouns connected by a form of the verb *to be* should always be in the nominative case. *Example*:

> It is *I*. (Not *me*.)

5 A pronoun that is the object of a preposition or of a transitive verb must be in the objective case. *Examples*:

> It would be impossible for *me* to do that job alone. (*Me* is the object of the preposition *for*.)
>
> The attendant gave *me* the keys to the locker. (*Me* is the indirect object of the verb *gave*.)

6 *Each, either, neither, anyone, anybody, somebody, someone, every, everyone, one, no one,* and *nobody* are singular pronouns. Each of these words takes a singular verb and a singular pronoun. *Examples*:

> *Neither likes* the pets of the other.
> *Everyone* must wait *his* turn.
> *Each* of the patients *carries* insurance.
> *Neither* of the women *has* completed *her* assignment.

7 When the correlative conjunctions *either/or* and *neither/nor* are used, the number of the verb agrees with the number of the last subject. *Examples*:

> Neither John nor Greg *eats* meat.
> Either the cat or the *mice take* charge in the barn.

8 A subject consisting of two or more nouns joined by a coordinating conjunction takes a plural verb. *Example*:

> Paul *and* Sue *were* the last to arrive.

9 The number of the verb is not affected by the addition to the subject of words introduced by *with, together with, no less than, as well as,* etc. *Example*:

> The *captain*, together with the rest of the team, *was delighted* by the victory celebration.

10 A verb agrees in number with its subject. A verb should not be made to agree with a noun that is part of a phrase following the subject. *Examples*:

> *Mount Snow*, one of my favorite ski areas, *is* in Vermont.
> The *mountains* of Colorado, like those of Switzerland, *offer* excellent skiing.

⑪ A verb should agree in number with the subject, not with the predicate noun or pronoun. *Examples*:

> Poor study *habits are* the leading cause of unsatisfactory achievement in school.
>
> The leading *cause* of unsatisfactory achievement in school *is* poor study habits.

⑫ A pronoun agrees with its antecedent in person, number, and gender. *Example*:

> Since you were absent on Tuesday, you will have to ask Mary or Beth for *her* notes on the lecture. (Use *her*, not *their*, because two singular antecedents joined by *or* take a singular pronoun.)

⑬ *Hardly, scarcely, barely, only*, and *but* (when it means *only*) are negative words. Do NOT use another negative in conjunction with any of these words. *Examples*:

> He *didn't have but* one hat. (WRONG)
>
> He had *but* one hat. OR: He had *only* one hat. (CORRECT)
>
> I *can't hardly* read the small print. (WRONG)
>
> I *can hardly* read the small print. OR: I *can't* read the small print. (CORRECT)

⑭ *As* is a conjunction introducing a subordinate clause, while *like* is a preposition. The object of a preposition is a noun or phrase. *Examples*:

> She did *as* she was told.
>
> He behaves *like* a fool.
>
> The gambler accepts only hard currency *like* gold coins.

⑮ When modifying the words *kind* and *sort*, the words *this* and *that* always remain in the singular. *Examples*:

> *This kind* of apple makes the best pie.
>
> *That sort* of behavior will result in severe punishment.

⑯ In sentences beginning with *there is* and *there are*, the verb should agree in number with the noun that follows it. *Examples*:

> There *isn't* an unbroken *bone* in her body. (The singular subject *bone* takes the singular verb *is*.)
>
> There *are* many *choices* to be made. (The plural subject *choices* takes the plural verb *are*.)

⑰ A noun or pronoun modifying a gerund should be in the possessive case. *Example*:

> Is there any criticism of *Arthur's* going? (*Going* is a gerund. It must be modified by *Arthur's*, not by Arthur.)

⑱ Do NOT use the possessive case when referring to an inanimate object. *Example*:

> He had difficulty with the *store's* management. (WRONG)
>
> He had difficulty with the management of the store. (CORRECT)

⑲ When expressing a condition contrary to fact or a wish, use the subjunctive form *were*. *Example*:

> I wish I *were* a movie star.

⑳ Statements equally true in the past and in the present are usually expressed in the present tense. The contents of a book are also expressed in the present tense. *Examples*:

> He said that Venus is a planet. (Even though he made the statement in the past, the fact remains that Venus *is* a planet.)
>
> In the book *Peter Pan*, Wendy says, "I can fly." (Every time one reads the book, Wendy *says* it again.)

ANTECEDENTS AND MODIFIERS

❶ *It*, when used as a relative pronoun, refers to the nearest noun. In your writing, you must be certain that the grammatical antecedent is indeed the intended antecedent. *Example*:

> Since the mouth of the cave was masked by underbrush, *it* provided an excellent hiding place. (Do you really mean that the underbrush is an excellent hiding place, or do you mean the cave?)

❷ *Which* and *that* also cause reference problems. In fact, whenever using pronouns, you must ask yourself whether or not the reference of the pronoun is clear. *Examples*:

> The first chapter awakens your interest in cloning, which continues to the end of the book. (What continues, cloning or your interest?)
>
> Jim told Bill that he was about to be fired. (Who is about to be fired? This sentence can be interpreted to mean that Jim was informing Bill about Bill's impending termination or about his, Jim's, own troubles.)

In your writing, you may find that the most effective way to clear up an ambiguity is to recast the sentence. *Examples*:

> The first chapter awakens your interest in cloning. The following chapters build upon this interest and maintain it throughout the book.
>
> Jim told Bill, "I am about to be fired." OR: Jim told Bill, "You are about to be fired."

❸ Adjectives modify only nouns and pronouns. Adverbs modify verbs, adjectives, and other adverbs. *Examples*:

> One can swim in a lake as *easy* as in a pool. (WRONG)
>
> One can swim in a lake as *easily* as in a pool. (CORRECT) (The adverb *easily* must modify the verb *can swim*.)
>
> I was *real* happy. (WRONG)
>
> I was *really* happy. (CORRECT) (The adverb *really* must be used to modify the adjective *happy*.)

Sometimes context determines the use of an adjective or adverb. *Examples*:

> The old man looked *angry*. (*Angry* is an adjective describing *the old* [angry old man].)
>
> The old man looked *angrily* out of the window. (*Angrily* is an adverb describing the man's manner of looking out the window.)

4 Phrases should be placed near the words they modify. *Examples*:

> The author says that he intends to influence your *life in the first chapter*. (WRONG)
>
> The *author in the first chapter* says . . . OR: *In the first chapter*, the author says . . .(CORRECT)
>
> He played the part in *Oklahoma* of Jud. (WRONG)
>
> He played the part of Jud in *Oklahoma*. (CORRECT)

5 Adverbs should be placed near the words they modify. *Examples*:

> The man was *only* willing to sell one horse. (WRONG)
>
> The man was willing to sell *only* one horse. (CORRECT)

6 Clauses should be placed near the words they modify. *Examples*:

> The man has an appointment *who is waiting in the office*. (WRONG)
>
> The man *who is waiting in the office* has an appointment. (CORRECT)

7 A modifier must modify something. *Examples*:

> Having excellent control, a no-hitter was pitched. (WRONG) (*Having excellent control* does not modify anything.)
>
> Having excellent control, the pitcher pitched a no-hitter. (CORRECT) (*Having excellent control* modifies *the pitcher*.)
>
> The day passed quickly, climbing the rugged rocks. (WRONG)
>
> The day passed quickly as we climbed the rugged rocks. (CORRECT)
>
> While away on vacation, the pipes burst. (WRONG) (The pipes were not away on vacation.)
>
> While we were away on vacation, the pipes burst. (CORRECT)
>
> To run efficiently, the technician should oil the lawnmower. (WRONG)
>
> The technician should oil the lawnmower to make it run efficiently. (CORRECT)

SENTENCE STRUCTURE

1 Every sentence must contain a verb. A group of words, no matter how long, without a verb is a sentence fragment, not a sentence. A verb may consist of one, two, three, or four words. *Examples*:

> The boy *studies* hard.
> The boy *will study* hard.

NOTE

The best test for the placement of a modifier is to read the sentence literally. If you read a sentence literally and it is literally ridiculous, it is WRONG. The meaning of a sentence must be clear to any reader. The words of the sentence *must make sense.*

The boy *has been studying* hard.

The boy *should have been studying* hard.

The words that make up the single verb may be separated. *Examples*:

It *is* not *snowing*.

It *will* almost certainly *snow* tomorrow.

❷   Every sentence must have a subject. The subject may be a noun, a pronoun, or a word or group of words functioning as a noun. *Examples*:

Fish swim. (noun)

Boats are sailed. (noun)

She is young. (pronoun)

Running is good exercise. (gerund)

To argue is pointless. (infinitive)

That he was tired was evident. (noun clause)

In commands, the subject is usually not expressed but is understood to be *You*. *Example*:

Mind your own business.

❸   A phrase cannot stand by itself as a sentence. A phrase is any group of related words that has no subject or predicate and that is used as a single part of speech. Phrases may be built around prepositions, particles, gerunds, or infinitives. *Examples*:

The boy *with curly hair* is my brother. (Prepositional phrase used as an adjective modifying *boy*.)

My favorite cousin lives *on a farm*. (Prepositional phrase used as an adverb modifying *lives*.)

Beyond the double white line is out of bounds. (Prepositional phrase used as a noun, subject of the sentence.)

A thunderstorm *preceding a cold front* is often welcome. (Participial phrase used as an adjective modifying *thunderstorm*.)

We eagerly awaited the pay envelopes *brought by the messenger*. (Participial phrase used as an adjective modifying *envelopes*.)

Running a day camp is an exhausting job. (Gerund phrase used as a noun, subject of the sentence.)

The director is paid well for *running the day camp*. (Gerund phrase used as a noun, the object of the preposition *for*.)

To breathe unpolluted air should be every person's birthright. (Infinitive phrase used as a noun, the subject of the sentence.)

The child began *to unwrap his gift*. (Infinitive phrase used as a noun, the object of the verb *began*.)

The boy ran away from home *to become a marine*. (Infinitive phrase use as an adverb modifying *ran away*.)

4 A *main, independent,* or *principal* clause can stand alone as a complete sentence or it may be combined with another clause. *Example*:

> The sky darkened ominously, and rain began to fall. (Two independent clauses joined by a coordinating conjunction.)

A *subordinate or dependent* clause must never stand alone. It is not a complete sentence despite the fact that it has a subject and a verb. A subordinate clause usually is introduced by a subordinating conjunction. Subordinate clauses may act as adverbs, adjectives, or nouns. *Example*:

> The witness said her name was Margaret Adams and *that she lived in Morganville.*

Subordinate adverbial clauses are generally introduced by the subordinating conjunction *when, while, because, as soon as, if after, although, as before, since, than, though, until,* or *unless. Examples*:

> *While we were waiting for the local,* the express roared past.
> The woman applied for a new job *because she wanted to earn more money.*

Although a subordinate clause contains both subject and verb, *it cannot stand alone* because it is introduced by a subordinating word.

> Subordinate adjective clauses may be introduced by the pronouns *who, which,* or *that. Examples*:

> The play *that he liked best* was a mystery.
> I have a neighbor *who served in the Peace Corps.*

Subordinate noun clauses may be introduced by *who, what,* or *that. Examples*:

> The station manager says *that the train will be late.*
> I asked the waiter *what the stew contained.*
> I wish I knew *who backed into my car.*

5 Two independent clauses cannot share one sentence without some form of connective. If they do, they form a run-on sentence. Two principal clauses may be joined by a coordinating conjunction, by a comma followed by a coordinating conjunction, or by a semicolon. They may form two distinct sentences. Two main clauses may NEVER be joined by a comma without a coordinating conjunction. This error is called a comma splice. *Examples*:

> A college education has never been more important than it is today it has never cost more. (WRONG—run-on sentence)
> A college education has never been more important than it is today, it has never cost more. (WRONG—comma splice)
> A college education has never been more important than it is today, and it has never cost more. (CORRECT)

A college education has never been more important than it is today; it has never cost more. (CORRECT)

A college education has never been more important than it is today. It has never cost more. (CORRECT)

A college education has never been more important than it is today. And it has never cost more. (CORRECT)

While a college education has never been more important than it is today, it has never cost more. (CORRECT)

6 Direct quotations are bound by all the rules of sentence formation. Beware of comma splices in divided quotations. *Examples*:

"Your total is wrong," he said, "add the column again." (WRONG)

"Your total is wrong," he said. "Add the column again." (CORRECT—The two independent clauses form two separate sentences.)

"Are you lost?" she asked, "may I help you?" (WRONG)

"Are you lost?" she asked. "May I help you?" (CORRECT—Two main clauses; two separate sentences.)

7 Comparisons must be logical and complete. Train yourself to concentrate on each sentence so that you can recognize errors. *Examples*:

Wilmington is larger than any city in Delaware. (WRONG)

Wilmington is larger than any *other* city in Delaware. (CORRECT)

He is as fat, if not fatter, than his uncle. (WRONG)

He is as fat *as*, if not fatter than, his uncle. (CORRECT)

I hope to find a summer job other than a lifeguard. (WRONG)

I hope to find a summer job other than *that of* lifeguard. (CORRECT)

Law is a better profession than an accountant. (WRONG)

Law is a better profession than *accounting*. (CORRECT)

8 Avoid the "is when" and "is where" construction. *Examples*:

A limerick is when a short poem has a catchy rhyme. (WRONG)

A limerick *is* a short poem with a catchy rhyme. (CORRECT)

To exile is where a person must live in another place. (WRONG)

To exile a person is to force him to live in another place. (CORRECT)

9 Errors in parallelism are often quite subtle, but you should learn to recognize and avoid them. *Examples*:

Skiing and to skate are both winter sports. (WRONG)

Skiing and *skating* are both winter sports. (CORRECT)

She spends all her time eating, asleep, and on her studies. (WRONG)

She spends all her time eating, *sleeping*, and *studying*. (CORRECT)

The work is neither difficult nor do I find it interesting. (WRONG)

The work is neither difficult nor *interesting*. (CORRECT)

His heavy drinking and the fact that he gambles makes him a poor role model. (WRONG)

His heavy *drinking* and *gambling make* him a poor role model. (CORRECT)

⑩ Avoid needless shifts in point of view. A shift in point of view is a change within the sentence from one tense or mood to another, from one subject or voice to another, or from one person or number to another. Shifts in point of view destroy parallelism within the sentence. *Examples*:

After he *rescued* the kitten, he rushes down the ladder to find its owner. (WRONG) (Shows a shift from past tense.)

After he *rescued* the kitten, he *rushed* down the ladder to find its owner. (CORRECT)

First stand at attention and then you *should salute* the flag. (WRONG) (Shows a shift from imperative to indicative mood.)

First *stand* at attention and then *salute* the flag. (CORRECT)

Mary especially likes math, but history is also enjoyed by her. (WRONG) (The subject shifts from *Mary* to *history*; the mood shifts from active to passive.)

Mary especially *likes* math, but *she* also *enjoys* history. (CORRECT)

George rowed around the island and soon the mainland came in sight. (WRONG) (The subject changes from *George* to *the mainland*.)

George rowed around the island and soon *came in sight* of the mainland. (CORRECT)

The captain welcomed us aboard, and the crew enjoyed showing *one* around the boat. (WRONG) (The object shifts from first to third person.)

The captain welcomed *us* aboard, and the crew enjoyed showing *us* around the boat. (CORRECT)

One should listen to the weather forecast so that *they* may anticipate a hurricane. (WRONG) (The subject shifts from singular to plural.)

One should listen to the weather forecast so that *he* may anticipate a hurricane. (CORRECT)

TROUBLESOME WORDS

There are a few groups of words that are often confused. You probably have many of these under control. Others may consistently give you trouble. Your choice of the best version of a sentence may hinge upon your understanding the correct uses of the words in these troublesome groups.

❶ **their, they're, there**

Their is the possessive of *they*. *Example*:
The Martins claimed *their* dog from the pound because it belonged to them.
They're is the contraction for *they are*. *Example*:
Tom and Marie said that *they're* going skiing in February.
There means *at that place*. *Example*:
You may park your car over *there*.

This last form is also used in sentences or clauses where the subject comes after the verb. *Example*:

There is no one here by that name.

2   **your, you're**

Your is the possessive of *you*. *Example*:

Didn't we just drive past *your* house?

You're is the contraction for *you are*. *Example*:

When we finish caroling, *you're* all coming inside for hot chocolate.

3   **whose, who's**

Whose is the possessive of *who*. *Example*:

The handwriting is very distinctive, but I cannot remember *whose* it is.

Who's is the contraction for *who is*. *Example*:

Who's calling at this hour of night?

4   **its, it's**

Its is the possessive of *it*. *Example*:

The injured dog is licking *its* wounds.

It's is the contraction for *it is*. *Example*:

It's much too early to leave for the airport.

5   **which, who, that**

Which as a relative pronoun that refers only to objects. *Example*:

The cat knocked over a vase, *which* fell and broke.

Who and *whom* refer only to people. *Examples*:

The boy *who* won the prize is over there.

To *whom* should we give the prize?

That may refer to objects or people. *That* is used only in restrictive clauses. *Examples*:

This is the vase *that* the cat knocked over.

The boy *that* won the prize is over there.

6   **learn, teach**

To *learn* is to *acquire* knowledge. To *teach* is to *impart* knowledge. *Example*: My mother *taught* me all that I have *learned*.

7   **between, among**

Between commonly applies to only two people or things. *Example*:

Let us keep this secret *between you and me*.

Among always implies that there are more than two. *Example*:

The knowledge is secure *among the members* of our club.

Exception: *Between* may be used with more than two objects to show the relationship of each object to each of the others, as in "The teacher explained the difference *between* adjective, adverb, and noun clauses."

8 **beside, besides**

Beside is a preposition meaning *by the side of it. Example*:

He sat *beside* his sick dog.

Besides is an adverb meaning *in addition to. Example*:

Besides his father, his mother also was ill.

9 **lay, lie**

The verb *to lay*, except when referring to hens, may be used only if you could replace it with the verb *to put*. At all other times, use a form of the verb *to lie*. *Examples*:

You may *lay* the books upon the table.

Let sleeping dogs *lie*.

10 **many/much, fewer/less, number/amount**

The rule of *many/much, fewer/less, number/amount* is governed by a simple rule of thumb. If the object can be counted, use *many, fewer, number*. If the object is thought of as a single mass or unit, use *much, less, amount*. *Examples*:

Many raindrops make *much* water.

If you have *fewer* dollars, you have *less* money.

The *amount* of property you own depends upon the *number* of acres in your lot.

11 **I, me**

The choice of *I or me* when the first-person pronoun is used with one or more proper names may be tested by eliminating the proper names and reading the sentence with the pronoun alone. *Examples*:

John, George, Marylou, and (me *or* I) went to the movies last night. (By eliminating the names you can readily choose *I went to the movies*.)

It would be very difficult for Mac and (I *or* me) to attend the wedding. (Without Mac it is clear that *difficult for me* is correct.)

12 **already, all ready**

Already means *prior to some specified time. Example*:

It is *already* too late to submit your application.

All ready means *completely ready. Example*:

The cornfield is *all ready* for the seed to be sown.

13 **altogether, all together**

Altogether means *entirely*.

Example: It is *altogether* too foggy to drive safely.

All together means *in sum* or *collectively*.

Example: The family will be *all together* at the Thanksgiving dinner table.

14 **two, to, too**

Two is the numeral 2. *Example*:

There are *two* sides to every story.
To means *in the direction of. Example*:
We shall go to school.
Too means *more than* or *also. Examples*:
It's *too* cold to go swimming today.
We shall go, *too*.

Test-Taking Techniques

MULTIPLE-CHOICE QUESTIONS

Almost all of the tests given on civil service exams are in a multiple-choice format. This means that you have four or five answer choices from which to select the correct answer. It's not something that should be overwhelming. There is a basic technique to answering these types of questions. Once you understand this technique, your test taking will be far less stressful.

First, there is only one correct answer. Since these tests have been given time and again, and the test developers have a sense of which questions work and which questions don't work, it is rare that your choices will be ambiguous. They may be complex and somewhat confusing, but there will still be only one right answer.

The first step is to look at the question, without looking at the answer choices. Now select the correct answer. That may sound somewhat simplistic, but it's usually the case that your first choice is the correct one. If you go back and change it, redo it again and again, it's more likely that you'll end up with the wrong answer. Thus, follow your instinct. Once you have come up with the answer, look at the answer choices. If your answer is one of the choices, you're probably correct. This technique is not 100 percent infallible, but it's a strong possibility that you've selected the right answer.

With math questions you should first solve the problem. If your answer is among the choices, you're probably correct. Don't ignore things like the proper function signs (adding, subtracting, multiplying, and dividing), negative and positive numbers, and so on.

But suppose you don't know the correct answer. You then use the "process of elimination." It's a time-honored technique for test takers. There is always one correct answer. There is usually one answer choice that is totally incorrect—a "distracter." If you look at that choice and it seems highly unlikely, then eliminate it. Depending on the number of choices (four or five), you've just cut down the number of choices to make. Now weigh the other choices. They may seem incorrect, or they may seem correct. If they seem incorrect, eliminate them. You've now increased your odds of finding the correct answer.

In the end, you may be left with only two choices. At that point, it's just a matter of guessing. But with only two choices left, you now have a 50 percent chance of getting it right. With four choices, you only have a 25 percent chance, and with five choices, only a 20 percent chance at guessing correctly. That's why the process of elimination is important.

"TEST-WISENESS"

NOTE

"Test-wiseness" is a general term that simply means being familiar with some good procedures to follow when getting ready for and taking a test. The procedures fall into four major areas: (1) being prepared, (2) avoiding careless errors, (3) managing your time, and (4) guessing.

Many factors enter into a test score. The most important factor should be the ability to answer the questions, which in turn indicates the ability to learn and perform the duties of the job. Assuming that you have this ability, knowing what to expect on the exam and familiarity with techniques of effective test taking should give you the confidence you need to do your best on the exam.

There is no quick substitute for long-term study and development of your skills and abilities to prepare you for doing well on tests. However, there are some steps you can take to help you do the very best you can. Some of these steps are done before the test, and some are performed when you are taking the test. Knowing these steps is often called being "test-wise." Following these steps may help you feel more confident as you take the actual test.

Being Prepared

Don't make the test harder than it has to be by not preparing yourself. You are taking a very important step in preparation by reading this book and taking the practice tests that are included. This will help you to become familiar with the tests and the kinds of questions you will have to answer.

As you use this book, carefully read the sample questions and directions for taking the test. Then, when you take the practice tests, time yourself as you will be timed for the real test.

As you are working on the sample questions, don't look at the correct answers before you try to answer them on your own. This can fool you into thinking you understand a question when you really don't. Try it on your own first, and then compare your answer with the one given. Remember, in a practice test, you are your own grader; you don't gain anything by pretending to understand something you really don't.

On the examination day assigned to you, allow the test itself to be the main attraction of the day. Do not squeeze it in between other activities. Be sure to bring your admission card, identification, and pencils, as instructed. Prepare these the night before so that you are not flustered by a last-minute search. Arrive rested, relaxed, and on time. In fact, plan to arrive a little bit early. Leave plenty of time for traffic tie-ups or other complications that might upset you and interfere with your test performance.

In the test room, the examiner will hand out forms for you to fill out. He or she will give you the instructions that you must follow in taking the examination. The examiner will tell you how to fill in the grids on the forms. Time limits and timing signals will be explained. If you do not understand any of the examiner's instructions, ASK QUESTIONS. It would be ridiculous to score less than your best because of poor communication.

At the examination, you must follow instructions exactly. Fill in the grids on the forms carefully and accurately. Misgridding may lead to losing veteran's credits to which you may be entitled or misaddressing of your test results. Do not begin until you are told to begin. Stop as soon as the examiner tells you to stop. Do not turn pages until you are told to do so. Do not go back to parts you have already completed. Any infraction of the rules is considered cheating. If you cheat, your test paper will not be scored, and you will not be eligible for appointment.

The answer sheet for most multiple-choice exams is machine scored. You cannot give any explanations to the machine, so you must fill out the answer sheet clearly and correctly.

To mark your answer sheet

1 **Blacken your answer space firmly and completely.**

2 **Mark only one answer for each question.** If you mark more than one answer, you will be considered wrong, even if one of the answers is correct.

3 **If you change your mind, you must erase your mark.** Attempting to cross out an incorrect answer will not work. You must erase any incorrect answer completely. An incomplete erasure might be read as a second answer.

4 **All of your answering should be in the form of blackened spaces.** The machine cannot read English. Do not write any notes in the margins.

5 **Answer each question in the right place.** Question 1 must be answered in space 1, for example, and question 52 in space 52. If you should skip an answer space and mark a series of answers in the wrong places, you must erase all those answers and do the questions over, marking your answers in the proper places. You cannot afford to use the limited time in this way. Therefore, as you answer each question, look at its number and check that you are marking your answer in the space with the same number.

Avoiding Careless Errors

Don't reduce your score by making careless mistakes. Always read the instructions for each test section carefully, even when you think you already know what the directions are. It's why we stress throughout this book that it's important to fully understand the directions for these different question-types before you go into the actual exam. It will not only reduce errors, but it will also save you time—time you will need for the questions.

What if you don't understand the directions? You will have risked getting the answers wrong for a whole test section. As an example, vocabulary questions can sometimes test synonyms (words with similar meanings) and sometimes test antonyms (words with opposite meanings). You can easily see how a mistake in understanding in this case could make a whole set of answers incorrect.

If you have time, reread any complicated instructions after you do the first few questions to check that you really do understand the directions. Of course, whenever you are allowed to, ask the examiner to clarify anything you don't understand.

Other careless mistakes affect only the response to particular questions. This often happens with arithmetic questions, but can happen with other questions as well. This type of error, called a "response error," usually stems from a momentary lapse of concentration.

A common error in reading interpretation questions is bringing your own information into the subject. For example, you may encounter a passage that discusses a subject you know something about. While this can make the passage easier to read, it can also tempt you to rely on your own knowledge about the subject. You must rely on information within the passage for your answers. In fact, sometimes the "wrong answers" to the questions are based on true information about the subject not given in the passage. Since the test makers are testing your reading ability, rather than your general knowledge of the subject, an answer based on information not contained in the passage is considered incorrect.

Managing Your Time

Before you begin, take a moment to plan your progress through the test. Although you are usually not expected to finish all of the questions given on a test, you should at least get an idea of how much time you should spend on each question in order to answer them all. For example, if there are 60 questions to answer and you have 30 minutes, you will have about one-half minute to spend on each question.

Keep track of the time on your watch or the room clock, but do not fixate on the time remaining. Your task is to answer questions. Do not spend too much time on any one question. If you find yourself stuck, do not take the puzzler as a personal challenge. Either guess and mark the question in the question booklet or skip the question entirely, marking the question as a skip and taking care to skip the answer space on the answer sheet. If there is time at the end of the exam or exam part, you can return and give marked questions another try.

Guessing

You may be wondering whether or not it is wise to guess when you are not sure of an answer (even if you've reduced the odds to 50 percent) or whether it is better to skip the question when you are not certain. The wisdom of guessing depends on the scoring method for the particular examination part. If the scoring is "rights only," that is, one point for each correct answer and no subtraction for wrong answers, then by all means you should guess. Read the question and all of the answer choices carefully. Eliminate those answer choices that you are certain are wrong. Then guess from among the remaining choices. You cannot gain a point if you leave the answer space blank; you may gain a point with an educated guess or even with a lucky guess. In fact, it is foolish to leave any spaces blank on a test that counts "rights only." If it appears that you are about to run out of time before completing such an exam, mark all the remaining blanks with the same letter. According to the law of averages, you should get some portion of those questions right.

If the scoring method is "rights minus wrongs," DO NOT GUESS. A wrong answer counts heavily against you. On this type of test, do not rush to fill answer spaces randomly at the end. Work as quickly as possible while concentrating on accuracy. Keep working carefully until time is called. Then stop and leave the remaining answer spaces blank.

For those tests that are scored by subtracting a fraction of a point for each wrong answer ("rights minus fraction of wrongs"), the decision as to whether or not to guess is really up to you. A correct answer gives you one point; a skipped space gives you nothing at all, but costs you nothing except the chance of getting the answer right; a wrong answer costs you 1/4 point. If you are really uncomfortable with guessing, you may skip a question, BUT you must then remember to skip its answer space as well. The risk of losing your place if you skip questions is so great that we advise you to guess even if you are not sure of the answer. Our suggestion is that you answer every question in order, even if you have to guess. It is better to lose a few 1/4 points for wrong guesses than to lose valuable seconds figuring where you started marking answers in the wrong place, erasing, and remarking answers. On the other hand, do not mark random answers at the end. Work steadily until time is up.

SCORING

If your exam is a short-answer exam, such as those often used by companies in the private sector, your answers will be graded by a personnel officer trained in grading test questions. If you blackened spaces on the separate answer sheet accompanying a multiple-choice exam, your answer sheet will be machine scanned or will be hand scored using a punched card stencil. Then a raw score will be calculated using the scoring formula that applies to that test or test portion—rights only, rights minus wrongs, or rights minus a fraction of wrongs. Raw scores on test parts are then added together for a total raw score.

A raw score is not a final score. The raw score is not the score that finds its way onto an eligibility list. The civil service testing authority converts raw scores to a scaled score according to an unpublicized formula of its own. The scaling formula allows for slight differences in difficulty of questions from one form of the exam to another and allows for equating the scores of all candidates. Regardless of the number of questions and possible different weights of different parts of the exam, most civil service test scores are reported on a scale of 1 to 10. The entire process of conversion from raw to scaled score is confidential information. The score you receive is not your number right, is not your raw score, and, despite being on a scale of 1 to 100, is not a percentage. It is a scaled score. If you are entitled to veteran's service points, these are added to your passing scaled score to boost your rank on the eligibility list. Veteran's points are added only to passing scores. A failing score cannot be brought to passing level by adding veteran's points. The score earned plus veteran's service points, if any, is the score that finds its place on the rank-order eligibility list.

TIP

One of the questions you should ask in the testing room is what scoring method will be used on your particular exam. You can then guide your guessing procedure accordingly.

PROMOTION EXAM

A Corrections Officer who plans a career in the corrections field can look forward to being promoted to positions of greater responsibility. In most corrections departments the job title directly above Corrections Officer is Corrections Captain. Other departments promote to Sergeant or Corporal. Whatever the intermediate titles, the final promotion goals are to the positions of Deputy Warden and Warden. Promotions are based on a combination of factors, including effectiveness as a Corrections Officer, attendance record, perceived enthusiasm, recommendations of supervisors, seniority, and the score earned on a promotion exam.

Just as initial entry-exams vary widely from jurisdiction to jurisdiction, promotion exams show a great deal of variation also. All promotion exams require the Corrections Officer to demonstrate a thorough knowledge of the field of corrections and of the daily duties of a Corrections Officer. In addition, most exams require total mastery of the rules and the ability to use sound judgment in corrections situations. Many exams attempt to measure the Corrections Officer's natural grasp of supervisory principles and methods. Beyond these basic topics tested by all promotion exams, many include questions that involve reading interpretation, report writing, scheduling, and mathematics. In some jurisdictions, Corrections Officers seeking advancement must take promotion courses. In these instances, the promotion exam will be based on course content. Other systems assume that a person who aspires to a corrections career has done extensive reading on the subject. These systems include questions based on correctional theory found in literature. Still other systems include "in-basket" tests that demonstrate administrative skills or situational role playing to show ability to deal with stressful situations.

INTERVIEW

If there is no exam and you are called directly to an interview, what you wear is more important. Take special care to look businesslike and professional. A neat dress, slacks and blouse, or skirted suit is fine for women; men should wear a suit or slacks, a jacket, shirt, and tie.

If you are called for an interview, you are most likely under serious consideration. There may still be competition for the job—someone else may be better suited than you—but you are qualified, and your skills and background have appealed to someone in the hiring office. The interview may be aimed at getting information about the following:

- **Your knowledge.** The interviewer wants to know what you know about the area in which you will work. You may also be asked questions probing your knowledge of the agency for which you are interviewing. Do you care enough to have educated yourself about the functions and role of the agency?

- **Your judgment.** You may be faced with hypothetical situations—job-related or interpersonal—and be asked questions like, "What would you do if . . .?" Think carefully before answering. Be decisive and diplomatic. There are no "right answers." The interviewer is aware that you are being put on the spot. How well you can handle this type of question is an indication of your flexibility and maturity.

- **Your personality.** You will have to be trained and supervised. You will have to work with others. What is your attitude? How will you fit in? The interviewer will make judgments in these areas on the basis of general conversation with you and from your responses to specific lines of questioning. Be pleasant, polite, and open with your answers, but do not volunteer a great deal of extra information. Stick to the subjects introduced by the interviewer. Answer fully, but resist the temptation to ramble on.

- **Your attitude toward work conditions.** These are practical concerns. If the job will require frequent travel for extended periods, how do you feel about it? What is your family's attitude? If you will be very unhappy about the travel, you may leave the job and your training will have been a waste of the taxpayers' money. The interviewer also wants to know how you will react to overtime or irregular shifts.

DRUG TEST

Most prisons and jails today test Corrections Officer applicants for drug use. Since close to 80 percent of the inmate population is prone to using drugs or alcohol, the agencies want to insure that the staff does not use drugs. An employee who uses drugs might tend to overlook an inmate's possession of drugs as minor misconduct; however, drugs and alcohol in prisons and jails are trouble. Most acts of violence in prison are a result of drug or alcohol use. As an applicant for the position of Corrections Officer, you will be required to take a test that will determine if you have any drugs or alcohol in your system. You will have the opportunity to explain the presence of any prescription drugs, and will probably have to get a note from the physician who prescribed them.

MEDICAL EXAMINATION

You'll be required to take a medical examination prior to employment as a Corrections Officer. The prison or jail agency will want to determine if you have any preexisting illnesses or problems that would prevent you from doing the job. They will also want to insure that you are physically able to undertake the training and can handle the work. Most agencies have a physician who will conduct the examination at no cost to the applicant; however, some agencies require that the applicant get a physical examination at his or her own expense.

PHYSICAL FITNESS TEST

Since the job of a Corrections Officer requires that you be able to carry or drag a human body in case of fire or emergency, and be able to run a certain distance, you may be required to take a physical fitness test prior to employment. The physical fitness test will normally be given during your initial training. It would be worthwhile for you to try to improve your health and strength before you have to take the fitness test.

BACKGROUND INVESTIGATION

If you work in corrections, you'll have to have a background check before you start to work. When you apply, you'll probably be fingerprinted, and the prints will be submitted to the FBI or the local law enforcement agency. It will take approximately a week to get the results back. If you have any felony convictions that were not disclosed at the time of your application, you will be questioned about them, and possibly risk being removed from consideration. It is best to be honest about a felony conviction when you apply. If the conviction was many years ago, the agency may allow you to work for them if you talk with them about it.

The application form may have a place to list as references relatives, previous employers, and neighbors whom you would want the employer to call. It is always a good idea to have people in mind whom you will use as references, and be able to provide a current address and phone number for each. It's always best to ask these people for permission before using their names. And let them know what kind of job you are applying for, so they can give it some thought before they talk with your prospective employer.

PSYCHOLOGICAL INTERVIEW

The psychological interview differs from the general information interview or the final hiring and placement interview in that it tries to assess your behavior under stress. Not all applicants for government jobs must be subjected to a psychological interview. It is usually limited to persons who will carry guns, to people who must make very quick decisions at moments of danger, and to people who might find themselves under interrogation by hostile forces. In other words, Corrections Officers must be able to do their jobs without "cracking" under the stress.

SUMMING IT UP

- The Corrections Officer screening process involves more than simply evaluating an application. Candidates are required to interview well and pass a written exam, drug screening, medical examination, physical fitness test, psychological interview, and a background investigation.

- There are three main components that make up the Corrections Officer Exam—Observation and Memory, Reading Comprehension, and English Grammar and Usage.

- Many factors enter into a test score. The most important factor should be the ability to answer the questions, which in turn indicates the ability to learn and perform the duties of the job.

PART II

SIX PRACTICE TESTS

ANSWER SHEET PRACTICE TEST 1

1. Ⓐ Ⓑ Ⓒ Ⓓ	20. Ⓐ Ⓑ Ⓒ Ⓓ	39. Ⓐ Ⓑ Ⓒ Ⓓ	57. Ⓐ Ⓑ Ⓒ Ⓓ	75. Ⓐ Ⓑ Ⓒ Ⓓ
2. Ⓐ Ⓑ Ⓒ Ⓓ	21. Ⓐ Ⓑ Ⓒ Ⓓ	40. Ⓐ Ⓑ Ⓒ Ⓓ	58. Ⓐ Ⓑ Ⓒ Ⓓ	76. Ⓐ Ⓑ Ⓒ Ⓓ
3. Ⓐ Ⓑ Ⓒ Ⓓ	22. Ⓐ Ⓑ Ⓒ Ⓓ	41. Ⓐ Ⓑ Ⓒ Ⓓ	59. Ⓐ Ⓑ Ⓒ Ⓓ	77. Ⓐ Ⓑ Ⓒ Ⓓ
4. Ⓐ Ⓑ Ⓒ Ⓓ	23. Ⓐ Ⓑ Ⓒ Ⓓ	42. Ⓐ Ⓑ Ⓒ Ⓓ	60. Ⓐ Ⓑ Ⓒ Ⓓ	78. Ⓐ Ⓑ Ⓒ Ⓓ
5. Ⓐ Ⓑ Ⓒ Ⓓ	24. Ⓐ Ⓑ Ⓒ Ⓓ	43. Ⓐ Ⓑ Ⓒ Ⓓ	61. Ⓐ Ⓑ Ⓒ Ⓓ	79. Ⓐ Ⓑ Ⓒ Ⓓ
6. Ⓐ Ⓑ Ⓒ Ⓓ	25. Ⓐ Ⓑ Ⓒ Ⓓ	44. Ⓐ Ⓑ Ⓒ Ⓓ	62. Ⓐ Ⓑ Ⓒ Ⓓ	80. Ⓐ Ⓑ Ⓒ Ⓓ
7. Ⓐ Ⓑ Ⓒ Ⓓ	26. Ⓐ Ⓑ Ⓒ Ⓓ	45. Ⓐ Ⓑ Ⓒ Ⓓ	63. Ⓐ Ⓑ Ⓒ Ⓓ	81. Ⓐ Ⓑ Ⓒ Ⓓ
8. Ⓐ Ⓑ Ⓒ Ⓓ	27. Ⓐ Ⓑ Ⓒ Ⓓ	46. Ⓐ Ⓑ Ⓒ Ⓓ	64. Ⓐ Ⓑ Ⓒ Ⓓ	82. Ⓐ Ⓑ Ⓒ Ⓓ
9. Ⓐ Ⓑ Ⓒ Ⓓ	28. Ⓐ Ⓑ Ⓒ Ⓓ	47. Ⓐ Ⓑ Ⓒ Ⓓ	65. Ⓐ Ⓑ Ⓒ Ⓓ	83. Ⓐ Ⓑ Ⓒ Ⓓ
10. Ⓐ Ⓑ Ⓒ Ⓓ	29. Ⓐ Ⓑ Ⓒ Ⓓ	48. Ⓐ Ⓑ Ⓒ Ⓓ	66. Ⓐ Ⓑ Ⓒ Ⓓ	84. Ⓐ Ⓑ Ⓒ Ⓓ
11. Ⓐ Ⓑ Ⓒ Ⓓ	30. Ⓐ Ⓑ Ⓒ Ⓓ	49. Ⓐ Ⓑ Ⓒ Ⓓ	67. Ⓐ Ⓑ Ⓒ Ⓓ	85. Ⓐ Ⓑ Ⓒ Ⓓ
12. Ⓐ Ⓑ Ⓒ Ⓓ	31. Ⓐ Ⓑ Ⓒ Ⓓ	50. Ⓐ Ⓑ Ⓒ Ⓓ	68. Ⓐ Ⓑ Ⓒ Ⓓ	86. Ⓐ Ⓑ Ⓒ Ⓓ
13. Ⓐ Ⓑ Ⓒ Ⓓ	32. Ⓐ Ⓑ Ⓒ Ⓓ	51. Ⓐ Ⓑ Ⓒ Ⓓ	69. Ⓐ Ⓑ Ⓒ Ⓓ	87. Ⓐ Ⓑ Ⓒ Ⓓ
14. Ⓐ Ⓑ Ⓒ Ⓓ	33. Ⓐ Ⓑ Ⓒ Ⓓ	52. Ⓐ Ⓑ Ⓒ Ⓓ	70. Ⓐ Ⓑ Ⓒ Ⓓ	88. Ⓐ Ⓑ Ⓒ Ⓓ
15. Ⓐ Ⓑ Ⓒ Ⓓ	34. Ⓐ Ⓑ Ⓒ Ⓓ	53. Ⓐ Ⓑ Ⓒ Ⓓ	71. Ⓐ Ⓑ Ⓒ Ⓓ	89. Ⓐ Ⓑ Ⓒ Ⓓ
16. Ⓐ Ⓑ Ⓒ Ⓓ	35. Ⓐ Ⓑ Ⓒ Ⓓ	54. Ⓐ Ⓑ Ⓒ Ⓓ	72. Ⓐ Ⓑ Ⓒ Ⓓ	90. Ⓐ Ⓑ Ⓒ Ⓓ
17. Ⓐ Ⓑ Ⓒ Ⓓ	36. Ⓐ Ⓑ Ⓒ Ⓓ	55. Ⓐ Ⓑ Ⓒ Ⓓ	73. Ⓐ Ⓑ Ⓒ Ⓓ	91. Ⓐ Ⓑ Ⓒ Ⓓ
18. Ⓐ Ⓑ Ⓒ Ⓓ	37. Ⓐ Ⓑ Ⓒ Ⓓ	56. Ⓐ Ⓑ Ⓒ Ⓓ	74. Ⓐ Ⓑ Ⓒ Ⓓ	92. Ⓐ Ⓑ Ⓒ Ⓓ
19. Ⓐ Ⓑ Ⓒ Ⓓ	38. Ⓐ Ⓑ Ⓒ Ⓓ			

answer sheet

Practice Test 1

92 QUESTIONS • 3 HOURS

Directions: You will be given 10 minutes to study the scene below and to try to notice and remember as many details as you can. You may not take any notes during this time. Then answer the 14 questions that follow.

1. The students in this classroom are seated at
   (A) arm chairs.
   (B) long tables.
   (C) individual desks.
   (D) desks for two persons.

2. The teacher is
   (A) saluting the flag.
   (B) wearing a short-sleeved shirt, vest, and bow tie.
   (C) not wearing glasses.
   (D) wearing a long-sleeved shirt and striped tie.

3. The time at which this hostage situation is occurring is
   (A) 4:10.
   (B) 2:25.
   (C) 4:20.
   (D) 1:35.

4. The person who is bald is
   (A) standing in the doorway.
   (B) requesting information.
   (C) seated in the middle row.
   (D) threatening the teacher.

5. What is the total number of people in this scene?
    (A) 11
    (B) 13
    (C) 14
    (D) 15

6. The person wearing a headscarf is
    (A) volunteering an answer.
    (B) wearing a dark shirt.
    (C) wearing a striped shirt.
    (D) left-handed.

7. Regardless of what else may be taught in this classroom, the room is specially equipped as a(n)
    (A) art room.
    (B) chemistry classroom.
    (C) computer laboratory.
    (D) music studio.

8. There is an empty desk
    (A) between the student wearing a sleeveless sweater and the person with the long braid.
    (B) at the left end of the third row.
    (C) in the front row directly in front of the teacher's outstretched arm.
    (D) nowhere in this room.

9. The person carrying the submachine gun is
    (A) looking at her watch.
    (B) standing beside the teacher.
    (C) aiming at the students.
    (D) looking out the window.

10. The person with light curly hair and a print blouse is
    (A) armed with a knife.
    (B) volunteering an answer.
    (C) standing.
    (D) seated in the front row.

11. An accurate statement about this scene is that
    (A) the students are inattentive.
    (B) one of the lights is not in good working order.
    (C) hats are not permitted in the classroom.
    (D) all of the chalkboards are clean.

12. The four dials behind the teacher
    (A) indicate the time in different time zones.
    (B) all appear to indicate the same thing.
    (C) are various weather instruments.
    (D) give different readings that cannot be determined.

13. The teacher's left hand is
    (A) resting on the counter in front of him.
    (B) raised as if fending off the gunman.
    (C) pointing to a student.
    (D) resting on a book.

14. The person wearing a plaid shirt is
    (A) sleeping.
    (B) writing.
    (C) looking to his left.
    (D) eyeing the gunman.

15. Corrections Officers are often required to search inmates and the various areas of the correctional institution for any items that may be considered dangerous or that are not permitted. In making a routine search, officers should not neglect to examine an item just because it is usually regarded as a permitted item. For instance, some innocent-looking object can be converted into a weapon by sharpening one of its parts or replacing a part with a sharpened or pointed blade. Which of the following objects could most easily be converted into a weapon in this way?
    (A) A ballpoint pen
    (B) A pad of paper
    (C) A crayon
    (D) A handkerchief

16. "Only authorized employees are permitted to handle keys. Under no circumstances should an inmate be permitted to use door keys. When not in use, all keys are to be deposited with the Security Officer." Which one of the following actions does NOT violate these regulations?

    (A) A Corrections Officer has given a trusted inmate the key to a supply room and sent the inmate to bring back a specific item from that room.

    (B) A priest comes to make authorized visits to inmates. The Corrections Officer is very busy, so he gives the priest the keys needed to reach certain groups of cells.

    (C) An inmate has a pass to go to the library. A Cell Block Officer examines the pass, then unlocks the door and lets the inmate through.

    (D) At the end of the day, a Corrections Officer puts his keys in the pocket of his street clothes and takes them home with him.

17. "Decisions about handcuffing or restraining inmates are often up to the Corrections Officers involved. An officer is legally responsible for exercising good judgment and for taking necessary precautions to prevent harm both to the inmate involved and to others." In which one of the following situations is handcuffing or other physical restraint most likely to be needed?

    (A) An inmate seems to have lost control of his senses and is banging his fists repeatedly against the bars of his cell.

    (B) During the past two weeks, an inmate has deliberately tried to start three fights with other inmates.

    (C) An inmate claims to be sick and refuses to leave his cell for a scheduled meal.

    (D) During the night an inmate begins to shout and sing, disturbing the sleep of other inmates.

18. "Some utensils that are ordinarily used in a kitchen can also serve as dangerous weapons—for instance, vegetable parers, meat saws, skewers, and ice picks. These should be classified as extremely hazardous." The most sensible way of solving the problem caused by the use of these utensils in a correctional institution is to

    (A) try to run the kitchen without using any of these utensils.

    (B) provide careful supervision of inmates using such utensils in the kitchen.

    (C) assign only trusted inmates to kitchen duty and let them use the tools without regular supervision.

    (D) take no special precautions, since inmates are not likely to think of using these commonplace utensils as weapons.

19. "Inmates may try to conceal objects that can be used as weapons or as escape devices. Therefore routine searches of cells or dormitories are necessary for safety and security." Of the following, it would probably be most effective to schedule routine searches to take place
    (A) on regular days and always at the same time of day.
    (B) on regular days but at different times of day.
    (C) at frequent but irregular intervals, always at the same time of day.
    (D) at frequent but irregular intervals and at different times of day.

20. "One of the purposes of conducting routine searches for forbidden items is to discourage inmates from acquiring such items in the first place. Inmates should soon come to realize that only possessors of these items have reason to fear or resent such searches." Inmates are most likely to come to this realization if
    (A) the searching officer leaves every inmate's possessions in a mess to make it clear that a search has taken place.
    (B) the searching officer confiscates something from every cell, though he may later return most of the items.
    (C) other inmates are not told when a forbidden item is found in an inmate's possession.
    (D) all inmates know that possession of a forbidden item will result in punishment.

21. Suppose you are a Corrections Officer supervising a work detail of 22 inmates. All 22 checked in at the start of the work period. Making an informal count an hour later, you count only 21 inmates. What is the first action to take?
    (A) Count again to make absolutely sure how many inmates are present.
    (B) Report immediately that an inmate has escaped.
    (C) Try to figure out where the missing inmate could be.
    (D) Wait until the end of the work period and then make a formal roll call.

22. "The officer who is making a count at night when inmates are in bed must make sure he sees each man. The rule 'See living breathing flesh' must be followed in making accurate counts." Of the following, which is the most likely reason for this rule?
    (A) An inmate may be concealing a weapon in the bed.
    (B) A bed may be arranged to give the appearance of being occupied even when the inmate is not there.
    (C) Waking inmates for the count is a good disciplinary measure because it shows them that they are under constant guard.
    (D) It is important for officers on duty at night to have something to do to keep them busy.

23. "When counting a group of inmates on a work assignment, great care should be taken to ensure accuracy. The count method should be adapted to the number of inmates and to the type of location." Suppose that you are supervising 15 inmates working in a kitchen. Most of them are moving about constantly, carrying dishes and equipment from one place to another. In order to make an accurate count, which of the following methods would be most suitable under these circumstances?

(A) Have the inmates "freeze" where they are whenever you call for a count, even though some of them may be carrying hot pans or heavy stacks of dishes.
(B) Have the inmates stop their work and gather in one place whenever it is necessary to make a count.
(C) Circulate among the inmates and make an approximate count while they are working.
(D) Divide the group into sections according to type of work and assign one inmate in each group to give you the number of his section.

24. "Officers on duty at entrances must exercise the greatest care to prevent movement of unauthorized persons. At vehicle entrances, all vehicles must be inspected and a record kept of their arrival and departure." Assume that, as a Corrections Officer, you have been assigned to duty at a vehicle entrance. Which of the following is probably the best method of preventing the movement of unauthorized persons in vehicles?

(A) If passenger identifications are checked when the vehicle enters, no check is necessary when the vehicle leaves.
(B) Passenger identifications should be checked for all vehicles when the vehicle enters and when it leaves.
(C) Passenger identifications need not be checked when the vehicle enters, but should always be checked when the vehicle leaves.
(D) Except for official vehicles, passenger identifications should be checked when the vehicle enters and when it leaves.

25. In making a routine search of an inmate's cell, an officer finds various items. Although there is no immediate danger, he is not sure whether the inmate is permitted to have one of the items. Of the following, the best action for the officer to take is to

(A) confiscate the item immediately.
(B) give the inmate the benefit of the doubt, and let her keep the item.
(C) consult his rule book or his supervising officer to find out whether the inmate is permitted to have the item.
(D) leave the item in the inmate's cell, but plan to report her for an infraction of the rules.

26. It is almost certain that there will be occasional escape attempts or an occasional riot or disturbance that requires immediate emergency action. A well-developed emergency plan for dealing with these events includes not only planning for prevention and control, and planning for action during the disturbance, but also planning steps that should be taken when the disturbance is over. When a disturbance is ended, which of the following steps should be taken first?

(A) Punish the ringleaders.

(B) Give first-aid to inmates or other persons who were injured.

(C) Make an institutional count of all inmates.

(D) Adopt further security rules to make sure such an incident does not occur again.

27. It is often important to make notes about an occurrence that will require a written report or personal testimony. Assume that a Corrections Officer has made the following notes for the warden of the institution about a certain occurrence: "10:45 a.m. March 16, 2006. Cellblock A. Robert Brown was attacked by another inmate and knocked to the floor. Brown's head hit the floor hard. He was knocked out. I reported a medical emergency. Dr. Thomas Nunez came and examined Brown. The doctor recommended that Brown be transferred to the infirmary for observation. Brown was taken to the infirmary at 11:15 a.m." Which of the following important items of information is missing or is incomplete in these notes?

(A) The time that the incident occurred

(B) The place where the incident occurred

(C) The names of both inmates involved in the fight

(D) The name of the doctor who made the medical recommendation

28. A Corrections Officer has made the following notes for the warden of his institution about an incident involving an infraction of the rules: "March 29, 2006. Cellblock B-4. Inmates involved were A. Whitman, T. Brach, M. Purlin, M. Verey. Whitman and Brach started the trouble about 7:30. I called for assistance. Officer Haley and Officer Blair responded. Officer Blair got cut, and blood started running down his face. The bleeding looked very bad. He was taken to the hospital and needed 8 stitches." Which of the following items of information is missing or is incomplete in these notes?

(A) The time and date of the incident

(B) The place of the incident

(C) Which inmates took part in the incident

(D) What the inmates did that broke the rules

29. Your Supervising Officer has instructed you to follow a new system for handling inmate requests. It seems to you that a new system is not going to work very well and that inmates may resent it. What should you do?

(A) Continue handling requests the old way, but do not let your Supervising Officer know you are doing this.

(B) Continue using the old system until you have a chance to discuss the matter with your Supervising Officer.

(C) Begin using the new system, but plan to discuss the matter with your Supervising Officer if the system really does not work well.

(D) Begin using the new system, but make sure the inmates know that it is not your idea and you do not approve of it.

30. Inmates who are prison-wise may know a good many tricks for putting something over. For instance, it is an officer's duty to stop fights among inmates. Therefore, inmates who want to distract the officer's attention from something that is going on in one place may arrange for a phony fight to take place some distance away. To avoid being taken in by a trick like this, a Corrections Officer should

(A) ignore any fights that break out among inmates.

(B) always make an inspection tour to see what is going on elsewhere before breaking up a fight.

(C) be alert for other suspicious activity when there is any disturbance.

(D) refuse to report inmates involved in a fight, if the fight seems to have been phony.

31. Copies of the regulations are posted at various locations in the cell block so that inmates can refer to them. Suppose that one of the regulations is changed and the Corrections Officers receive revised copies to post in their cell blocks. Of the following, the most effective way of informing the inmates of the revision is to

(A) let the inmates know that you are taking down the old copies and putting up new ones in their place.

(B) post the new copies next to the old ones, so that inmates will be able to compare them and learn about the change for themselves.

(C) leave the old copies up until you have had a chance to explain the change to each inmate.

(D) post the new copies in place of the old ones and also explain the change orally to the inmates.

32. A fracture is a broken bone. In a simple fracture, the skin is not broken. In a compound fracture, a broken end of the bone pierces the skin. Whenever a fracture is feared, the first thing to do is to prevent motion of the broken part. Suppose that an inmate has just tripped on a stairway and twisted his ankle. He says it hurts badly, but you cannot tell what is wrong merely by looking at it. Of the following, the best action to take is to

(A) tell the inmate to stand up and see whether he can walk.

(B) move the ankle gently to see whether you can feel any broken ends of bones.

(C) tell the inmate to rest a few minutes and promise to return later to see whether his condition has improved.

(D) tell the inmate not to move his foot and put in a call for medical assistance.

33. "It is part of institutional procedure that at specified times during each 24-hour period all inmates in the institution are counted simultaneously. Each inmate must be counted at a specific time. All movement of inmates ceases from the time the count starts until it is finished and cleared as correct." Assume that, as a Corrections Officer, you are making such a count when an inmate in your area suddenly remembers he has an important 9 a.m. clinic appointment. You check his clinic pass and find that this is true. What should you do?

(A) Let him go to the clinic even though he may be counted again there.

(B) Take him off your count and tell him to be sure he is included in the count being made at the clinic.

(C) Keep him in your count and tell him to inform the officer at the clinic that he has already been counted.

(D) Ask him to wait a few minutes until the counting period is over and then let him go to the clinic.

34. "Except in the case of a serious illness or injury (when a doctor should see the inmate immediately), emergency sick calls should be kept to a minimum, and inmates should be encouraged to wait for regular sick-call hours." In which of the following cases is an emergency sick call most likely to be justified?

(A) An inmate has had very severe stomach pains for several hours.

(B) An inmate has cut his hand, and the bleeding has now stopped.

(C) An inmate's glasses have been broken, and he is nearly blind without them.

(D) A normally healthy inmate has lost his appetite and does not want to eat.

35. "People who have lost their freedom are likely to go through periods of depression, or to become extremely resentful or unpleasant. A Corrections Officer can help inmates who are undergoing such periods of depression by respecting their feelings and treating them in a reasonable and tactful manner." Suppose that an inmate reacts violently to a simple request made in a normal, routine manner by a Corrections Officer. Of the following, which is likely to be the most effective way of handling the situation?

(A) Point out to the inmate that it is his own fault that he is in jail, and he has nobody to blame for his troubles but himself.

(B) Tell the inmate that he is acting childishly and that he had better straighten out.

(C) Tell the inmate in a friendly way that you can see he is feeling down, but that he should comply with your request.

(D) Let the inmate know that you are going to report his behavior unless he changes.

36. An inmate tells you, a Corrections Officer, of his concern about the ability of his wife and children to pay for rent and food while he is in the institution. Of the following, which is the best action to take?

(A) Assure him that his wife and children are getting along fine, although you do not actually know this.

(B) Put him in touch with the social worker or the correctional employee who handles such problems.

(C) Offer to lend him money yourself if his family is really in need.

(D) Advise him to forget about his family and start concentrating on his own problems.

37. "It is particularly important to notice changes in the general pattern of an inmate's behavior. When an inmate who has been generally unpleasant and who has not spoken to an officer unless absolutely necessary becomes very friendly and cooperative, something has happened, and the officer should take steps to make sure what." Of the following possible explanations for this change in behavior, which one is the LEAST likely to be the real cause?

(A) The inmate may be planning some kind of disturbance or escape attempt and is trying to fool the officer.

(B) The inmate may be trying to get on the officer's good side for some reason of her own.

(C) Her friendliness and cooperation may indicate a developing mental illness.

(D) She may be overcoming his initial hostile reactions to her imprisonment.

38. As a Corrections Officer, you have an idea about a new way for handling a certain procedure. Your method would require a minor change in the regulations, but you are sure it would be a real improvement. The best thing for you to do is to

(A) discuss the idea with your Supervising Officer, explaining why it would work better than the present method.

(B) try your idea on your own cell block, telling inmates that it is just an experiment and not official.

(C) attempt to get officers on other cell blocks to use your methods on a strictly unofficial basis.

(D) forget the whole thing, since it might be too difficult to change the regulations.

39. "Corrections Officers assigned to visiting areas have a dual supervisory function, since their responsibilities include receiving persons other than inmates as well as handling inmates. Here, of all places, it is important for an officer to realize that she is acting as a representative of her institution and that what she is doing is very much like public relations work." Assume that you are a Corrections Officer assigned to duty in a visiting area. Which of the following ways of carrying out this assignment is most likely to result in good public relations?

(A) You should treat inmates and visitors sternly, because this will let them know that the institution does not put up with any nonsense.

(B) You should be friendly to inmates, but suspicious of visitors.

(C) You should be stern with inmates, but polite and tactful with visitors.

(D) You should treat both inmates and visitors in a polite and tactful way.

QUESTIONS 40-44 ARE BASED ON THE FOLLOWING PASSAGE.

The handling of supplies is an important part of correctional administration. A good deal of planning and organization is involved in the purchase, stock control, and issue of bulk supplies to the cell block. This planning is meaningless, however, if the final link in the chain—the Cell Block Officer who is in charge of distributing supplies to the inmates—does not do his job in the proper way. First, when supplies are received, the officer himself should immediately check them or should personally supervise the checking, to make sure the count is correct. Nothing but trouble will result if an officer signs for 200 towels and discovers hours later that he is 20 towels short. Did the 20 towels "disappear," or did they never arrive in the first place? Second, all supplies should be locked up until they are actually distributed. Third, the officer must keep accurate records when supplies are issued. Complaints will be kept to a minimum if the officer makes sure that each inmate has received the supplies to which he is entitled, and if the officer can tell from his records when it is time to reorder to prevent a shortage. Fourth, the officer should either issue the supplies himself or else personally supervise the issuing. It is unfair and unwise to put an inmate in charge of supplies without giving him adequate supervision. A small thing like a bar of soap does not mean much to most people, but it means a great deal to the inmate who cannot even shave or wash up unless he receives the soap that is supposed to be issued to him.

40. Which one of the following jobs is NOT mentioned by the passage as the responsibility of a Cell Block Officer?

(A) Purchasing supplies

(B) Issuing supplies

(C) Counting supplies when they are delivered to the cell block

(D) Keeping accurate records when supplies are issued

41. The passage says that supplies should be counted when they are delivered. Of the following, which is the best way of handling this job?

(A) The Cell Block Officer can wait until he has some free time and then count them himself.

(B) An inmate can start counting them right away, even if the Cell Block Officer cannot supervise his work.

(C) The Cell Block Officer can personally supervise an inmate who counts the supplies when they are delivered.

(D) Two inmates can count them when they are delivered, supervising each other's work.

42. The passage gives an example concerning a delivery of 200 towels that turned out to be 20 towels short. The author of the passage uses this example to show that

(A) the missing towels were stolen.

(B) the missing towels never arrived in the first place.

(C) it is impossible to tell what happened to the missing towels because no count was made when they were delivered.

(D) it does not matter that the missing towels were not accounted for because it is never possible to keep track of supplies accurately.

43. The main reasons given by the passage for making a record when supplies are issued is that keeping records

(A) will discourage inmates from stealing supplies.

(B) is a way of making sure that each inmate receives the supplies to which he is entitled.

(C) will show the officer's superiors that he is doing his job in the proper way.

(D) will enable the inmates to help themselves to any supplies they need.

44. The passage says that it is unfair to put an inmate in charge of supplies without giving him adequate supervision. Which of the following is the most likely explanation of why it would be "unfair" to do this?

(A) A privilege should not be given to one inmate unless it is given to all the other inmates too.

(B) It is wrong to make one inmate work when all the others can sit in their cells and do nothing.

(C) The Cell Block Officer should not be able to get out of doing a job by making an inmate do it for him.

(D) The inmate in charge of supplies could be put under pressure by other inmates to do them "special favors."

QUESTIONS 45–49 ARE BASED ON THE FOLLOWING PASSAGE.

The typical Corrections Officer must make predictions about the probable future behavior of his charges in order to make judgments affecting those individuals. In learning to predict behavior, the results of scientific studies of inmate behavior can be of some use. Most studies that have been made show that older men tend to obey rules and regulations better than younger men and tend to be more reliable in carrying out assigned jobs. Men who had good employment records on the outside also tend to be more reliable than men whose records show haphazard employment or unemployment. Oddly enough, men convicted of crimes of violence are less likely to be troublemakers than men convicted of burglary or other crimes involving stealth. While it might be expected that first offenders would be much less likely to be troublemakers than men with previous convictions, the difference between the two groups is not very great. It must be emphasized, however, that predictions based on a man's background are only likelihoods—they are never certainties. A successful Corrections Officer learns to give some weight to a man's background, but he should rely even more heavily on his own personal judgment of the individual in ques-

tion. A good officer will develop in time a kind of sixth sense about human beings that is more reliable than any statistical prediction.

45. The passage suggests that knowledge of scientific studies of inmate behavior would probably help the Corrections Officer to

(A) make judgments that affect the inmates in his charge.

(B) write reports on all major infractions of the rules.

(C) accurately analyze how an inmate's behavior is determined by his background.

(D) change the personalities of the individuals in his charge.

46. According to the information in the passage, which one of the following groups of inmates would tend to be most reliable in carrying out assigned jobs?

(A) Older men with haphazard employment records

(B) Older men with regular employment records

(C) Younger men with haphazard employment records

(D) Younger men with regular employment records

47. According to the information in the passage, which of the following are most likely to be troublemakers?

(A) Older men convicted of crimes of violence

(B) Younger men convicted of crimes of violence

(C) Younger men convicted of crimes involving stealth

(D) First offenders convicted of crimes of violence

48. The passage indicates that information about a man's background is
- **(A)** a sure way of predicting his future behavior.
- **(B)** of no use at all in predicting his future behavior.
- **(C)** more useful in predicting behavior than a Corrections Officer's expert judgment.
- **(D)** less reliable in predicting behavior than a Corrections Officer's expert judgment.

49. The passage names two groups of inmates whose behavior might be expected to be quite different, but who in fact behave only slightly differently. The two groups are
- **(A)** older men and younger men.
- **(B)** first offenders and men with previous convictions.
- **(C)** men with good employment records and men with records of haphazard employment or unemployment.
- **(D)** men who obey the rules and men who do not.

QUESTIONS 50–54 ARE BASED ON THE FOLLOWING PASSAGE.

A large proportion of the people who are behind bars are not convicted criminals but are people who have been arrested and are being held until their trial in court. Experts have often pointed out that this detention system does not operate fairly. For instance, a person who can afford to pay bail usually will not stay locked up. The theory of the bail system is that the person will make sure to show up in court on time because otherwise he will forfeit his bail—he will lose the money he has put up. Sometimes a person who can show that he is a stable citizen with a job and a family will be released on "personal recognizance" (without bail). The result is that well-to-do, employed, or family people often avoid the detention system. The people who do wind up in detention tend to be poor, unemployed, single, and young.

50. According to the above passage, people who are put behind bars
- **(A)** are almost always dangerous criminals.
- **(B)** include many innocent people who have been arrested by mistake.
- **(C)** are often people who have been arrested but have not yet come to trial.
- **(D)** are all poor people who tend to be young and single.

51. The passage says that the detention system works unfairly against people who are
- **(A)** rich.
- **(B)** married.
- **(C)** old.
- **(D)** unemployed.

52. The passage uses the expression "forfeit his bail." Even if you had not seen the word *forfeit* before, you could figure out from the way it is used in the passage that forfeiting probably means
- **(A)** losing track of something.
- **(B)** giving up something.
- **(C)** finding something.
- **(D)** avoiding something.

53. When someone is released on "personal recognizance," this means that the
- **(A)** judge knows that the person is innocent.
- **(B)** person does not have to show up for a trial.
- **(C)** person has a record of previous convictions.
- **(D)** person does not have to pay bail.

54. Suppose that two men were booked on the same charge at the same time and that the same bail was set for both of them. One man was able to put up bail, and he was released. The second man was not able to put up bail, and he was held in detention. The writer of the passage would most likely feel that this result is

(A) unfair, because it does not have any relation to guilt or innocence.

(B) unfair, because the first man deserves severe punishment.

(C) fair, because the first man is obviously innocent.

(D) fair, because the law should be tougher on poor people than on rich people.

QUESTIONS 55–59 ARE BASED ON THE FOLLOWING NAMES AND NUMBERS FOR NINE INMATES. EACH QUESTION CONSISTS OF THREE SETS OF NUMBERS AND LETTERS. EACH SET SHOULD CONSIST OF THE NUMBERS OF THREE INMATES AND THE FIRST LETTER OF EACH OF THEIR NAMES. THE LETTERS SHOULD BE IN THE SAME ORDER AS THE NUMBERS. IN AT LEAST TWO OF THE THREE CHOICES, THERE WILL BE AN ERROR. MARK ONLY THAT CHOICE IN WHICH THE LETTERS CORRESPOND WITH THE NUMBERS AND ARE IN THE SAME ORDER. IF ALL THREE SETS ARE WRONG, MARK (D).

1-Johnson	4-Thompson	7-Gordon
2-Smith	5-Frank	8-Porter
3-Edwards	6-Murray	9-Lopez

55. (A) 382 EGS
(B) 461 TMJ
(C) 875 PLF

56. (A) 549 FLT
(B) 692 MJS
(C) 758 GFP

57. (A) 936 LEM
(B) 253 FSE
(C) 147 JTL

58. (A) 569 PML
(B) 716 GJP
(C) 842 PTS

59. (A) 356 FEM
(B) 198 JPL
(C) 637 MEG

QUESTIONS 60–64 ARE BASED ON THE FOLLOWING PASSAGE.

Mental disorders are found in a fairly large number of the inmates in correctional institutions. There are no figures as to the number of inmates who are mentally disturbed—partly because it is hard to draw a precise line between "mental disturbance" and "normality"—but experts find that somewhere between 15% and 25% of inmates are suffering from disorders that are obvious enough to show up in routine psychiatric examinations. Society has not yet come to grips with the problem of what to do with mentally disturbed offenders. There is not enough money available to set up treatment programs for all the people identified as mentally disturbed; and there would probably not be enough qualified psychiatric personnel available to run such programs even if they could be set up. Most mentally disturbed offenders are therefore left to serve out their time in correctional institutions, and the burden of dealing with them falls on Corrections Officers. This means that a Corrections Officer must be sensitive enough to human behavior to know when he is dealing with a person who is not mentally normal and that the officer must be imaginative enough to be able to sense how an abnormal individual might react under certain circumstances.

60. According to the above passage, mentally disturbed inmates in correctional institutions

    (A) are usually transferred to mental hospitals when their condition is noticed.

    (B) cannot be told from other inmates, because tests cannot distinguish between insane people and normal people.

    (C) may constitute as much as 25% of the total inmate population.

    (D) should be regarded as no different from all the other inmates.

61. The passage says that today the job of handling mentally disturbed inmates is mainly up to

    (A) psychiatric personnel.

    (B) other inmates.

    (C) Corrections Officers.

    (D) administrative officials.

62. Of the following, which is a reason given in the passage for society's failure to provide adequate treatment programs for mentally disturbed inmates?

    (A) Law-abiding citizens should not have to pay for fancy treatment programs for criminals.

    (B) A person who breaks the law should not expect society to give him special help.

    (C) It is impossible to tell whether an inmate is mentally disturbed.

    (D) There are not enough trained people to provide the kind of treatment needed.

63. The expression "abnormal individual," as used in the last sentence of the passage, refers to an individual who is

    (A) of average intelligence.

    (B) of superior intelligence.

    (C) completely normal.

    (D) mentally disturbed.

64. The author of the passage would most likely agree that

    (A) Corrections Officers should not expect mentally disturbed persons to behave the same way a normal person would behave.

    (B) Corrections Officers should not report infractions of the rules committed by mentally disturbed persons.

    (C) mentally disturbed persons who break the law should be treated exactly the same way as anyone else.

    (D) mentally disturbed persons who have broken the law should not be imprisoned.

QUESTIONS 65–71 ARE BASED ON THE ROSTER OF INMATES, THE INSTRUCTIONS, THE TABLE, AND THE PASSAGE BELOW.

Twelve inmates of a correctional institution are divided into three permanent groups in their workshop. They must be present and accounted for in these groups at the beginning of each workday. During the day, the inmates check out of their groups for various activities. They check back in again when those activities have been completed. Assume that the day is divided into three activity periods.

Roster of Inmates

Group X	Ted	Frank	George	Harry
Group Y	Jack	Ken	Larry	Mel
Group Z	Phil	Bob	Sam	Vic

The following table shows the movements of these inmates from their groups during the day. Assume that all were present and accounted for at the beginning of Period I.

		Group X	Group Y	Group Z
Period I	Check-outs:	Ted, Frank	Ken, Larry	Phil
Period II	Check-ins:	Frank	Ken, Larry	Phil
	Check-outs:	George	Jack, Mel	Bob, Sam, Vic
Period III	Check-ins:	George	Mel, Jack	Sam, Bob, Vic
	Check-outs:	Frank, Harry	Ken	Vic

65. At the end of Period I, what was the total number of inmates remaining in their own permanent groups?
- **(A)** 8
- **(B)** 7
- **(C)** 6
- **(D)** 5

66. At the end of Period I, the inmates remaining in Group Z were
- **(A)** George and Harry.
- **(B)** Jack and Mel.
- **(C)** Bob, Sam, and Vic.
- **(D)** Phil.

67. At the end of Period II, the inmates remaining in Group Y were
- **(A)** Ken and Larry.
- **(B)** Jack, Ken, and Mel.
- **(C)** Jack and Ken.
- **(D)** Ken, Mel, and Larry.

68. At the end of Period II, what was the total number of inmates remaining in their own permanent groups?
- **(A)** 8
- **(B)** 7
- **(C)** 6
- **(D)** 5

69. At the end of Period II, the inmates who were NOT present in Group Z were
- **(A)** Phil, Bob, and Sam.
- **(B)** Sam, Bob, and Vic.
- **(C)** Sam, Vic, and Phil.
- **(D)** Vic, Phil, and Bob.

70. At the end of Period III, the inmates remaining in Group Y were
- **(A)** Ted, Frank, and George.
- **(B)** Jack, Mel, and Ken.
- **(C)** Jack, Larry, and Mel.
- **(D)** Frank and Harry.

71. At the end Period III, what was the total number of inmates NOT present in their own permanent groups?

(A) 4
(B) 5
(C) 6
(D) 7

72. Add $51.79, $29.39, and $8.98.

(A) $78.97
(B) $88.96
(C) $89.06
(D) $90.16

73. Add $72.07 and $31.54; then subtract $25.75.

(A) $77.86
(B) $82.14
(C) $88.96
(D) $129.36

74. Start with $82.47, then subtract $25.50, $4.75, and $0.35.

(A) $30.60
(B) $51.87
(C) $52.22
(D) $65.25

75. Add $19.35 and $37.75; then subtract $9.90 and $19.80.

(A) $27.40
(B) $37.00
(C) $37.30
(D) $47.20

76. Multiply $38.85 by 2; then subtract $27.90.

(A) $21.90
(B) $48.70
(C) $49.80
(D) $50.70

77. Add $53.66, $9.27, and $18.75; then divide by 2.

(A) $35.84
(B) $40.34
(C) $40.84
(D) $41.34

78. Out of 192 inmates in a certain cell block, 96 are to go on a work detail, and another 32 are to report to a vocational class. All the rest are to remain in the cell block. How many inmates should be left in the cell block?

(A) 48
(B) 64
(C) 86
(D) 128

79. Assume that you, as a Corrections Officer, are responsible for seeing that the right number of utensils are counted out for a meal. You need enough utensils for 620 women. One fork and one spoon are needed for each woman. In addition, one ladle is needed for each group of 20 women. How many utensils will be needed altogether?

(A) 1,240
(B) 1,271
(C) 1,550
(D) 1,860

80. Assume that you, as a Corrections Officer, are supervising the inmates who are assigned to a dishwashing detail. There is a direct relationship between the amount of time it takes to do all the dishwashing and the number of inmates who are washing dishes. When two inmates are washing dishes, the job takes 6 hours. If there are four inmates washing dishes, how long should the job take?

(A) 1 hour
(B) 2 hours
(C) 3 hours
(D) 4 hours

81. Assume that you, as a Corrections Officer, are in charge of supervising the laundry sorting and counting. You expect that on a certain day there will be nearly 7,000 items to be sorted and counted. If one inmate can sort and count 500 items in an hour, how many inmates are needed to sort all 7,000 items in one hour?

    (A) 2
    (B) 5
    (C) 7
    (D) 14

82. A carpentry course is being given for inmates who want to learn a skill. The course will be taught in several different groups. Each group should contain at least 12 but no more than 16 men. The smaller the group the better, as long as there are at least 12 men per group. If 66 inmates are going to take the course, they should be divided into

    (A) 4 groups of 16 men.
    (B) 4 groups of 13 men and 1 group of 14 men.
    (C) 3 groups of 13 men and 2 groups of 14 men.
    (D) 6 groups of 11 men.

83. Of the 100 inmates in a certain cell block, one half were assigned to cleanup work, and one fifth were assigned to work in the laundry. How many inmates were NOT assigned for cleanup work or laundry work?

    (A) 30
    (B) 40
    (C) 50
    (D) 60

84. A certain cell block has a maximum capacity of 250 inmates. On March 26, there were 200 inmates housed in the cellblock, 12 inmates were added on that day, and 17 inmates were added on the following day. No inmates left on either day. How many more inmates could this cell block have accommodated on the second day?

    (A) 11
    (B) 16
    (C) 21
    (D) 28

85. A certain cell block has 240 inmates. From 8 a.m. to 9 a.m. on March 25, 120 inmates were assigned to cleanup work and 25 inmates were sent for physical examinations. All the other inmates remained in their cells. How many inmates should have been in their cells during this hour?

    (A) 65
    (B) 85
    (C) 95
    (D) 105

86. There were 254 inmates in a certain cell block at the beginning of the day. At 9:30 a.m., 12 inmates were checked out to the dispensary. At 10:00 a.m., 113 inmates were checked out to work details. At 10:30 a.m., 3 inmates were checked out to another cell block. How many inmates were present in this cell block at 10:45 a.m. if none of the inmates who were checked out had returned?

    (A) 116
    (B) 126
    (C) 136
    (D) 226

87. There were 242 inmates in a certain cell block at the beginning of the day. At 9:00 a.m., 116 inmates were checked out to a recreational program. At 9:15, 36 inmates were checked out to an educational program. At 9:30, 78 inmates were checked out on a work detail. By 10:15, the only inmates who had returned were 115 inmates who had been checked back in from the recreational program. A count made at 10:15 should show that the number of inmates present in the cell block is

    (A) 127.
    (B) 128.
    (C) 135.
    (D) 137.

QUESTIONS 88–92 ARE BASED ON THE FACT SITUATION AND THE REPORT OF INMATE INJURY FORM BELOW.

Fact Situation

Peter Miller is a Corrections Officer assigned to duty in cell block A. His superior officer is John Doakes. Miller was on duty at 1:30 p.m. on March 21 when he heard a scream for help from cell 12. He hurried to cell 12 and found inmate Richard Rogers stamping out a flaming book of matches. Inmate John Jones was screaming. It seems that Jones had accidentally set fire to the entire book of matches while lighting a cigarette, and had burned his left hand. Smoking was permitted at this hour. Miller reported the incident by phone, and Jones was escorted to the dispensary, where his hand was treated at 2:00 p.m. by Dr. Albert Lorillo. Dr. Lorillo determined that Jones could return to his cell block, but that he should be released from work for four days. The doctor scheduled a reexamination for March 22. A routine investigation of the incident was made by James Lopez. Jones confirmed to this officer that the above statement of the situation was correct.

REPORT OF INMATE INJURY

(1) Name of inmate _____   (2) Assignment _____

(3) Number _____   (4) Location _____

(5) Nature of injury _____   (6) Date _____

(7) Details (how, when, where injury was incurred) _____

_____

(8) Received medical attention: date _____ time _____

(9) Treatment _____

(10) Disposition (check one or more):   ____ (10-2) Return to duty
     ____ (10-1) Return to housing area

     ____ (10-3) Work release ____ days   ____ (10-4) Reexamine in ____ days

(11) Employee reporting injury _____

(12) Employee's supervisor or superior officer _____

(13) Medical officer treating injury _____

(14) Investigating officer _____

(15) Head of institution _____

88. Which of the following should be entered in Item 1?
- **(A)** Peter Miller
- **(B)** John Doakes
- **(C)** Richard Rogers
- **(D)** John Jones

89. Which of the following should be entered in Item 11?
- **(A)** Peter Miller
- **(B)** James Lopez
- **(C)** Richard Rogers
- **(D)** John Jones

90. Which of the following should be entered in Item 8?
    (A) 2/21, 1:30 p.m.
    (B) 2/21, 2:00 p.m.
    (C) 3/21, 1:30 p.m.
    (D) 3/21, 2:00 p.m.

91. For Item 10, which of the following should be checked?
    (A) 10-4 only
    (B) 10-1 and 10-4
    (C) 10-1, 10-3, and 10-4
    (D) 10-2, 10-3, and 10-4

92. Of the following items, which one cannot be filled in on the basis of the information given in the Fact Situation?
    (A) Item 12
    (B) Item 13
    (C) Item 14
    (D) Item 15

practice test

ANSWER KEY AND EXPLANATIONS

1. C	20. D	39. D	57. A	75. A
2. D	21. A	40. A	58. C	76. C
3. A	22. B	41. C	59. C	77. C
4. D	23. B	42. C	60. C	78. B
5. B	24. B	43. B	61. C	79. B
6. B	25. C	44. D	62. D	80. C
7. B	26. B	45. A	63. D	81. D
8. D	27. C	46. B	64. A	82. B
9. C	28. D	47. C	65. B	83. A
10. D	29. C	48. D	66. C	84. C
11. B	30. C	49. B	67. A	85. C
12. D	31. D	50. C	68. D	86. B
13. A	32. D	51. D	69. B	87. A
14. C	33. D	52. B	70. C	88. D
15. A	34. A	53. D	71. B	89. A
16. C	35. C	54. A	72. D	90. D
17. A	36. B	55. B	73. A	91. C
18. B	37. C	56. C	74. B	92. D
19. D	38. A			

1. **The correct answer is (C).** As far as we can see, each student is seated at an individual desk.

2. **The correct answer is (D).** The teacher is wearing round frame glasses, a long-sleeved white shirt, vest, and striped tie. He is gesturing with his right hand, not saluting the flag.

3. **The correct answer is (A).** The time indicated on the clock is 4:10. If there is a clock, expect a time question.

4. **The correct answer is (D).** The bald black man has his handgun aimed directly at the teacher.

5. **The correct answer is (B).** There are 13 people in the scene. Always count people in a memory picture.

6. **The correct answer is (B).** The woman wearing a headscarf is sitting at the far left in the third row and is wearing a dark shirt.

7. **The correct answer is (B).** The long counter at the front of the room, where the teacher is standing, has a sink with two faucets at one end and two gas jets as well. Clearly, the room is equipped as a chemistry classroom.

8. **The correct answer is (D).** Nowhere in this room.

9. **The correct answer is (C).** The woman in the doorway wearing a camouflage-design jumpsuit is aiming her submachine gun at the roomful of students.

10. **The correct answer is (D).** The woman in the second seat from the left in the front row has light-colored curly hair and is wearing a print blouse.

11. **The correct answer is (B).** The students are either taking notes or watching the teacher; one person is wearing a baseball cap; writing can be seen on the chalkboard. However, the dark area on the ceiling indicates that a light is not in good working order.

12. **The correct answer is (D).** The dial faces are illegible, but each has a single pointer pointing in a different direction, so we know that they are not clocks.

13. **The correct answer is (A).** The teacher's left hand is on the counter in front of him. His right hand is raised, but not toward the gunman.

14. **The correct answer is (C).** The student in the far left seat in the front row is wearing a plaid shirt and is looking off to his left.

15. **The correct answer is (A).** While the corner of a pad of paper might serve as a blunt instrument, actual conversion into a weapon is most feasible with a ballpoint pen.

16. **The correct answer is (C).** In choice (A) an inmate is handed a key, clearly a violation. In choice (B), the priest, though not an inmate, is also not an authorized employee, so his being handed a key is in violation. The Corrections Officer who takes home the keys in choice (D) is violating the regulation that keys must be deposited with the Security Officer when not in use.

17. **The correct answer is (A).** The inmate who repeatedly bangs his fists against the bars of his cell is in danger of causing himself bodily harm. This inmate must be restrained.

18. **The correct answer is (B).** A kitchen cannot be operated without certain utensils that have the potential of use as dangerous weapons. The sensible cautionary procedure is to maintain careful supervision in the kitchen.

19. **The correct answer is (D).** The element of surprise is necessary for effective searches. Any pattern to the searches would serve as warning to inmates to temporarily stash weapons or escape devices in an area not subject to search.

20. **The correct answer is (D).** Choices (A) and (B) would have the reverse effect. Inmates would come to fear searches even if not guilty. Choice (C) does not serve the purpose at all since inmates would not learn of the punishment that follows possession of a forbidden item.

21. **The correct answer is (A).** Don't jump the gun and sound the alarm on the basis of an informal count, but do make the formal count right away; then act on the basis of fact, if indeed an inmate is missing.

22. **The correct answer is (B).** Cover of darkness is best for escape, so the officer must be certain that the blanketed heap in the bed is really the inmate.

23. **The correct answer is (B).** To insure accuracy you must count inmates yourself, and you must count them when they are not in motion. Endangering their safety is not necessary; let the inmates put things down before you count.

24. **The correct answer is (B).** Accomplices may be smuggled into the prison, so vehicles must be checked at entry as well as at exit. Official vehicles are not immune from escapees hiding themselves inside, so they must also be searched.

25. **The correct answer is (C).** A Corrections Officer should not act rashly, but should always follow through with research and consultations whenever there is a doubt.

26. **The correct answer is (B).** Health and safety always come first. Tend to the injured party.

27. **The correct answer is (C).** The reporting officer has forgotten to name the inmate who attacked Brown.

28. **The correct answer is (D).** The officer has neglected to state the nature of the trouble and what rules were broken.

29. **The correct answer is (C).** You must follow your supervisor's instructions. If you have an opportunity to discuss the new methods before they are to go into effect, by all means raise your questions with your supervisor. If not, go to the new procedures; they may work well. If they do not work well, speak to your supervisor. Professional behavior dictates that you NEVER discuss your misgivings with the inmates.

30. **The correct answer is (C).** The rule is that you must act to stop the fight, but, knowing that the fight might be a diversionary tactic, keep alert.

31. **The correct answer is (D).** Never assume literacy. Always explain changes along with your posting.

32. **The correct answer is (D).** Since there is the possibility of a fracture, and a fracture must not be moved, the best policy is to have the inmate sit still and send for medical assistance.

33. **The correct answer is (D).** This prison rule is stated very clearly. The clinic can wait. Count the prisoner in the proper place at the proper time.

34. **The correct answer is (A).** Severe stomach pains may indicate appendicitis or some other true medical emergency. The other three choices describe problems that can wait until morning.

35. **The correct answer is (C).** Within prison limits, try tact and kindness first.

36. **The correct answer is (B).** The well-being of dependents is a very real concern. The inmate should be introduced to professionals who can contact the family and take necessary steps to assist them.

37. **The correct answer is (C).** Sudden cooperativeness is not a common sign of impending mental illness. Look for other causes.

38. **The correct answer is (A).** Innovation and initiative are fine qualities, but get permission from your supervisor before making changes.

39. **The correct answer is (D).** You should treat everyone in a polite and tactful way.

40. **The correct answer is (A).** The Cell Block Officer enters the supplies picture after the purchasing stage.

41. **The correct answer is (C).** The Cell Block Officer is responsible; therefore, he should count the supplies himself or personally supervise the inmate who does the counting.

42. **The correct answer is (C).** The only way to know how many items were actually delivered is to make a count upon receipt.

43. **The correct answer is (B).** Choice (D) is wrong. Choices (A) and (C) are correct statements, but they are not supported by the passage.

44. **The correct answer is (D).** The unfairness is putting an inmate in a position where other inmates might take advantage of him.

45. **The correct answer is (A).** The scientific studies of inmate behavior may help the officer to understand and broadly predict specific behaviors, but will not give deep understanding of individuals nor assist in making significant changes in personalities.

46. **The correct answer is (B).** The passage states that older men and men who had good employment records tend to be the most reliable within a prison setting.

47. **The correct answer is (C).** The passage states that the troublemakers tend to be the younger men convicted of crimes involving stealth.

48. **The correct answer is (D).** The passage states that information about a man's background is helpful but no substitute for the Corrections Officer's expert judgment based upon experience.

49. **The correct answer is (B).** Surprisingly, first offenders and men with previous convictions behave similarly in prison.

50. **The correct answer is (C).** The first sentence tells us that many people behind bars are simply awaiting trial.

51. **The correct answer is (D).** The unemployed tend to have neither bail money nor proof of stability, so they cannot be released on personal recognizance.

52. **The correct answer is (B).** The passage tells us that when the person forfeits his bail, he loses the money he put up.

53. **The correct answer is (D).** The person who is released on personal recognizance does not have to pay bail, but he must show up for trial and be judged innocent or guilty.

54. **The correct answer is (A).** The writer clearly feels that the bail system is unfair because it is based on economic status rather than upon guilt or innocence.

55. **The correct answer is (B).** Choice (A) should read 382 EPS; choice (C) should read 875 PGF.

56. **The correct answer is (C).** Choice (A) should read 549 FTL; choice (B) should read 692 MLS.

57. **The correct answer is (A).** Choice (B) should read 253 SFE; choice (C) should read 147 JTG.

58. **The correct answer is (C).** Choice (A) should read 569 FML; choice (B) should read 716 GJM.

59. **The correct answer is (C).** Choice (A) should ready 356 EFM; choice (B) should read 198 JLP.

60. **The correct answer is (C).** The passage suggests that 15% to 25% of prison inmates may be mentally disturbed.

61. **The correct answer is (C).** The burden of dealing with mentally disturbed prison inmates falls mainly upon Corrections Officers.

62. **The correct answer is (D).** The passage mentions both the costs and the lack of trained personnel as reasons for failure to provide treatment programs.

63. **The correct answer is (D).** In this passage, "abnormal individual" means one who is mentally disturbed.

64. **The correct answer is (A).** The last sentence of the passage means that the Corrections Officer must understand that a mentally disturbed person may not behave in the same way that a normal, healthy person behaves.

65. **The correct answer is (B).** There are 12 inmates. Five check out during Period I, leaving 7 in their permanent groups.

66. **The correct answer is (C).** Phil checked out, leaving Bob, Sam, and Vic.

67. **The correct answer is (A).** During Period II, Jack and Mel checked out, but Ken and Larry returned.

68. **The correct answer is (D).** In Group X, Ted stayed out, and George checked out; 2 remained. In group Y, 2 checked out, but the 2 who had been out during Period I returned. In Group Z, 3 checked out while one returned. Group X (2) plus Group Y (2) plus Group Z (1) equals 5.

69. **The correct answer is (B).** Bob, Sam, and Vic checked out during Period II.

70. **The correct answer is (C).** Larry returned during Period II and did not leave. Mel and Jack checked back in during Period III. Only Ken checked out.

71. **The correct answer is (B).** In Group X, Ted had never returned after checking out in Period I; Frank and Harry both checked out during Period III. In Group Y, as mentioned in question 83, only Ken was missing. In Group Z, Phil remained since his return in Period II; Sam, Bob, and Vic all returned, but Vic checked out again. So, 3 were not present in Group X, and 1 each out in Groups Y and Z make a total of 5.

72. **The correct answer is (D).**

$$
\begin{array}{r}
\$51.79 \\
29.39 \\
+\quad 8.98 \\
\hline
\$90.16
\end{array}
$$

73. **The correct answer is (A).**

$$
\begin{array}{r}
\$72.07 \\
+\quad 31.54 \\
\hline
103.61 \\
-\quad 25.75 \\
\hline
\$77.86
\end{array}
$$

74. **The correct answer is (B).**

		OR		
	$82.47			$25.50
−	25.50			4.75
	56.97		+	0.35
−	4.75			$30.60
	52.22			
−	0.35			$82.47
	$51.87		−	30.60
				$51.87

75. **The correct answer is (A).**

		OR		
	$19.35			$9.90
+	37.75		+	19.80
	57.10			$29.70
−	9.90			
	47.20			$57.10
−	19.80		−	29.70
	$27.40			$27.40

76. **The correct answer is (C).**

	$38.85
×	2
	77.70
−	27.90
	$49.80

77. **The correct answer is (C).**

	$53.66
	9.27
+	18.75
	$81.68 ÷ 2 = $40.84

78. **The correct answer is (B).**

			OR		
	192	inmates		96	to work detail
−	96	on work detail		+ 32	to class
	96			128	out of cell block
				192	total
−	32	to class		− 128	out of cell block
	64	remaining		64	remaining

79. **The correct answer is (B).** 620 women × 2 utensils per woman = 1,240 personal utensils;

620 ÷ 20 31 groups of 20 each requiring a ladle

1,240	forks and spoons
+ 31	ladles
1,271	utensils

80. **The correct answer is (C).** Two inmates take 6 hours to wash the dishes. Four inmates is twice as many as two inmates. Since there is a direct relationship between the time it takes to do the dishes and the number of inmates, twice the inmates should wash the dishes in half the time. Half of 6 hours is 3 hours.

81. **The correct answer is (D).** 7,000 items ÷ 500 items per inmate = 14 inmates to do the job.

82. **The correct answer is (B).** Choice (A) does not place all 66 men; choice (C) provides for 67 men; the groups in choice (D) are smaller than regulation.

83. **The correct answer is (A).** One half of 100 = 50 assigned to cleanup; one fifth of 100 = 20 assigned to the laundry; 70 inmates assigned; 100 − 70 = 30 not assigned.

84. **The correct answer is (C).** 200 + 12 + 17 = 229 inmates in the cell block; 250 − 229 = 21 remaining places.

85. **The correct answer is (C).** 240 − 120 to cleanup = 120 − 25 for physicals = 95 remaining.

86. **The correct answer is (B).** 12 inmates to dispensary + 113 to work + 3 to another cell block = 128 checked out; 254 − 128 = 126 remaining.

87. **The correct answer is (A).** 242 − 116 to recreation = 126 − 36 to education = 90 − 78 to work detail = 12 + 115 returned from recreation = 127 in the cell block.

88. **The correct answer is (D).** The injured inmate is John Jones.

89. **The correct answer is (A).** Peter Miller, the Corrections Officer on duty at the time of the injury, reported the injury.

90. **The correct answer is (D).** Jones was treated on March 21 at 2:00 p.m. (The injury occurred at 1:30.)

91. **The correct answer is (C).** Jones was returned to his cell block, released from work for four days, and scheduled for reexamination the next day.

92. **The correct answer is (D).** The name of the head of the institution is not given in the Fact Situation.

ANSWER SHEET PRACTICE TEST 2

1. Ⓐ Ⓑ Ⓒ Ⓓ	14. Ⓐ Ⓑ Ⓒ Ⓓ	27. Ⓐ Ⓑ Ⓒ Ⓓ	40. Ⓐ Ⓑ Ⓒ Ⓓ	53. Ⓐ Ⓑ Ⓒ Ⓓ
2. Ⓐ Ⓑ Ⓒ Ⓓ	15. Ⓐ Ⓑ Ⓒ Ⓓ	28. Ⓐ Ⓑ Ⓒ Ⓓ	41. Ⓐ Ⓑ Ⓒ Ⓓ	54. Ⓐ Ⓑ Ⓒ Ⓓ
3. Ⓐ Ⓑ Ⓒ Ⓓ	16. Ⓐ Ⓑ Ⓒ Ⓓ	29. Ⓐ Ⓑ Ⓒ Ⓓ	42. Ⓐ Ⓑ Ⓒ Ⓓ	55. Ⓐ Ⓑ Ⓒ Ⓓ
4. Ⓐ Ⓑ Ⓒ Ⓓ	17. Ⓐ Ⓑ Ⓒ Ⓓ	30. Ⓐ Ⓑ Ⓒ Ⓓ	43. Ⓐ Ⓑ Ⓒ Ⓓ	56. Ⓐ Ⓑ Ⓒ Ⓓ
5. Ⓐ Ⓑ Ⓒ Ⓓ	18. Ⓐ Ⓑ Ⓒ Ⓓ	31. Ⓐ Ⓑ Ⓒ Ⓓ	44. Ⓐ Ⓑ Ⓒ Ⓓ	57. Ⓐ Ⓑ Ⓒ Ⓓ
6. Ⓐ Ⓑ Ⓒ Ⓓ	19. Ⓐ Ⓑ Ⓒ Ⓓ	32. Ⓐ Ⓑ Ⓒ Ⓓ	45. Ⓐ Ⓑ Ⓒ Ⓓ	58. Ⓐ Ⓑ Ⓒ Ⓓ
7. Ⓐ Ⓑ Ⓒ Ⓓ	20. Ⓐ Ⓑ Ⓒ Ⓓ	33. Ⓐ Ⓑ Ⓒ Ⓓ	46. Ⓐ Ⓑ Ⓒ Ⓓ	59. Ⓐ Ⓑ Ⓒ Ⓓ
8. Ⓐ Ⓑ Ⓒ Ⓓ	21. Ⓐ Ⓑ Ⓒ Ⓓ	34. Ⓐ Ⓑ Ⓒ Ⓓ	47. Ⓐ Ⓑ Ⓒ Ⓓ	60. Ⓐ Ⓑ Ⓒ Ⓓ
9. Ⓐ Ⓑ Ⓒ Ⓓ	22. Ⓐ Ⓑ Ⓒ Ⓓ	35. Ⓐ Ⓑ Ⓒ Ⓓ	48. Ⓐ Ⓑ Ⓒ Ⓓ	61. Ⓐ Ⓑ Ⓒ Ⓓ
10. Ⓐ Ⓑ Ⓒ Ⓓ	23. Ⓐ Ⓑ Ⓒ Ⓓ	36. Ⓐ Ⓑ Ⓒ Ⓓ	49. Ⓐ Ⓑ Ⓒ Ⓓ	62. Ⓐ Ⓑ Ⓒ Ⓓ
11. Ⓐ Ⓑ Ⓒ Ⓓ	24. Ⓐ Ⓑ Ⓒ Ⓓ	37. Ⓐ Ⓑ Ⓒ Ⓓ	50. Ⓐ Ⓑ Ⓒ Ⓓ	63. Ⓐ Ⓑ Ⓒ Ⓓ
12. Ⓐ Ⓑ Ⓒ Ⓓ	25. Ⓐ Ⓑ Ⓒ Ⓓ	38. Ⓐ Ⓑ Ⓒ Ⓓ	51. Ⓐ Ⓑ Ⓒ Ⓓ	64. Ⓐ Ⓑ Ⓒ Ⓓ
13. Ⓐ Ⓑ Ⓒ Ⓓ	26. Ⓐ Ⓑ Ⓒ Ⓓ	39. Ⓐ Ⓑ Ⓒ Ⓓ	52. Ⓐ Ⓑ Ⓒ Ⓓ	65. Ⓐ Ⓑ Ⓒ Ⓓ

answer sheet

Practice Test 2

65 QUESTIONS • 3 HOURS

Directions: You will be given 10 minutes to study the five scenes that follow and to try to notice and remember as many details as you can. You may not take any notes during this time. Then answer the 30 questions that follow.

A Courtroom Scene

117

A Portion of a Cell Block

At the Bank

At the Office

Student Session

practice test

QUESTIONS 1–6 ARE BASED ON THE PHOTOGRAPH OF A COURTROOM SCENE.

1. The judge is
   - (A) watching court testimony.
   - (B) conferring with the attorney.
   - (C) looking over some papers.
   - (D) handing documents to a court officer.

2. The person standing is
   - (A) waving papers at the judge.
   - (B) curly haired.
   - (C) wearing a dark coat.
   - (D) looking at the witness.

3. The woman at the table is holding her glasses.
   - (A) True
   - (B) False

4. Two people can be seen seated at the table.
   - (A) True
   - (B) False

5. The judge is NOT wearing glasses.
   - (A) True
   - (B) False

6. An American flag is to the left of the judge.
   - (A) True
   - (B) False

QUESTIONS 7–12 ARE BASED ON THE PHOTOGRAPH OF "A PORTION OF A CELL BLOCK."

7. The lighting in the cell block is provided by
   - (A) skylights.
   - (B) fluorescent tubes.
   - (C) spotlights that are not visible in the picture.
   - (D) a single light bulb.

8. The officer is
   - (A) talking to the inmate.
   - (B) unlocking the cell.
   - (C) looking down at an open book.
   - (D) smiling.

9. The officer is wearing glasses.
   - (A) True
   - (B) False

10. The officer is clean shaven.
    - (A) True
    - (B) False

11. This photograph was taken with the cell doors open.
    - (A) True
    - (B) False

12. An inmate is sticking both hands through the cell bars.
    - (A) True
    - (B) False

QUESTIONS 13–17 ARE BASED ON THE PHOTOGRAPH "AT THE BANK."

13. The teller is
    - (A) wearing a tie.
    - (B) wearing glasses.
    - (C) making change.
    - (D) left-handed.

14. The female customer is wearing
    - (A) a floral dress.
    - (B) light-colored pants.
    - (C) short sleeves.
    - (D) a plaid skirt.

15. The male customer is
    - (A) handing money to the teller.
    - (B) wearing a bow tie.
    - (C) talking to another man in line.
    - (D) writing a check.

16. The number of computer terminals visible in the picture is
    - (A) 3
    - (B) 5
    - (C) 6
    - (D) 4

17. The floral arrangement in the picture is
    - (A) in front of the teller.
    - (B) behind the male customer.
    - (C) next to the computer terminal.
    - (D) next to the window.

QUESTIONS 18–22 ARE BASED ON THE PHOTOGRAPH "AT THE OFFICE."

18. The ratio of women to men in the picture is
    (A) 3:4.
    (B) 5:4.
    (C) 4:3.
    (D) 3:5.

19. The item NOT shown on the table is
    (A) a laptop computer.
    (B) a vase.
    (C) a water pitcher.
    (D) a glass of water.

20. The woman directly in front of the laptop computer is
    (A) pointing to the computer screen.
    (B) reading the papers in front of her.
    (C) typing on the keyboard.
    (D) taking notes.

21. The man speaking to the woman in the background is
    (A) holding a pencil.
    (B) wearing glasses.
    (C) drinking a glass of water.
    (D) wearing a dark suit.

22. All of the following statements are true EXCEPT
    (A) There are seven people at the table.
    (B) The pitcher of water is at the head of the table.
    (C) One person is holding a pencil.
    (D) Three people are standing.

QUESTIONS 23–27 ARE BASED ON THE PHOTOGRAPH "STUDENT SESSION."

23. The number of people in this picture is
    (A) 6.
    (B) 5.
    (C) 7.
    (D) 4.

24. The student wearing sunglasses
    (A) is sitting cross-legged.
    (B) has blond hair.
    (C) is wearing shorts.
    (D) is reading a book.

25. The item in the far left background is likely a
    (A) hockey stick.
    (B) guitar.
    (C) tennis racket.
    (D) none of these.

26. Of the female students in the group,
    (A) two are speaking to each other.
    (B) all are taking notes.
    (C) two are wearing ponytails.
    (D) one is wearing a hat.

27. The time of day is likely
    (A) early evening.
    (B) mid afternoon.
    (C) morning.
    (D) cannot tell from the picture.

QUESTIONS 28–30 ARE BASED ON THE FOLLOWING PRISON RULES.

Transport of prisoners from one institution to another constitutes a risky maneuver that must be accomplished strictly according to established procedure. Strip-search all prisoners prior to loading them on the bus. If transporting an even number of prisoners, handcuff the prisoners in pairs. If transporting only one prisoner and in the case of the final prisoner in an odd count, cuff together the hands of that prisoner behind his or her back. Apply leg irons to the outer leg of each prisoner cuffed to another prisoner, that is, shackle the leg opposite the hand that is cuffed to the bracket in the floor of the bus at the end of the bench on which that prisoner is seated. Shackle prisoners who are cuffed with their hands behind their backs by their left legs. At boarding, verify identities of prisoners and double-check all restraints. Seat prisoners on the bus in alternate rows so that there is an empty bench between rows of prisoners.

Corrections Officers accompanying prisoners being transported are assigned to the bus in the ratio of one officer, not including the driver, for each group of four prisoners, but in no instance may fewer than two officers accompany prisoners being transferred between prisons. At least one officer must be stationed in front of the prisoners and facing them. At least one officer must be stationed to the rear of all prisoners where activity may be observed from behind. Officers must maintain easy clearance so as to be able to move within the bus as needed. Under no circumstances may any officer, with the exception of the driver, be so positioned as to present his or her back to any prisoner.

28. Cooper, Johns, Lorant, Frusciante, Chavez, Sweeny, and Hammer have all been sentenced to prison terms of longer than one year and must now be transferred from the county jail, where they had been held pending sentencing, to the upstate penitentiary. Corrections Officer Krupka has strip-searched each of these prisoners and has handcuffed the right hand of Cooper to the left hand of Johns, the left hand of Lorant to the right hand of Chavez, the right hand of Frusciante to the left hand of Hammer, and the two hands of Sweeny behind Sweeny's back. Officer Fielding is attaching leg irons to the prisoners. Which of the following actions should Fielding take?

    (A) Attach a leg iron to Lorant's left leg.
    (B) Attach a leg iron to Sweeny's right leg.
    (C) Attach a leg iron to Cooper's left leg.
    (D) Attach leg irons to both of Sweeny's legs.

29. The maximum security Lakeside Penitentiary has become dangerously overcrowded, so the superintendent has selected nine inmates who have proven to be untroublesome for transfer to a medium-security institution in another county. The inmates have been strip-searched, handcuffed, and placed in leg irons according to procedure and have been seated on the bus. Officer Tolbert, the driver, gets into the driver's seat. Officer Graves stands at the front of the bus facing the seated prisoners. Officer Schlesinger stands at the back of the bus to observe the prisoners from behind. Officer Cronin should

    (A) sit in the empty seat beside the ninth prisoner.
    (B) get off the bus, because she is not needed.
    (C) sit on an empty bench between rows of prisoners.
    (D) station herself at an empty corner of the bus.

30. Officer Yeager is standing outside the bus at the foot of the steps, checking on prisoners as they board. Officer Yeager verifies names and serial numbers of prisoners being transported and notes date and time on the official list. She tests handcuffs to be certain that they are securely locked and makes sure that leg irons are in place. Then Officer Yeager pats down each prisoner before allowing them to board the bus. Officer Yeager is taking a nonstandard action by

    (A) patting down the prisoners.
    (B) checking off names and serial numbers on a list.
    (C) standing outside the bus at the foot of the steps.
    (D) testing handcuffs.

QUESTIONS 31 AND 32 ARE BASED ON THE FOLLOWING PRISON RULES.

Religious observance by prison inmates may not be infringed unless a religious practice is in conflict with prison safety or security rules. The faith of an inmate must not be questioned or ridiculed. Wherever possible, encourage religious practice. Officers should take steps to accommodate specific reasonable requests.

31. Father Flaherty, a Roman Catholic priest, comes every Saturday afternoon to hear confession from inmates. One Saturday, inmate Mohammed Mahmoud requests permission to go to confession. Officer Trotsky knows that Mahmoud turns toward Mecca and prays five times every day. Officer Trotsky should

    (A) ask Mahmoud why he, a devout Moslem, wants to confess to a Catholic priest.
    (B) turn down the request as totally out of order.
    (C) grant permission while laughing.
    (D) schedule a time for Mahmoud to go to confession.

32. Inmate Ratner approaches Officer Hill and tells Hill that Wednesday night is the anniversary of his father's death. Ratner would like to light a 24-hour memorial candle for his father on that night. Officer Hill should

    (A) tell Ratner that lighting a candle is impossible, because prisoners are not permitted to use matches or lighters.
    (B) permit Ratner to light a candle in his cell under supervision, because this observance is very meaningful to the prisoner.
    (C) arrange for Ratner to observe an officer's lighting of a candle in the supervisor's office and for Ratner to say a prayer while there.
    (D) tell Ratner that he, Officer Hill, will light a candle for him at his home and will be certain that it burns for 24 hours.

QUESTION 33 IS BASED ON THE FOLLOWING PRISON RULES.

A prisoner held under minimum security who has served more than two thirds of his or her sentence with no rules violations may be awarded a weekend pass for a visit to the home of his or her parents or spouse. The prisoner must register the telephone number of the home he or she will be visiting and must call the prison's toll-free monitoring number at noon and at 9:00 p.m. of the first day of the visit and at 8:00 a.m. and 2:00 p.m. of the second day of the visit. The monitoring telephone has a display that indicates the phone number from which the call is originating. A call originating from any number other than that registered is cause for immediate revocation of the pass and retrieval of the prisoner.

33. Inmate Zakris has served 18 months of a 21-month sentence and requests a weekend pass to the home she shares with her husband and 5-year-old son. She registers her home telephone number and is granted the pass, which begins at 9:00 a.m. Saturday. Promptly at 8:00 a.m. on Sunday, Zakris telephones the prison, but the number displayed on the monitor is not the number she had registered. Zakris tells Officer Right, who takes the call, that she has taken her son to visit with her parents at their home. Officer Right should

    (A) ask for the phone number at her parents' home.
    (B) revoke her pass and send a Correction Officer to bring Zakris back to prison immediately.
    (C) tell Zakris to return to her own home at once and to call in as soon as she gets there.
    (D) accept the call and explanation.

QUESTIONS 34 AND 35 ARE BASED ON THE FOLLOWING PRISON RULES.

Considering the number of prison inmates and the violent character of many of these inmates, prison riots are a very rare occurrence. However, even a minor disturbance in a prison tends to have a contagious effect and must be instantly contained before it expands into a major riot. An incipient riot is broadcast throughout the prison by an alarm signal of one long and two short blasts. Alarm signal buttons are placed along all prison walls at 35-foot intervals and are activated by insertion of a special key carried by all Corrections Officers.

At the first sign of unrest, all prisoners throughout the prison must immediately be returned to and confined in their cells. Classes, work assignments, and recreation are all canceled. Meals are to be delivered to the cells. Routine sick call is suspended, but inmates who are under treatment or who become visibly ill or injured must receive treatment. Where feasible, prison doctors will attend to prisoners in their cells. Where facilities of the infirmary are imperative for treatment, prisoners may be individually escorted to the infirmary one at a time. Such prisoners must be handcuffed with both hands behind their backs. The only exception to this rule is such instance when the prisoner's injury is such as to make handcuffing behind the back hazardous to the condition being treated. If a prisoner cannot be handcuffed from behind, an attempt should be made to handcuff the hands in front. The escorting officer must be armed, alert, and positioned behind the prisoner for rapid response.

34. The prisoners from cell block 3, tier 2, north wing of the prison have been shooting baskets in the gym. Suddenly inmate Lyons wheels around and throws a basketball with great force directly at Correction Officer Bryant. Immediately other inmates begin pelting Officer Bryant with basketballs. Officer Glidden, observing this activity, turns his key in the nearest alarm signal device. On hearing the alarm, Officer Ring, overseeing preparation of lunch by prisoners in the south wing kitchen, should

   (A) begin assigning delivery of meals to the cells.
   (B) organize the prompt return of all inmate kitchen workers to their cells.
   (C) handcuff all inmates in the kitchen with their hands behind their backs preparatory to return to their cells.
   (D) continue to supervise the preparation of lunch.

35. In response to an alarm that has sounded signaling a disturbance in a remote section of the penitentiary, all prisoners have been returned to their cells. Officer Umeh, patrolling a walkway in cell block D, comes upon inmates Hughes and Mazza fighting in the cell they share. Hughes is bleeding from a gash in his scalp, and his right arm, also bleeding, is awkwardly distorted with the hand in front of Hughes's waist and with bone protruding. Officer Umeh has good reason to suspect that the arm is broken. Officer Umeh should

   (A) send for a doctor.
   (B) cuff Hughes's hands behind his back and march him to the infirmary.
   (C) cuff Hughes's hands in front of him and march him to the infirmary.
   (D) cuff his own right hand to Hughes's left hand and march him to the infirmary.

QUESTIONS 36–38 ARE BASED ON THE FOLLOWING PRISON RULES.

Except in the instance of prisoners under sentence of death or sentence of life imprisonment with no opportunity for parole, preparation for parole should begin upon admittance to the prison and must be ongoing throughout the duration of incarceration. Preparation for parole should consist of, but not be limited to, literacy education, courses preparatory to the GED, college courses by correspondence or television, industrial training, health and family life education, socialization, and psychological assistance with personal adjustment difficulties. While all of these measures in preparation for parole are mandated to be available to prospective parolees, they may not be denied to any prisoner.

At the intake interview, the Admitting Officer must advise each new inmate of the various services and opportunities available to him or her. During the evaluation period, administer to each new inmate batteries of aptitude, achievement, and interest tests. If appropriate, supplement psychological tests and diagnostic interviews with projective techniques in order to complete a profile of each inmate and to plan a comprehensive program of preparation for release to parole. Refusal of a prospective parolee to accept the program of preparation will weigh negatively among factors being considered by the parole board. Any prisoner who declines parole preparation must be advised that such refusal may lead to delay or denial of parole.

The Admitting Officer should briefly describe work and volunteer activities that are available to prisoners who exhibit good behavior and attitudes after their first six months in the prison.

36. Upon entering the Women's Correctional Facility, new inmate Joan Harrison learns that she may enroll for two academic courses and one industrial course, each meeting five days a week for 45 minutes. In addition, she may take her choice among recreational arts and crafts and sports and fitness offerings and a facilitated group-therapy session that meets twice weekly. Harrison, an educated woman, eagerly signs up for two college courses and joins the softball team. However, she still protests her innocence and bitterly declines any counseling or group therapy of a rehabilitative nature. Officer Gladstone, who is in charge of tailoring a program for Harrison, should

(A) tell Harrison that she will never be paroled if she doesn't go for rehabilitation.

(B) suggest that Harrison add a handicraft, such as quilting, to her program.

(C) accept Harrison's choices without comment for the moment, but note the need for follow-up on getting Harrison into some form of therapy later on.

(D) urge Harrison to volunteer to help out in the prison library.

37. Logan Chambers, who raped and murdered five women, has been sentenced to death. At his intake interview, Chambers tells Admitting Officer Simon that he would like to earn a GED diploma in prison and is eager to learn typesetting and printing. Chambers would also like to be a member of a group that meets twice weekly to learn budgeting and household management. Officer Simon should tell Chambers that

(A) his positive attitude is sure to win him early parole.

(B) his requests are ridiculous, since he will soon be dead and will have no use for the knowledge and skills he develops.

(C) he may learn typesetting and printing, because these skills may be useful within the prison community, but that he may not take up valuable space in the GED classroom nor in any group developing skills useful only to free individuals.

(D) he has made solid choices and will be enrolled as he wishes.

38. Bram Byrd dropped out of school at the age of 16 after having completed slightly fewer than eight years of school. He has been in and out of jail and prison over the last six years and is now serving time for drug sales. Testing indicates that Byrd is not very intelligent, but that he certainly can accept and profit from education and training. Byrd is not ambitious, submits to testing and interviews lethargically answering in monosyllables, and makes no inquiries of what training or activities are open to him. At the end of the evaluation period, Officer Selicki should

(A) assign Byrd to a cell block and tell him to stay out of trouble.

(B) describe the options open to Byrd and urge him to get education and training so that he does not need to run drugs for a living.

(C) send Byrd for drug detox and rehabilitation.

(D) tell Byrd that he will not get out of prison until he has a high school education and a skill.

QUESTIONS 39 AND 40 ARE BASED ON THE FOLLOWING PRISON RULES.

No matter how carefully the inmates are supervised, contraband still manages to find its way into the hands of prison inmates. Some contraband items, most notably drugs and escape plans, enter on the persons of visitors. Other contraband items, especially ingeniously crafted escape implements, are created or stolen within the prison itself. Frequent, periodic searches of the cells must be carried out according to specified procedures.

Searches should be unannounced and should occur at irregularly spaced intervals and at varying times of day. Officers should take advantage of times that large groups of inmates are out of their cells at meals, recreation, work detail, or classes.

In searching a cell, methodically start with the bed, lifting and turning mattress and pillow, squeezing and shaking all bedding. Lift and turn all books and papers and carefully flip between all pages of all books. Inspect clothing for signs of seams that may have been opened to conceal objects slipped into linings or folds, along with the obvious search of pockets. Inspect all fixtures in the cell by inserting a gloved hand into faucets and drains. Finally, tap gently on all surfaces—walls, floors, and ceilings—to listen for hollowed-out areas. Follow any hollow sound at once by cutting out a portion of that surface.

If you discover contraband or any sign of prohibited activity, immediately place the inmate or inmates assigned to that cell into solitary confinement cells with restricted activity. If the hollow sound produces no evidence, assign the inmate or inmates who had been occupying that cell to an empty cell with all surfaces intact pending replastering and total integrity of all surfaces of the disturbed cell.

39. It is 10:00 a.m. on Thursday, and the inmates of cell block G are all out of their cells and accounted for at various assigned activities. Officers Zingler and Rhee are on routine cell inspection. They enter cell G 5 c, occupied by inmate Whistler, and lift, squeeze, punch, and shake the mattress and pillow. Officer Zingler lifts and turns papers and books while Officer Rhee turns his attention to Whistler's clothing. Rhee feels an unusual stiffness in the lining behind a pocket of Whistler's jacket and tears open the lining. There he finds an envelope of crack cocaine. The next action Officers Zingler and Rhee should take is to

- **(A)** search the sink and toilet drains.
- **(B)** tap the wall, ceiling, and floor surfaces for hollowed-out areas that might contain more crack.
- **(C)** collect Whistler from his activity and place him in solitary confinement.
- **(D)** send for Whistler and ask him where he got the crack.

40. In a search of the cell occupied by inmate Flak, Officers Broward and Lee check bedding, books and papers, and clothing and find nothing suspicious. Then Officer Broward pokes her finger into the faucet and down the sink drain. Officer Broward does not feel any foreign object in either faucet or drain, but she sees a discolored spot on the wall just beside the sink and becomes suspicious. Officer Lee taps the area and hears nothing unusual, but agrees that the discolored spot must be investigated. Officer Lee uses a small saw to cut out the discolored area. She discovers that the water pipe behind the cutout area is leaking very slightly. Officer Broward notes on the inspection report that this cell has a leaky pipe and that a plumber should be summoned and returns to the office to file her report. Officer Lee should

- **(A)** immediately have Flak placed into solitary confinement as punishment for damaging her cell.
- **(B)** take steps to reassign Flak to another cell with an intact wall.
- **(C)** move on to inspect the next cell.
- **(D)** find another officer to join her on cell inspection.

QUESTION 41 IS BASED ON THE FOLLOWING PRISON RULES.

Even the best-run prisons suffer from occasional escapes. Escaped prisoners present a real danger to the public. Generally prisoners who escape are among the most desperate of criminals facing very long or capital sentences and having nothing to lose if they are recaptured. Usually they have managed to arm themselves and will not hesitate to use those arms. Often they are charming as well, to get cooperation from unsuspecting members of the public.

At the instant that any prisoner or prisoners cannot be accounted for, prison officials must consider that the prisoner or prisoners have escaped and must act to protect the public. Various measures must be taken simultaneously.

In the prison: Return all prisoners to their cells. Count. Search all possible hiding places within the prison buildings and grounds. Consider all possible points of exit from the prison and inspect carefully. Interview all personnel who might be aware of means of exit.

Outside the prison: Search the periphery of the prison walls. Deploy search teams, each accompanied by a dog, in all directions fanning out from the prison.

In the community: Request that local radio stations broadcast a warning to the public and supply the radio station with full physical descriptions of all escapees. Broadcast warnings should also include useful background information about each escapee along with mention of personal habits and unique identifying characteristics. Submit the same descriptions to television stations and police departments along with faxes of prison photos of the escapees. Request assistance of community and state police.

41. Doing a routine bed-check at 2:00 a.m., Corrections Officer Towson senses that the mound in inmate Nilson's bed is not breathing. Officer Towson reaches for the gate to the cell and discovers that it is not locked. Indeed, the mound is a mere jumble of bedding and clothing. Officer Towson sounds an alarm. The superintendent alerts the press and surrounding police forces of the circumstances of the escape and supplies a description of inmate Nilson. Search teams get to work looking for Nilson inside and outside the prison. What other step should be taken?

    (A) Rouse all the inmates and count them while they are awake.

    (B) Cancel classes and recreation.

    (C) Interview other prisoners to learn if they knew of Nilson's plans.

    (D) No additional steps are needed at this time.

QUESTIONS 42–45 CONSIST OF SHORT STATEMENTS GIVING INFORMATION ABOUT EVENTS. CHOOSE THE PARAGRAPH THAT CONVEYS THE INFORMATION MOST CLEARLY AND ACCURATELY.

42. A complaint of prison brutality:
    Complainant: Pedro Perez, #754098
    Accused: Corrections Officer Brophy
    Date of Complaint: January 4
    Date of alleged brutality: December 25
    Location: County Correctional Institute
    Alleged action: rough handling, ethnic slurs and obscene language, pistol whipping, and denial of access to Christmas services and festivities
    Complainant's representative: John VanDam, Attorney-at-Law

    (A) In a complaint filed January 4 by Attorney John VanDam, Pedro Perez, #754098, alleges that Corrections Officer Brophy beat him up and called him names and refused to let him celebrate Christmas.

    (B) Pedro Perez complains that Corrections Officer Brophy is a racist because he beat him up and called him names and wouldn't let him have Christmas at the County Correctional Institution, says John VanDam.

    (C) John VanDam, a lawyer, says that on January 4, Pedro Perez says that Officer Brophy hit him and cursed at him on Christmas. His number is #754098.

    (D) Attorney VanDam has filed a complaint for Pedro Perez, #745098, in which Perez says he had a fight with Officer Brophy on Christmas in the County Correctional Institution. He didn't let him go to church.

43. A jailhouse suicide:
Institution: Women's House of Detention
Location: cell block A, tier 1, cell #45
Date: July 23
Time of discovery: 4:42 a.m.
Inmate: Jennifer Mohan, #8603
Reporter: Corrections Officer Francois

(A) Corrections Officer Francois found Jennifer Mohan, #8603, hanging in her cell on July 23 at the Women's House of Detention at 4:42 a.m.

(B) Jennifer Mohan, #8603, killed herself by hanging at 4:42 a.m. in cell block A, tier 1, cell #45 in the Women's House of Detention by Corrections Officer Francois.

(C) On July 23 at 4:42 a.m., Corrections Officer Francois discovered Jennifer Mohan, #8603, hanging in cell #45, cellblock A, tier 1, of the Women's House of Detention.

(D) Corrections Officer Francois reported at 4:42 a.m. in the Women's House of Detention that Jennifer Mohan was dead in cell #45, cell block A, tier 1. She was hanging.

44. Off-duty Corrections Officer McKenzie notices an apparently unsupervised small boy wandering aimlessly on White Road between Locust Lane and Sprague Avenue. He asks the child his name and is told "Bobby." The child, who appears to be no more than three years old, has curly blond hair and is wearing striped pants and a white T-shirt with Mickey Mouse on the front. The youngster cannot tell his last name or where he lives. Officer McKenzie calls the police dispatcher from the nearest call box and asks the dispatcher to check with the local precinct, and possibly other precincts as well, to see if a child matching this description has been reported missing. Which of the following statements expresses this information most clearly and accurately?

(A) Bobby is all alone on White Road between Locust Lane and Sprague Avenue. Has anyone missed him?

(B) A small blond boy wearing striped pants and a Mickey Mouse T-shirt and identifying himself as "Bobby" is wandering on White Road between Locust Lane and Sprague Avenue. Has he been reported missing?

(C) Correction Officer McKenzie, who is not on duty, has little Bobby on White Road between Locust Lane and Sprague Avenue in striped pants. He is blond and missing.

(D) An off-duty little boy named Bobby is with Correction Officer McKenzie at a call box on White Road between Locust Lane and Sprague Avenue. He likes Mickey Mouse and wears striped pants.

45. Dorothy Hultz of 17-12 Highland Way stops in at the precinct house and complains to the desk officer, Sergeant Tortino, that she has been receiving obscene telephone calls. She tells the officer that the calls come in to her telephone—824-6686—between 7 and 9 p.m., and that the caller, an unknown male with a husky voice and no particular accent, breathes heavily, asks obscene questions, and makes obscene suggestions to any female answering the phone. Sergeant Tortino instructs Ms. Hultz that all household members should hang up promptly when receiving such calls. By which of the following reports will Sergeant Tortino convey the information to the telephone company most clearly and accurately?

(A) An unidentified male with a husky voice has been making obscene phone calls to 824-6686, the home of Dorothy Hultz at 17-12 Highland Way, between 7 and 9 p.m.

(B) Dorothy Hultz gets obscene calls from a husky man at 824-6686 at 17-12 Highland Way between 7 and 9 p.m.

(C) A husky voice breathes hard and is obscene between 7 and 9 p.m., says Dorothy Hultz over the telephone of 824-6686 at 17-12 Highland Way.

(D) Between 7 and 9 p.m., any female receives a husky obscene voice at 824-6686 from 17-12 Highland Way by Dorothy Hultz.

QUESTIONS 46–50 CONSIST OF FIVE SENTENCES, NUMBERED 1 TO 5. SELECT THE MOST REASONALBE ORDER OF THE SENTENCES TO FORM A LOGICAL, COHESIVE STORY.

46. 1. Cartons of cigarettes, some burst open, were scattered all over the highway.
2. One of the trucks overturned.
3. One police officer called for an ambulance for the driver of the overturned truck, who appeared to be seriously injured.
4. Another police officer noticed that the federal tax stamps on the cigarettes were counterfeit.
5. There was a turnpike crash between two trucks.

(A) 5–2–3–4–1
(B) 5–1–2–3–4
(C) 5–2–1–3–4
(D) 1–5–2–3–4

47. 1. Everyone entering the elevators for the upper floors of the municipal building must pass through a metal detector.
2. A sign in the lobby read "All applicants for the Corrections Officer exam must check their weapons."
3. As the man approached the elevator, the alarm began to sound.
4. The Corrections Officer exam was being given on the seventh floor.
5. The man was not permitted to take the exam.

(A) 4–2–3–1–5
(B) 2–4–1–3–5
(C) 1–2–3–4–5
(D) 2–1–4–5–3

48. 1. An off-duty Corrections Officer was seated in a restaurant.

2. Two men entered, drew guns, and robbed the cashier.

3. The officer made no attempt to stop the robbery.

4. He justified his conduct by claiming that an officer, when off duty, is a private citizen.

5. He finished his meal and walked out of the restaurant.

(A) 1–2–5–3–4

(B) 2–1–5–4–3

(C) 1–2–3–4–5

(D) 1–2–3–5–4

49. 1. Upon their arrival at the scene, the officers could not find evidence of a break-in.

2. The officers climbed over the fence and observed two people running into an alleyway.

3. Two people disappeared into the darkness.

4. However, as the officers continued their investigation, they heard noises coming from the rear of the building.

5. As the officers raced to the rear of the building, they saw four people alighting from the roof by way of a ladder.

(A) 1–4–5–2–3

(B) 5–1–4–2–3

(C) 1–2–3–4–5

(D) 5–1–2–3–4

50. 1. The Corrections Officer noticed a ticking suitcase under a workbench in the boiler room.

2. The suitcase was clean of any dust.

3. The boiler room was hot and dusty.

4. The Corrections Officer opened the suitcase and found pajamas and an alarm clock inside.

5. The Corrections Officer was searching the prison in response to a bomb threat.

(A) 1–2–3–4–5

(B) 5–4–3–2–1

(C) 5–1–3–2–4

(D) 1–5–3–2–4

QUESTIONS 51–65 ARE BASED ON READING PASSAGES. READ EACH PASSAGE AND ANSWER THE QUESTION THAT FOLLOWS IT ACCORDING TO WHAT WAS STATED OR IMPLIED IN THE PASSAGE.

51. Unfortunately, specialization in industry creates workers who lack versatility. When a laborer is trained to perform only one task, she is almost entirely dependent for employment on the demand for that particular skill. If anything happens to interrupt that demand, she is unemployed.

The passage best supports the statement that

(A) the demand for labor of a particular type is constantly changing.

(B) the average laborer is not capable of learning more than one task at a time.

(C) some cases of unemployment are due to a laborers' lack of versatility.

(D) too much specialization is as dangerous as too little.

52. The indiscriminate or continual use of any drug without medical supervision is dangerous. Even drugs considered harmless may result in chronic poisoning if used for a period of years. Pharmacists should not renew prescriptions without consulting the doctor. The doctor prescribed a given amount because he or she wished to limit use of the drug to a certain time. Never use a drug prescribed for someone else just because your symptoms appear similar. There may be differences, apparent to an expert but hidden from you, that indicate an entirely different ailment requiring different medication.

The passage best supports the statement that

(A) the use of drugs is very dangerous.
(B) once a physician has prescribed a drug, it is safe to renew the prescription.
(C) people with similar symptoms are usually suffering from the ailment.
(D) a drug considered harmless may be dangerous if taken over a long period of time without supervision.

53. The storage battery is a lead-acid, electrochemical device used for storing energy in its chemical form. The battery does not actually store electricity, but converts an electrical charge into chemical energy that is stored until the battery terminals are connected to a closed external circuit. When the circuit is closed, the chemical energy inside the battery is transformed back into electrical energy through a chemical action, and, as a result, current flows through the circuit.

The passage best supports the statement that a lead-acid battery stores

(A) current.
(B) electricity.
(C) atomic energy.
(D) chemical energy.

54. The term "custody," as used in the criminal-treatment system, means control, under law, over an individual who has committed a criminal act. Probation, imprisonment, and parole are types of custody. Historically, imprisonment was viewed as punishment, and parole developed as a means of relieving the punishment of prison.

The passage best supports the statement that

(A) parole is generally unrelated to the punishment process.
(B) probation and parole do not involve custody of the individual.
(C) violent inmates are rarely under control.
(D) probation developed as an alternative to punishment.

55. I consider that man's brain originally is like a little empty attic, and you have to stock it with such furniture as you choose. A fool takes in all the lumber of every sort that he comes across. The knowledge that might be useful to him gets crowded out or is jumbled up with a lot of other things so that he has difficulty laying his hands on it. It is a mistake to think that the little room has elastic walls and can distend to any size. Depend upon it, there comes a time when for every addition of knowledge you forget something that you knew before.

The passage best supports the statement that knowledge

(A) should be sought for its own sake.
(B) should be avoided.
(C) should be acquired only if it is necessary.
(D) may be acquired without limitation.

56. It's dangerous to change the weather and the climate. We do not know enough about how such changes will affect the earth. What may seem good for one area may be bad for another. If you change a grassland into a vegetable farm, where will the cattle in the area graze? Before we tinker with our natural environment, we should be very sure of what we are doing.

The passage best supports the statement that the writer believes that

(A) changes in climate and weather may be harmful.

(B) changing climate and weather will improve the earth's surface.

(C) people should never meddle with the natural environment.

(D) it's easy to figure out what will happen when you change the weather.

57. In many states, criminal responsibility extends to persons 16 years of age or more who are not, by reason of mental disease or defect, deprived of substantial capacity to know or appreciate either the nature and consequences of their conduct or that such conduct is wrong.

The most reasonable implication of this statement is that a

(A) person 15 years and 11 months old who stabs a 17-year-old is not criminally responsible.

(B) 16-year-old who commits a robbery is rarely considered criminally responsible.

(C) 15-year-old who is considered a danger to society may not be placed in official custody.

(D) 15-year-old cannot be placed under parole supervision.

58. During the last century and a half, the economic life of the Western world has been transformed by a series of remarkable inventions and the general application of science to the productive process. A revolution more profound in its effects than any armed revolt that ever shook the foundations of a political state has been achieved in the three realms of manufacturing, agriculture, and communication.

The passage best supports the statement that science

(A) has shaken the foundations of manufacturing, agriculture, and communication.

(B) has revolutionized the productive process.

(C) is the tool of the inventor.

(D) has been an important factor in the founding of the agricultural process.

59. Since duplicating machines are being changed constantly, the person who is in the market for such a machine should not purchase offhand the kind with which he or she is most familiar or the one recommended by the first salesperson who calls. Instead, the purchaser should analyze the particular equipment situation and then investigate all the possibilities.

The passage best supports the statement that when duplicating equipment is being purchased, the

(A) purchaser should choose equipment that can be used with the least extra training.

(B) needs of the purchaser's office should determine the selection.

(C) buyer should have his or her needs analyzed by an office equipment salesperson.

(D) recommendations of salespeople should usually be ignored.

60. Those correction theorists who are in agreement with severe and rigid controls as a normal part of the correctional process are confronted with a contradiction: this is so because responsibility that is consistent with freedom cannot be developed in a repressive atmosphere. They do not recognize this contradiction when they carry out their programs with dictatorial force and expect convicted criminals exposed to such programs to be reformed into free and responsible citizens.

The passage best supports the statement that a repressive atmosphere in a prison

(A) does not conform to present-day ideas of freedom of the individual.

(B) is admitted by correction theorists to be in conflict with the basic principles of the normal correctional process.

(C) is advocated as the best method of maintaining discipline when rehabilitation is of secondary importance.

(D) is not suitable for the development of a sense of responsibility consistent with freedom.

61. For the United States, Canada has become the most important country in the world, yet there are few countries about which Americans know less. Canada is the third largest country in the world; only Russia and China are larger. The area of Canada is more than a quarter of the whole British Empire.

The passage best supports the statement that

(A) the British Empire is smaller than Russia or China.

(B) the territory of China is greater than that of Canada.

(C) Americans know more about Canada than about China or Russia.

(D) the United States is the most important nation in the world as far as Canada is concerned.

62. There has been a slump in first-aid training in the industries, and yet one should not think there is less interest in first-aid in industry. The falling off has been in the number of new employees needing such training. It appears that in industries interested in first-aid training, there is now a higher percentage of people so trained than there ever were before.

The passage best supports the statement that first-aid training is

(A) a means of avoiding the most serious effects of accidents.

(B) being abandoned because of expense.

(C) sometimes given to new workers in industry.

(D) of great importance to employees.

63. A recently published article states: "Weight for height and age is, as many have previously held, an inadequate index of the 'nutritional status' of a child. It is unscientific and unfair to set average weight as a goal for all children or for an individual child. Weighing and measuring, however, should be continued as a record of the trend of individual growth that is of value to the physician in relation to other findings and to interest the child in his or her growth."

   The passage implies that weighing and measuring the height of children

   (A) are useful to the physician.
   (B) are of no value and should be stopped.
   (C) are of no value but give interesting information.
   (D) indicate the nutritional status of the child.

64. Neither immediate protection for the community nor long-range reformation of the prisoner can be achieved by prison personnel who express toward the offender whatever feelings of frustration, fear, jealousy, or hunger for power they may have.

   The significance of this statement for Corrections Officers is that they should

   (A) be on the constant lookout for opportunities to prove their courage to inmates.
   (B) not allow deeply personal problems to affect their relations with the inmates.
   (C) not try to advance themselves on the job because of personal motives.
   (D) spend a good part of their time examining their own feelings in order to understand better those of the inmates.

65. Since 95% of prison inmates are released, and a great majority of these within two to three years, a prison that does nothing more than separate the criminal from society offers little promise of real protection to society.

   The passage best supports the inference that

   (A) once it has been definitely established that a person has criminal tendencies, that person should be separated for the rest of his or her life from ordinary society.
   (B) prison sentences in general are much too short and should be lengthened to afford greater protection to society.
   (C) punishment, rather than separation of the criminal from society, should be the major objective of a correctional system.
   (D) when a prison system produces no change in prisoners and the period of imprisonment is short, the period during which society is protected is also short.

ANSWER KEY AND EXPLANATIONS

1. A	14. D	27. B	40. B	53. D
2. C	15. D	28. C	41. A	54. D
3. B	16. B	29. D	42. B	55. C
4. A	17. B	30. A	43. C	56. A
5. A	18. C	31. D	44. B	57. A
6. A	19. B	32. C	45. A	58. B
7. D	20. C	33. B	46. C	59. B
8. C	21. D	34. B	47. B	60. D
9. B	22. D	35. C	48. D	61. B
10. B	23. B	36. C	49. A	62. C
11. B	24. B	37. D	50. C	63. A
12. A	25. B	38. B	51. C	64. B
13. A	26. C	39. C	52. D	65. D

1-27. **If you missed any of these questions, look back at the pictures and observe more closely.**

28. **The correct answer is (C).** Cooper's right hand is cuffed, so he must be shackled by the left leg.

29. **The correct answer is (D).** Officer Cronin must stay on the bus because nine prisoners require three guards, not counting the driver. Cronin must position himself where he can observe all prisoners, with his back to none, and ready to move quickly if needed.

30. **The correct answer is (A).** The prisoners should have been strip searched before cuffing. The pat-down at boarding is not specified in the boarding procedure.

31. **The correct answer is (D).** The rules are clear: Officer Trotsky must not question or ridicule the request and must take steps to accommodate Mahmoud.

32. **The correct answer is (C).** The request is reasonable, but prison safety must remain paramount. The creative solution offered by choice (C) allows the prisoner maximum participation in this observance while maintaining strict adherence to the prison fire regulations.

33. **The correct answer is (B).** The rules are clear. Zakris has violated the conditions of her pass and must be returned at once to the prison.

34. **The correct answer is (B).** Safety and discipline are the first concern. The inmates will not starve if lunch is served late. According to the rules, Officer Ring must get the inmates back to their cells.

35. **The correct answer is (C).** The nature of the injury suggests that the doctor will need X-ray and other infirmary-based equipment. Since the injured hand is in front of the prisoner's waist, cuffing the hands at the front is feasible.

36. **The correct answer is (C).** Harrison has just entered the facility. Counseling and therapy can be added when she has become more reconciled. Choice (A) is incorrect because the word never is much too strong; Choice (D) is incorrect because volunteer activities are open only to inmates who have exhibited good behavior and attitudes in their first six months.

37. **The correct answer is (D).** The rule is clear: "...these measures in preparation for parole...may not be denied to any prisoner."

38. **The correct answer is (B).** The rules require that the new prisoner be advised of the options open to him whether or not he requests this information. Choice (D) is an overstatement. Lack of cooperation may negatively affect parole, but the prisoner will surely be released when he has completed his full sentence. Further, the prisoner should accept training, but there is no requirement that he profit from it.

39. **The correct answer is (C).** Further search and questioning can be done later. The rules require that the inmate be immediately placed into solitary confinement.

40. **The correct answer is (B).** Flak has done nothing wrong and should not be punished. However, she is entitled to undamaged quarters. She should be assigned to another cell.

41. **The correct answer is (A).** The count is very important and must be done swiftly and accurately. This is the best way to avoid being duped by dummies in the beds.

42. **The correct answer is (A).** Choice (B) is a childish statement omitting all details. Choices (C) and (D) lead to confusions: Whose number is 754098? Who didn't let whom go to church?

43. **The correct answer is (C).** Choices (A) and (D) leave out important identifying details. Choice (B) is not incorrect but is poorly stated.

44. **The correct answer is (B).** Choice (A) is an inadequate description of the child; choices (C) and (D) are garbled.

45. **The correct answer is (A).** In choice (B) the man is husky rather than his voice; choices (C) and (D) are garbled.

46. **The correct answer is (C).** 5–2–1–3–4

47. **The correct answer is (B).** 2–4–1–3–5

48. **The correct answer is (D).** 1–2–3–5–4

49. **The correct answer is (A).** 1–4–5–2–3

50. **The correct answer is (C).** 5–1–3–2–4

51. **The correct answer is (C).** Workers with limited, specialized skills are limited to employment where the specific skills are needed. The paragraph does not address the problems of workers whose skills are not sufficiently specialized.

52. **The correct answer is (D).** This is stated in the first two sentences. The paragraph states that persons with similar symptoms *may* have different ailments, not that they necessarily *do*.

53. **The correct answer is (D).** So stated in the second sentence.

54. **The correct answer is (D).** This is the meaning of the last sentence.

55. **The correct answer is (C).** The paragraph advocates selective learning. The author suggests that unnecessary learning leads to forgetting of more important information.

56. **The correct answer is (A).** See the first sentence. On the other hand, choice (C) is too emphatic. The paragraph does not say *never;* it just says to be careful.

57. **The correct answer is (A).** A person fifteen years and eleven months old is under the age of sixteen and thus is not criminally responsible even though he or she commits a criminal act.

58. **The correct answer is (B).** Read carefully. The answer is stated in the first sentence. The second sentence is commentary.

59. **The correct answer is (B).** The last sentence gives this answer. The paragraph specifically cautions against choosing equipment on the sole basis of familiarity with its operation.

60. **The correct answer is (D).** This is a restatement of the theme of the paragraph.

61. **The correct answer is (B).** The paragraph is very short, but it requires careful reading. The only statement supported by the paragraph is that China is larger than Canada.

62. **The correct answer is (C).** If fewer new employees need such training now, clearly the training is being given to some new workers.

63. **The correct answer is (A).** The last sentence says that weighing and measuring are of value to the physician.

64. **The correct answer is (B).** Frustrations, fears, jealousies, and hunger for power fall into the category of deeply personal problems. Correction Officers must not allow such problems to affect their relations with prison inmates nor to distract them from their responsibilities.

65. **The correct answer is (D).** A short period of incarceration protects society for only a short time. If rehabilitation occurs during the imprisonment, the protection of society is extended into the time that the rehabilitated prisoner is released.

ANSWER SHEET PRACTICE TEST 3

1. Ⓐ Ⓑ Ⓒ Ⓓ	13. Ⓐ Ⓑ Ⓒ Ⓓ	25. Ⓐ Ⓑ Ⓒ Ⓓ	37. Ⓐ Ⓑ Ⓒ Ⓓ	49. Ⓐ Ⓑ Ⓒ Ⓓ
2. Ⓐ Ⓑ Ⓒ Ⓓ	14. Ⓐ Ⓑ Ⓒ Ⓓ	26. Ⓐ Ⓑ Ⓒ Ⓓ	38. Ⓐ Ⓑ Ⓒ Ⓓ	50. Ⓐ Ⓑ Ⓒ Ⓓ
3. Ⓐ Ⓑ Ⓒ Ⓓ	15. Ⓐ Ⓑ Ⓒ Ⓓ	27. Ⓐ Ⓑ Ⓒ Ⓓ	39. Ⓐ Ⓑ Ⓒ Ⓓ	51. Ⓐ Ⓑ Ⓒ Ⓓ
4. Ⓐ Ⓑ Ⓒ Ⓓ	16. Ⓐ Ⓑ Ⓒ Ⓓ	28. Ⓐ Ⓑ Ⓒ Ⓓ	40. Ⓐ Ⓑ Ⓒ Ⓓ	52. Ⓐ Ⓑ Ⓒ Ⓓ
5. Ⓐ Ⓑ Ⓒ Ⓓ	17. Ⓐ Ⓑ Ⓒ Ⓓ	29. Ⓐ Ⓑ Ⓒ Ⓓ	41. Ⓐ Ⓑ Ⓒ Ⓓ	53. Ⓐ Ⓑ Ⓒ Ⓓ
6. Ⓐ Ⓑ Ⓒ Ⓓ	18. Ⓐ Ⓑ Ⓒ Ⓓ	30. Ⓐ Ⓑ Ⓒ Ⓓ	42. Ⓐ Ⓑ Ⓒ Ⓓ	54. Ⓐ Ⓑ Ⓒ Ⓓ
7. Ⓐ Ⓑ Ⓒ Ⓓ	19. Ⓐ Ⓑ Ⓒ Ⓓ	31. Ⓐ Ⓑ Ⓒ Ⓓ	43. Ⓐ Ⓑ Ⓒ Ⓓ	55. Ⓐ Ⓑ Ⓒ Ⓓ
8. Ⓐ Ⓑ Ⓒ Ⓓ	20. Ⓐ Ⓑ Ⓒ Ⓓ	32. Ⓐ Ⓑ Ⓒ Ⓓ	44. Ⓐ Ⓑ Ⓒ Ⓓ	56. Ⓐ Ⓑ Ⓒ Ⓓ
9. Ⓐ Ⓑ Ⓒ Ⓓ	21. Ⓐ Ⓑ Ⓒ Ⓓ	33. Ⓐ Ⓑ Ⓒ Ⓓ	45. Ⓐ Ⓑ Ⓒ Ⓓ	57. Ⓐ Ⓑ Ⓒ Ⓓ
10. Ⓐ Ⓑ Ⓒ Ⓓ	22. Ⓐ Ⓑ Ⓒ Ⓓ	34. Ⓐ Ⓑ Ⓒ Ⓓ	46. Ⓐ Ⓑ Ⓒ Ⓓ	58. Ⓐ Ⓑ Ⓒ Ⓓ
11. Ⓐ Ⓑ Ⓒ Ⓓ	23. Ⓐ Ⓑ Ⓒ Ⓓ	35. Ⓐ Ⓑ Ⓒ Ⓓ	47. Ⓐ Ⓑ Ⓒ Ⓓ	59. Ⓐ Ⓑ Ⓒ Ⓓ
12. Ⓐ Ⓑ Ⓒ Ⓓ	24. Ⓐ Ⓑ Ⓒ Ⓓ	36. Ⓐ Ⓑ Ⓒ Ⓓ	48. Ⓐ Ⓑ Ⓒ Ⓓ	60. Ⓐ Ⓑ Ⓒ Ⓓ

answer sheet

Practice Test 3

60 QUESTIONS • 3 HOURS

Directions: You will be given 10 minutes to study the four scenes that follow and to try to notice and remember as many details as you can. You may not take any notes during this time. Then answer the questions that follow.

On the Beat

Security Control Post

Hospital Ward

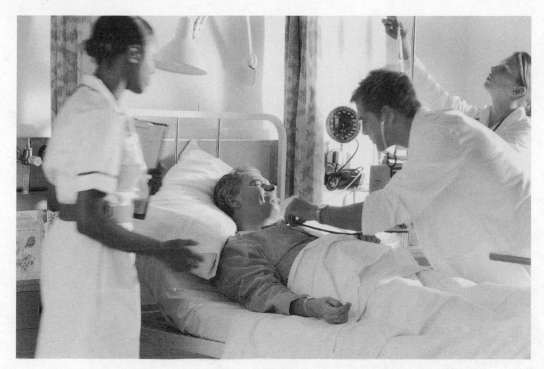

practice test

A View Inside Prison

QUESTIONS 1–3 ARE BASED ON THE PHOTOGRAPH "ON THE BEAT."

1. The people in the photograph are
   (A) one man and one women.
   (B) three men.
   (C) two men.
   (D) not looking at the camera.

2. What can be seen behind the people?
   (A) athletic fields.
   (B) an airport.
   (C) a police car.
   (D) a delivery truck.

3. The uniforms consist of
   (A) dark slacks and dark long-sleeved shirts.
   (B) dark slacks and light short-sleeved shirts.
   (C) dark slacks and light long-sleeved shirts.
   (D) dark slacks and dark short-sleeved shirts.

QUESTIONS 4 AND 5 ARE BASED ON THE PHOTOGRAPH "SECURITY CONTROL POST."

4. The number of active TV monitors visible in the photograph is
   (A) 8.
   (B) 15.
   (C) 21.
   (D) 25.

5. Which of the following statements is NOT correct?
   (A) There are three telephones on the table.
   (B) There is a pencil holder on the table.
   (C) The man is wearing a watch.
   (D) The man has one arm resting on the table.

QUESTIONS 6–8 ARE BASED ON THE PHOTOGRAPH "HOSPITAL WARD."

6. The doctor is
   (A) writing on the patient's chart.
   (B) using a stethoscope.
   (C) talking to the patient.
   (D) speaking to the nurse.

7. The patient is
   (A) talking to the nurse.
   (B) out of bed.
   (C) lying down.
   (D) sitting up.

8. The nurse next to the patient is
   (A) holding a stethoscope.
   (B) holding the patient's hand.
   (C) wearing glasses.
   (D) holding a clipboard.

QUESTIONS 9 AND 10 ARE BASED ON THE PHOTOGRAPH "A VIEW INSIDE PRISON."

9. The officer is
   (A) smiling.
   (B) serious.
   (C) laughing.
   (D) confused.

10. Which one of the following statements is correct?
    (A) The officer is holding handcuffs in his hand.
    (B) The officer is carrying a clipboard.
    (C) The officer is carrying handcuffs attached to his belt.
    (D) There is a light fixture visible between the front two cells.

11. You, a Corrections Officer, notice something unusual in the cell block under your care. You should immediately
    (A) report the matter in writing to your superior officer.
    (B) investigate the matter.
    (C) wait for a time to see whether anything happens.
    (D) blow your whistle and sound a general alarm.

12. A prison inmate asks you to recommend a good lawyer to him. You should
    (A) comply with his request.
    (B) tell him you wish to consult your superior officer before making your suggestion.
    (C) tell him that it would be undesirable for you as a Corrections Officer to make such recommendation.
    (D) suggest that he study the law himself, since he has plenty of time.

13. An inmate under your care is epileptic. You should
    (A) pay no attention to her.
    (B) take special care that she does not work in such a place as to make it easy for her to hurt herself.
    (C) endeavor to make her comfortable at all times.
    (D) take special care that she does not escape.

14. Of the following, you, a Corrections Officer, will most likely find it necessary to be able to
    (A) shoot accurately to halt a prisoner's escape.
    (B) subdue prisoners with physical strength.
    (C) keep your temper when insulted by a prisoner.
    (D) speak the vernacular commonly used by prison inmates.

15. You receive instructions from your supervisor that you do not fully understand. For you to ask for a further explanation would be
    (A) good; chiefly because your supervisor will be impressed by your interest in your work.
    (B) poor; chiefly because the time of your supervisor will be needlessly wasted.
    (C) good; chiefly because proper performance depends on full understanding of the work to be done.
    (D) poor; chiefly because officers should be able to think for themselves.

16. An inmate tells you that the prisoner in the cell next to hers has stolen her pocket radio. Of the following, the best action for you to take *first* is to
    (A) ask the inmate on what she bases her accusation.
    (B) ask the inmate to put her complaint in writing, including a description of the stolen article.
    (C) search the cell of the accused.
    (D) report the accusation to your supervisor.

17. "*Prison Rule*: A Corrections Officer must be in control of all of his or her keys at all times. *Prison Rules*: Under no circumstances may a prisoner be unsupervised." You are escorting a prisoner to a dental appointment in another part of the prison. As you pass through a gate from one section to another, your key breaks in the lock. You are unable to remove the portion of the key from the lock. You should

    (A) continue with the prisoner, since the key is stuck and useless.
    (B) stay with the key and send the prisoner along to the dental appointment.
    (C) send the prisoner back to get another Corrections Officer as escort.
    (D) remain with the prisoner beside the gate until another Corrections Officer appears to escort the prisoner and to send for the locksmith, even though it will make the prisoner late for the dentist.

18. As a Corrections Officer, the best action for you to take with respect to complaints made by inmates is to

    (A) ignore these complaints, since it is only natural for prison inmates to complain.
    (B) investigate all complaints thoroughly.
    (C) tell the inmates to submit all complaints to your superior officer whose responsibility it is to handle such matters.
    (D) weigh the merit of each complaint before you take further action.

19. At times you, in your capacity as a Corrections Officer, may he expected to testify in court about a prisoner. In preparation for such testimony, the most important of the following actions for you to take is to

    (A) wear your newest uniform so as to create a good impression.
    (B) refresh your memory about the facts of the case before going to court.
    (C) discuss what you are going to say with the head of the organization representing Corrections Officers.
    (D) talk to the prisoner about the testimony he or she is going to give.

20. As a Corrections Officer supervising a prisoner who operates a piece of dangerous machinery, you should NOT

    (A) keep an account of the amount of work the prisoner turns out.
    (B) tell the prisoner about problems that might arise in operating the machine.
    (C) answer the prisoner's questions about written operational instructions that the prisoner should have read.
    (D) allow the prisoner to make mistakes for a day or two before correcting the mistakes.

21. You observe that George and Henry, who previously had been rather cool toward one another, suddenly seem to have a lot to say to each other. They spend a great deal of time talking, whispering, and laughing together. You should

    (A) ask them to share their joke with you.
    (B) tell them that whispering is prohibited and all communication must be made in a normal voice.
    (C) report their unusual behavior to your supervisor.
    (D) watch them carefully to be certain that nothing more than friendship is developing.

practice test

22. The Department of Corrections has a regulation that prohibits socializing between Corrections Officers and prison inmates. The *best* reason for this rule is that

(A) a Corrections Officer who socializes with inmates may be tempted to help them escape.

(B) socializing with prisoners leads them to the mistaken impression that the Corrections Officer is "on their side."

(C) the Corrections Officer may become lax in his or her duties of guarding the prisoners.

(D) prisoners who socialize with the Corrections Officers will be beaten by the other prisoners.

23. A prisoner goes berserk in the dining room of a prison. He begins to complain loudly and profanely about the quality of the food. Of the following, the Corrections Officer in charge of the dining room should *immediately*

(A) tell the prisoner to calm down and to be happy he is eating a meal.

(B) get the inmate to stop by asking the other prisoners to ignore him.

(C) have the prisoner removed from the dining hall.

(D) inspect the food to find out whether anything is wrong with it.

24. Giving the prisoners job training in their assigned tasks is one of the duties of the Correction Officer. When giving this training, the officer should be sensitive to the fact that

(A) a prisoner who learns quickly will become a model prisoner.

(B) a prisoner who learns slowly has no interest in learning.

(C) one prisoner can learn a job just as fast as any other prisoner.

(D) a prisoner may lack confidence in his or her ability to learn the job.

25. A prison regulation prohibits a Corrections Officer from individually punishing a prisoner, even though the prisoner is caught breaking the rule, and requires instead that the infraction be reported to a superior officer. The *most* likely reason for such a rule is that

(A) Corrections Officers cannot judge the effects of punishment.

(B) most Corrections Officers would give punishment that is too severe.

(C) if punishment is given, it should be administered by the institution itself in line with correctional policy.

(D) additional punishment is bad policy in a rehabilitation setting.

26. One inmate, Helen, has attracted your attention because she reminds you so much of your own younger sister. The *best* way for you to deal with your feelings toward Helen is to

(A) grant her little favors and explain to the other inmates how Helen resembles your sister.

(B) suppress your feelings and treat Helen like everyone else.

(C) ask that Helen be transferred to the care of another Corrections Officer.

(D) treat Helen a bit more harshly than other prisoners because you are so disappointed in her.

27. A prisoner regulation requires that a doctor prescribing medicine for a prisoner must personally observe the prisoner taking the medicine in his or her presence. The most fundamental reason for this rule in a prison is to

(A) enable the doctor to give prompt treatment if the prisoner has an unexpected reaction to the medication.

(B) keep prisoners from saving up the medicine and from using it for improper purposes.

(C) be certain that the medicine is taken so that the prisoner will soon get well.

(D) discourage prisoners from pretending illnesses in order to avoid work assignments.

28. A prisoner who has a reputation as a liar comes to you with a story that an escape is being planned by several other inmates. He names the inmates and gives details of their plans. The *best* action for you to take is to

(A) take him to your superior officer.

(B) tell him that you know of his reputation and that there is no use in his trying to win favor with you.

(C) ask some other prisoners, not the named, if there is any truth to his story.

(D) alert your fellow Corrections Officers to keep a special eye on the named inmates.

29. Alicia, a new prisoner in your care, is especially lethargic and unresponsive. She refuses to participate or to follow instructions. The *first* thing you should do in your management of Alicia is

(A) lock her in her cell.

(B) request a suicide watch.

(C) ask another officer who is fluent in Spanish to try to reason with her.

(D) check her records to see if there is any notation about physical or language limitations or about her mental state.

30. A Corrections Officer, alone on duty, sees two of several prisoners in a work detail under his supervision suddenly begin to beat each other with their fists. The Officer immediately wades in and attempts to forcibly separate the two enraged prisoners. In most instances, an action like this by a Corrections Officer would be

(A) desirable; such prompt movement by the officer will prevent the fight from spreading.

(B) undesirable; since other prisoners would be unsupervised while the officer acts, the two should be allowed to fight it out.

(C) desirable; seeing an officer act so quickly, other prisoners will be hesitant to start fights in the future.

(D) undesirable; an immediate call for help should be made before the officer takes personal action.

31. In recreation yard conversation, José learns that Bill, who committed essentially the same crime that José committed, is serving a much shorter sentence. José becomes sullen and hostile and complains bitterly to you about injustices and prejudice in the criminal justice system. The *best* way to calm José is to

(A) suggest that he ask Bill what defense tactics he used in order to draw a lighter sentence.

(B) tell José that since criminals have committed crimes, there is no requirement that they be treated fairly.

(C) assure José that he had a wise judge and got what he deserved.

(D) explain to José that sentencing is based not only upon the nature of the crime but also on previous records and special circumstances surrounding the crime at the time.

32. It is absolutely forbidden for Corrections Officers to accept any gifts from prisoners or their families. The most important reason for this rule is that
(A) favors would be expected in return.
(B) the gifts may have been stolen.
(C) prison populations and their families generally cannot afford gifts.
(D) prisoners who had not given gifts might turn against the gift givers.

33. You are in charge of a group of inmates who work in a shop where they use several tools. The most practical method for making sure that no tools are smuggled out at the end of the work day is to
(A) assign a special place to each tool mid-check to see that each tool is in its assigned place before you and the inmates leave.
(B) chain each tool to the work bench with a long chain.
(C) search the inmates before they leave the shop.
(D) have each inmate give you a receipt for each tool he uses and return the receipt to the inmate when the tool is returned.

34. While walking through a prison corridor, you come upon an unfamiliar inmate lying on the floor unconscious with blood on his face. The *first* action for you to take is to
(A) examine the inmate to see what first-aid assistance you can give.
(B) go through the inmate's pockets to see what identification he has on his person.
(C) go to the warden's office to get assistance.
(D) ask the prisoners in the area what happened.

35. It is prison regulation that a Corrections Officer who is escorting a group of prisoners must always walk at the back of the group. The *best* reason for this regulation is that
(A) the officer can keep the stragglers from falling behind.
(B) no fights can develop behind the officer.
(C) there is no opportunity for the officer to be attacked from behind.
(D) the officer can see in which direction escapees run.

36. A Corrections Officer should shoot if
(A) he observes an inmate in the act of stealing from another inmate.
(B) he observes one inmate about to strike another.
(C) an inmate armed with a pick attacks another officer.
(D) An officer should never shoot.

37. Every Monday the prison office issues a bulletin telling of changes in rules and regulations, new educational and social programs that are being offered, and special events for the week. Your *best* action with respect to this bulletin is to
(A) post it on the bulletin board and tell prisoners that the bulletin is there for all to read.
(B) read the bulletin aloud to the prisoners and then post it.
(C) have the same prisoner, the one with the commanding voice, read the bulletin aloud each week, then post it.
(D) choose a different prisoner each week to read the bulletin aloud before posting.

38. A large group of prisoners, larger than usual, is congregated in the center of the exercise area talking quietly but with great animation. A couple of prisoners keep looking furtively over their shoulders at you. The *first* thing you should do is

(A) summon some other Corrections Officers to join you in observing these prisoners.

(B) call aside one of the prisoners whom you know by experience to be cooperative and forthright and ask her what is going on.

(C) notify the warden of this unusual congregation.

(D) step up to the group and tell the prisoners to disperse and get back to their exercise and recreation.

39. A new prisoner, a Sikh, insists upon wearing a tightly wound turban on his head at all times, in defiance of prison regulations but in accordance with his religion. Your *best* action would be to

(A) confiscate the turban; rules are rules.

(B) ask a couple of other prisoners to jump the Sikh and snatch the turban and bring it to you.

(C) send the Sikh to solitary confinement.

(D) privately ask the Sikh to unwind his turban for you so that you may be satisfied that no weapon is involved; then consult the warden.

40. Frank and Nick, two prisoners who have never distinguished themselves in any way, approach you and tell you that they have information about a gambling ring in their cell block. They offer to amass details for you and to name names, asking for nothing in return. You should

(A) thank them and tell them that you eagerly await their full report.

(B) thank them for alerting you to the situation, but assure them that you and your fellow officers will pick up the surveillance from there.

(C) reprimand them for carrying tales.

(D) report them to the warden as participants in a gambling ring.

FOR QUESTIONS 41–50, CHOOSE THE ANSWER THAT BEST COMBINES THE THREE SHORT SENTENCES. YOUR CHOICE SHOULD CONVEY ALL THE INFORMATION IN A CLEAR, SUCCINCT, AND GRAMMATICALLY CORRECT MANNER.

41. Zirconium is considered to be a rare metal.
Copper, tin, and lead are mined from the earth's crust.
There is more zirconium than copper, tin, and lead in the earth's crust.

(A) Zirconium is a metal rarely found in the earth's crust, with copper, tin, and lead.

(B) Copper, tin, and lead are abundant in the earth's crust, as is zirconium.

(C) Copper, tin, and lead are metals found in the earth's crust, unlike zirconium.

(D) Although zirconium is classified as a rare metal, it is more abundant in the earth's crust than copper, tin, or lead.

42. Male mosquitos feed on vegetable juice.
    Female mosquitos drink animal blood.
    Only female mosquitos are equipped to draw blood.
    - **(A)** Mosquitos cause distress to humans because of their feeding habits, which are painful and bloodthirsty.
    - **(B)** Mosquitos have a liquid diet.
    - **(C)** Male mosquitos are incapable of drawing blood. Only female mosquitos drink animal blood.
    - **(D)** People are bitten by female mosquitos that drink their blood and have ability to draw it and are not bitten by male mosquitos that don't have the ability to draw blood but drink vegetable juice.

43. A police dog must accept food only from its trainer.
    Poisoned meat causes painful death.
    Strict discipline is part of a police dog's training.
    - **(A)** Part of the discipline in a police dog's training is learning to accept food only from its master. Thus the police dog is not lured to a painful death from eating poisoned meat.
    - **(B)** A disciplined police dog eats poisoned meat only when it is served by its trainer.
    - **(C)** A police dog is disciplined to eat only food given by their trainer. This way they don't die from eating poisoned meat.
    - **(D)** The police dog is disciplined to know what is poisoned meat and eats only food that is not poisoned by its trainer.

44. Before World War II, Dutch elm disease was controlled and limited.
    During the war, quarantines and tree sanitation measures were relaxed.
    Dutch elm disease is a fatal fungus infection.
    - **(A)** Dutch elm disease, which is a fatal fungus infection, used to be controlled by quarantines and tree sanitation measures and was curtailed during World War II.
    - **(B)** Before World War II, Dutch elm disease, a fatal fungus infection, was controlled by quarantines and tree sanitation.
    - **(C)** Relaxation of quarantines and tree sanitation during World War II caused Dutch elm disease to be fatal fungus infection.
    - **(D)** The fatal fungus infection, Dutch elm disease, relaxed quarantines and tree sanitation during World War II.

45. John has a bag of marbles.
    Mary and I have no marbles.
    John is willing to share equally.
    - **(A)** Mary and I want John's marbles, but John won't give them to us.
    - **(B)** Mary and me will each get some of John's marbles.
    - **(C)** John will divide his marbles between Mary and I.
    - **(D)** When the marbles are shared, John, Mary, and I will each have one third.

46. There are three salespersons in the store.
    Lois, one of the salespersons, is 5'9" tall.
    Neither Bob nor Alice, both of whom sell in the store, is as tall as 5'9".
    - **(A)** Of all the salespersons in the store, Lois is taller.
    - **(B)** Lois is taller than any salesperson in the store.
    - **(C)** Lois is taller than any other salesperson in the store.
    - **(D)** Of all the salespersons, neither Bob nor Alice are as tall as Lois.

47. Backgammon is a complex game.
You must be able to change strategies often to play it well.
It is easy to learn.

   (A) Backgammon is a complex game, and you must change strategies often to learn it well.
   (B) Though backgammon is easy to learn, it is a complex game that requires frequent shifts of strategy when played well.
   (C) To learn to play backgammon you must shift complex strategies easily.
   (D) You must easily learn to shift strategies to play the complex game of backgammon well.

48. Fish in tropical waters are colorful.
They swim among coral reefs.
You can see them from glass-bottomed boats.

   (A) You can swim in tropical waters and see glass-bottomed boats, colorful fish, and coral reefs.
   (B) You can see glass-bottomed fish swimming among coral reefs and colorful boats in tropical waters.
   (C) In tropical waters, you can see glass-bottomed boats, colorful fish, and coral reefs swimming.
   (D) From glass-bottom boats, you can see colorful fish swimming in tropical waters among coral reefs.

49. The hiker was lost.
A St. Bernard rescued him.
It happened in the Alps.

   (A) The hiker was rescued by a St. Bernard lost in the Alps.
   (B) The lost Alpine hiker was rescued by a St. Bernard.
   (C) The hiker in the lost Alps was rescued by a St. Bernard.
   (D) In the Alps the hiker was rescued by a lost St. Bernard.

50. Taxes are deducted from all wages.
Workers who must work at night are paid overtime.
The rate of tax to be withheld is fixed by law.

   (A) The law requires that people who are paid overtime must pay taxes.
   (B) According to the law, people who work at night must be paid overtime and deduct taxes.
   (C) The tax rate on overtime pay is deducted from wages by law and is paid at night.
   (D) By law a fixed rate of taxes is deducted from all wages, including those paid as overtime for night work.

FOR QUESTIONS 51–60, READ EACH PASSAGE, THE QUESTION THAT FOLLOWS IT, AND THE FOUR ANSWER CHOICES. CHOOSE THE ANSWER THAT BEST CONVEYS THE MEANING OF THE PASSAGE.

51. At times it has been suggested that it is incongruous for the government to employ one lawyer to prosecute and another to defend the same prisoner. This is a superficial point of view, for it overlooks the principle that the government should be as anxious to shield the innocent as it is to punish the guilty.

The passage best supports the statement that

(A) it is not properly within the scope of the government to provide criminals with both prosecuting and defending lawyers.

(B) a person held for a crime, if he be poor, need never fear that he will not be adequately defended, because the government makes provision for competent lawyers to aid him in his defense.

(C) although sometimes criticized, it is governmental policy to shield the innocent by providing legal defense for indigent persons accused of crime.

(D) it is an incongruous point of view that the government should concurrently shield the innocent and punish the guilty.

52. The capacity of banks to grant loans depends, in the long run, on the amount of money deposited with them by the public. In the short run, however, it is a well-known fact that banks not only can, but do, lend more than is deposited with them. If such lending is carried to excess, it leads to inflation.

The passage best supports the statement that

(A) banks often indulge in the vicious practice of lending more than is deposited with them.

(B) in the long run, a sound banking policy operates for the mutual advantage of the bankers and the public.

(C) inflation is sometimes the result of excess lending by the banks.

(D) bank lending is always in direct ratio with bank deposits.

53. There exists a false but popular idea that a clue is a mysterious fact that most people overlook but that some very keen investigator easily discovers and recognizes as having, in itself, a remarkable meaning. The clue is most often an ordinary fact that an observant person picks up—something that gains its significance when, after a long series of careful investigations, it is connected with a network of other clues.

To be of value, clues must be

(A) discovered by skilled investigators.

(B) found under mysterious circumstances.

(C) connected with other facts.

(D) discovered soon after the crime.

54. Certain chemical changes, such as fermentation, are due to the action of innumerable living microorganisms known as bacteria. Bacteria also cause the decomposition of sewage.

Certain chemical changes are due to

(A) bacteria.
(B) oxidation.
(C) fermentation.
(D) decomposition.

55. Any business not provided with capable substitutes to fill all important positions is a weak business. Therefore, a foreman should train each man not only to perform his own particular duties, but also to do those of two or three positions.

The passage best supports the statement that

(A) dependence on substitutes is a sign of a weak organization.
(B) training will improve the strongest organization.
(C) the foreman should be the most expert at any particular job under him.
(D) vacancies in vital positions should be provided for in advance.

56. The coloration of textile fabrics composed of cotton and wool generally requires two processes, as the process used in dyeing wool is seldom capable of fixing the color upon cotton. The usual method is to immerse the fabric in the requisite baths to dye the wool and then to treat the partially dyed material in the manner found suitable for cotton.

The dyeing of textile fabrics composed of cotton and wool is

(A) more successful when the material contains more cotton than wool.
(B) not satisfactory when solid colors are desired.
(C) restricted to two colors for any one fabric.
(D) based upon the methods required for dyeing the different materials.

57. The increased size of business organizations has resulted in less personal contact between superior and subordinate. Consequently, business executives today depend more upon records and reports to secure information and exercise control over the operations of various departments.

The increased size of business organizations has

(A) caused a complete cleavage between employer and employee.
(B) resulted in less personal contact between superior and subordinate.
(C) tended toward class distinctions in large organizations.
(D) resulted in a better means of controlling the operations of various departments.

practice test

58. Most solids, like most liquids, expand when heated and contract when cooled. To allow for this, roads, sidewalks, and railroad tracks are constructed with spacings between sections so that they can expand during the hot weather.

If roads, sidewalks, and railroad tracks were not constructed with spacings between sections,

(A) nothing would happen to them when the weather changed.

(B) they could not be constructed as easily as they are now.

(C) they would crack or break when the weather changed.

(D) they would not appear to be even.

59. In a lightning-like military advance, similar to that used by the Germans, the use of persistent chemicals is unnecessary. It might even be a detriment to a force advancing over a broad front.

The passage best supports the statement that

(A) chemicals should not be used by a defending army.

(B) the Germans advanced in a narrow area.

(C) an advancing army may harm itself through the use of chemicals.

(D) chemical warfare is only effective if used by an advancing army.

60. It is probably safe to assume that for most people, mental growth ceases somewhere between ages 14½ and 16. After that, any increase in ability to meet novel situations is gained from experience. Intellectual growth is likewise ascribed to wider experience and more information, rather than to an increase in mental capacity.

Most individuals somewhere between 14½ and 16

(A) make demands on mere experience rather than on native ability.

(B) show an increase rather than a decrease in general mental capacity.

(C) have achieved their total mental growth.

(D) cease to show increased capacity to meet novel situations.

ANSWER KEY AND EXPLANATIONS

1. C	13. B	25. C	37. B	49. B
2. C	14. C	26. B	38. C	50. D
3. D	15. C	27. B	39. D	51. C
4. C	16. A	28. A	40. B	52. C
5. A	17. D	29. D	41. D	53. C
6. B	18. D	30. D	42. C	54. A
7. C	19. B	31. D	43. A	55. D
8. D	20. D	32. A	44. B	56. D
9. B	21. D	33. A	45. D	57. B
10. C	22. C	34. A	46. C	58. C
11. B	23. C	35. C	47. B	59. C
12. C	24. D	36. C	48. D	60. C

1-10. **If you missed any of these questions, look back at the pictures and observe more closely.**

11. **The correct answer is (B).** Something that appears to be unusual may or may not have any great significance. Certainly, you should not just ignore it and wait for further developments. On the other hand, do not be an alarmist and do not jump to conclusions. Go ahead and investigate; then act on the basis of real knowledge or justified suspicions.

12. **The correct answer is (C).** You must keep your distance from the prisoners. It is not your place to recommend a lawyer or even a choice of lawyers. You might recommend the prison library and its directories of attorneys.

13. **The correct answer is (B).** During an epileptic attack, the epileptic loses consciousness, falls to the floor, and may flail his or her arms and legs. The epileptic should not work in a place where an epileptic attack might present real danger to him or her. In all other respects, the epileptic should be treated like everyone else.

14. **The correct answer is (C).** You will often find prisoners to be insolent and insulting, and you will have to control your temper under such verbal attack. Having to subdue prisoners with physical strength and having to shoot to thwart an escape are rare occurrences. The Corrections Officer should not stoop to the language of the prisoners, but should speak clearly and correctly at all times.

15. **The correct answer is (C).** Obviously, you must fully understand instructions to do a good job. The time spent getting the instructions straight is time well spent.

16. **The correct answer is (A).** Since the inmate has accused a specific other inmate, there should be some basis to the accusation. You must find the basis for the specific accusation before proceeding with any action.

17. **The correct answer is (D).** You are obliged to follow all rules exactly. A dental appointment is not a life-or-death matter, so you have no room to make your own judgment as to the inaccessibility of the key or the reliability of the prisoner.

18. **The correct answer is (D).** As a Corrections Officer, you will hear many complaints from inmates. You listen to each complaint before deciding which ones merit thorough investigation and referral to your superior.

19. **The correct answer is (B).** You should know the whole picture—be aware of the background of the prisoner, the nature of the crime, and the individual's prison behavior—before attempting to answer questions.

20. **The correct answer is (D).** You are in charge of the prisoner's safety. You must instruct, observe, and correct to assure safe operation of dangerous machinery.

21. **The correct answer is (D).** Prisoners are permitted to make new friends. Corrections Officers are permitted to take note and monitor the direction of new friendships.

22. **The correct answer is (C).** It is important that lines of authority be maintained at all times. If the Corrections Officer becomes "one of the boys," he is likely to let down his guard and become lax in his duties.

23. **The correct answer is (C).** Any bizarre behavior disrupts routine and may lead to disorder or worse. The disruptive prisoner must be removed quickly and quietly.

24. **The correct answer is (D).** Many factors contribute to criminal behavior, and there are many individual differences among criminals. One known contributing factor to criminal behavior is a feeling of inferiority and lack of self-confidence. You must consider this possibility when giving training.

25. **The correct answer is (C).** Prisoners can easily sense capricious behavior on the part of Corrections Officers, so it is best for all punishment to be a matter of policy, not judgment on the part of any officer.

26. **The correct answer is (B).** You are an adult and must behave as an adult. Suppress your feelings and treat Helen like any other inmate.

27. **The correct answer is (B).** Many medicines that are highly effective in proper doses have very different qualities and effects when given in massive doses. It is therefore important that prisoners take the prescribed medications at the prescribed times for maximum effectiveness and to preclude their hoarding them for abusive purposes.

28. **The correct answer is (A).** A prospective escape is not a matter to be trifled with. You cannot delay and observe. Since the inmate has names and details, he should be thoroughly interviewed by your superior officer. Under no circumstances should you discuss this information with other prisoners.

29. **The correct answer is (D).** It is possible that Alicia is deaf, physically disabled, ill, or depressed, or that English is unintelligible to her. Check the records; then proceed on the basis of the problem. Punishment is called for only if there are no other reasons for her noncompliance.

30. **The correct answer is (D).** There is no way of knowing how a fight will develop. An inmate may have a homemade weapon; other prisoners might join in. The officer must summon reinforcements before placing himself into the fight.

31. **The correct answer is (D).** Calm reasoning and logical explanation may not work, but this certainly is the avenue to take.

32. **The correct answer is (A).** All the answer choices may be true, but the most important reason for the Corrections Officer to not accept gifts is so that he or she avoids being in a position of obligation to the prisoner.

33. **The correct answer is (A).** All the choices would work, but the most practical and orderly method is that described in choice (A). This is also the most dignified method and the least demeaning to the prisoners.

34. **The correct answer is (A).** Health and safety come first.

35. **The correct answer is (C).** Protect yourself. You must be able to see all of the inmates at all times.

36. **The correct answer is (C).** Shooting is justified when the life of a fellow officer is clearly in danger.

37. **The correct answer is (B).** You must not assume literacy among all the prisoners. The bulletin must be read aloud. Choosing the same prisoner each week smacks of favoritism and would put that prisoner in a difficult position among his peers. In choosing a different prisoner each week, you run the risk of choosing a prisoner who will be embarrassed by poor reading skills.

38. **The correct answer is (C).** When behavior is alarmingly out of the ordinary and gives the appearance of leading to a dangerous situation within a short period, it is best to let the warden know about it right away. The warden will undoubtedly send other Corrections Officers to back you up.

39. **The correct answer is (D).** Choice (B) is clearly the worst option. You must balance the rules themselves with the reasons for the rules and for your obligation to respect the religious practices of inmates. By privately checking for weapons, you are satisfying the reason for this particular rule. The problem of religious privileges is a sticky one and is best relegated to the warden.

40. **The correct answer is (B).** You are not in the position of employing inmates, and you do not want to put yourself into a position of obligation to Frank and Nick. You should most certainly avail yourself of the information they have given and follow through with your own observation.

41. **The correct answer is (D).** Choice (A) inserts an extra dimension, that of the metals being found together. Choice (B) assumes an unstated abundance of the metals and contradicts the rarity of zirconium. Choice (C) denies that zirconium exists in the earth's crust.

42. **The correct answer is (C).** Choice (A) leaves out the sex distinctions entirely. Choice (B) is true but inadequate. Choice (D) is factually correct but is an unwieldy run-on sentence.

43. **The correct answer is (A).** Choice (B) is true but ridiculous. Choice (D) is only ridiculous. Choice (C) is grammatically incorrect. "A police dog" is singular, so all pronouns referring to the dog must also be singular.

44. **The correct answer is (B).** Choice (A), when extricated from the run-on sentence, states that Dutch elm disease was curtailed during Word War II. Choice (C) states that relaxation of quarantines caused the disease to become a fatal fungus infection. The disease always was fatal. Choice (D) makes no sense at all.

45. **The correct answer is (D).** Choice (A) is false. In choice (B), the subject should read "Mary and I." In Choice (C), "Mary and me" is the object of the preposition *between*.

46. **The correct answer is (C).** In choice (A), since the comparison is among three persons, "Lois is tallest." Choice (B) is impossible. Lois cannot be taller than any salesperson in the store because she is one of the salespersons and cannot be taller than herself. Choice (D) must read "neither Bob nor Alice *is*."

47. **The correct answer is (B).** Read carefully. Each of the wrong choices misses the full meaning of the three sentences.

48. **The correct answer is (D).** Choice (A) is correct, but the point is that one should observe the scene from glass-bottomed boats. Choice (B) is ridiculous. As for choice (C), coral reefs are stationary.

49. **The correct answer is (B).** The modifier must be carefully placed so as to leave no doubt as to who or what was lost.

50. **The correct answer is (D).** Choice (A) is true but inadequate in covering the message. Choice (B) incorrectly suggests that workers deduct their own taxes. Choice (C) is ridiculous.

51. **The correct answer is (C).** The passage states the principle that the government must shield the innocent. Ordinarily this is done through the establishment of trial machinery whereby the accused may present his case to a jury of his peers. Since, under this principle, every accused is entitled to trial, the government provides counsel for indigent defendants. Choice (B) is incorrect because the government does not guarantee the competence of the lawyers it provides. Choice (D) contradicts the passage. Choice (A) is incorrect because the government provides prosecuting lawyers for its own benefits, not for the benefit of the accused.

52. **The correct answer is (C).** This is the best interpretation of the passage. While the passage is cautionary, it is not judgmental, so choice (A) is incorrect. Choice (D) is directly contradicted by the passage. Choice (B) is not discussed in the passage.

53. **The correct answer is (C).** The passage tells us that the value of the clue lies in its relationship to all the other clues.

54. **The correct answer is (A).** Fermentation and decomposition are chemical changes brought about by the action of bacteria.

55. **The correct answer is (D).** The point of this passage is that a business should be prepared to fill unexpected vacancies with pretrained staff members.

56. **The correct answer is (D).** The passage tells us that the dyeing of wool requires a process quite different from that for dyeing cotton. Fabric that contains both wool and cotton fibers must go through both processes, one after the other.

57. **The correct answer is (B).** See the first sentence.

58. **The correct answer is (C).** The spaces allow roads, sidewalks, and railroad tracks to expand in summer and contract in winter without cracking or breaking.

59. **The correct answer is (C).** In stating that the use of chemicals might be a detriment to an advancing force, the paragraph means that an advancing army might cause harm to itself with its own chemicals.

60. **The correct answer is (C).** The first sentence states that for most people, mental growth ceases between the ages of 14½ and 16. The remainder of the paragraph explains that what may later appear to be increased capacity must be ascribed to greater experience and information.

ANSWER SHEET PRACTICE TEST 4

1. Ⓐ Ⓑ Ⓒ Ⓓ	21. Ⓐ Ⓑ Ⓒ Ⓓ	41. Ⓐ Ⓑ Ⓒ Ⓓ	61. Ⓐ Ⓑ Ⓒ Ⓓ	81. Ⓐ Ⓑ Ⓒ Ⓓ
2. Ⓐ Ⓑ Ⓒ Ⓓ	22. Ⓐ Ⓑ Ⓒ Ⓓ	42. Ⓐ Ⓑ Ⓒ Ⓓ	62. Ⓐ Ⓑ Ⓒ Ⓓ	82. Ⓐ Ⓑ Ⓒ Ⓓ
3. Ⓐ Ⓑ Ⓒ Ⓓ	23. Ⓐ Ⓑ Ⓒ Ⓓ	43. Ⓐ Ⓑ Ⓒ Ⓓ	63. Ⓐ Ⓑ Ⓒ Ⓓ	83. Ⓐ Ⓑ Ⓒ Ⓓ
4. Ⓐ Ⓑ Ⓒ Ⓓ	24. Ⓐ Ⓑ Ⓒ Ⓓ	44. Ⓐ Ⓑ Ⓒ Ⓓ	64. Ⓐ Ⓑ Ⓒ Ⓓ	84. Ⓐ Ⓑ Ⓒ Ⓓ
5. Ⓐ Ⓑ Ⓒ Ⓓ	25. Ⓐ Ⓑ Ⓒ Ⓓ	45. Ⓐ Ⓑ Ⓒ Ⓓ	65. Ⓐ Ⓑ Ⓒ Ⓓ	85. Ⓐ Ⓑ Ⓒ Ⓓ
6. Ⓐ Ⓑ Ⓒ Ⓓ	26. Ⓐ Ⓑ Ⓒ Ⓓ	46. Ⓐ Ⓑ Ⓒ Ⓓ	66. Ⓐ Ⓑ Ⓒ Ⓓ	86. Ⓐ Ⓑ Ⓒ Ⓓ
7. Ⓐ Ⓑ Ⓒ Ⓓ	27. Ⓐ Ⓑ Ⓒ Ⓓ	47. Ⓐ Ⓑ Ⓒ Ⓓ	67. Ⓐ Ⓑ Ⓒ Ⓓ	87. Ⓐ Ⓑ Ⓒ Ⓓ
8. Ⓐ Ⓑ Ⓒ Ⓓ	28. Ⓐ Ⓑ Ⓒ Ⓓ	48. Ⓐ Ⓑ Ⓒ Ⓓ	68. Ⓐ Ⓑ Ⓒ Ⓓ	88. Ⓐ Ⓑ Ⓒ Ⓓ
9. Ⓐ Ⓑ Ⓒ Ⓓ	29. Ⓐ Ⓑ Ⓒ Ⓓ	49. Ⓐ Ⓑ Ⓒ Ⓓ	69. Ⓐ Ⓑ Ⓒ Ⓓ	89. Ⓐ Ⓑ Ⓒ Ⓓ
10. Ⓐ Ⓑ Ⓒ Ⓓ	30. Ⓐ Ⓑ Ⓒ Ⓓ	50. Ⓐ Ⓑ Ⓒ Ⓓ	70. Ⓐ Ⓑ Ⓒ Ⓓ	90. Ⓐ Ⓑ Ⓒ Ⓓ
11. Ⓐ Ⓑ Ⓒ Ⓓ	31. Ⓐ Ⓑ Ⓒ Ⓓ	51. Ⓐ Ⓑ Ⓒ Ⓓ	71. Ⓐ Ⓑ Ⓒ Ⓓ	91. Ⓐ Ⓑ Ⓒ Ⓓ
12. Ⓐ Ⓑ Ⓒ Ⓓ	32. Ⓐ Ⓑ Ⓒ Ⓓ	52. Ⓐ Ⓑ Ⓒ Ⓓ	72. Ⓐ Ⓑ Ⓒ Ⓓ	92. Ⓐ Ⓑ Ⓒ Ⓓ
13. Ⓐ Ⓑ Ⓒ Ⓓ	33. Ⓐ Ⓑ Ⓒ Ⓓ	53. Ⓐ Ⓑ Ⓒ Ⓓ	73. Ⓐ Ⓑ Ⓒ Ⓓ	93. Ⓐ Ⓑ Ⓒ Ⓓ
14. Ⓐ Ⓑ Ⓒ Ⓓ	34. Ⓐ Ⓑ Ⓒ Ⓓ	54. Ⓐ Ⓑ Ⓒ Ⓓ	74. Ⓐ Ⓑ Ⓒ Ⓓ	94. Ⓐ Ⓑ Ⓒ Ⓓ
15. Ⓐ Ⓑ Ⓒ Ⓓ	35. Ⓐ Ⓑ Ⓒ Ⓓ	55. Ⓐ Ⓑ Ⓒ Ⓓ	75. Ⓐ Ⓑ Ⓒ Ⓓ	95. Ⓐ Ⓑ Ⓒ Ⓓ
16. Ⓐ Ⓑ Ⓒ Ⓓ	36. Ⓐ Ⓑ Ⓒ Ⓓ	56. Ⓐ Ⓑ Ⓒ Ⓓ	76. Ⓐ Ⓑ Ⓒ Ⓓ	96. Ⓐ Ⓑ Ⓒ Ⓓ
17. Ⓐ Ⓑ Ⓒ Ⓓ	37. Ⓐ Ⓑ Ⓒ Ⓓ	57. Ⓐ Ⓑ Ⓒ Ⓓ	77. Ⓐ Ⓑ Ⓒ Ⓓ	97. Ⓐ Ⓑ Ⓒ Ⓓ
18. Ⓐ Ⓑ Ⓒ Ⓓ	38. Ⓐ Ⓑ Ⓒ Ⓓ	58. Ⓐ Ⓑ Ⓒ Ⓓ	78. Ⓐ Ⓑ Ⓒ Ⓓ	98. Ⓐ Ⓑ Ⓒ Ⓓ
19. Ⓐ Ⓑ Ⓒ Ⓓ	39. Ⓐ Ⓑ Ⓒ Ⓓ	59. Ⓐ Ⓑ Ⓒ Ⓓ	79. Ⓐ Ⓑ Ⓒ Ⓓ	99. Ⓐ Ⓑ Ⓒ Ⓓ
20. Ⓐ Ⓑ Ⓒ Ⓓ	40. Ⓐ Ⓑ Ⓒ Ⓓ	60. Ⓐ Ⓑ Ⓒ Ⓓ	80. Ⓐ Ⓑ Ⓒ Ⓓ	100. Ⓐ Ⓑ Ⓒ Ⓓ

answer sheet

Practice Test 4

> **Directions:** Each question has four suggested answers. Decide which one is the best answer.

1. "Certain inmate types are generally found in prisons. These types are called gorillas, toughs, hipsters, and merchants. Gorillas deliberately use violence to intimidate fearful inmates into providing favors. Toughs are swift to explode into violence against prisoners because of real or imagined insult. Exploitation of others is not their major goal. Hipsters are bullies who choose victims with caution in order to win acceptance among inmates by demonstrating physical bravery. Their bravery, however, is false. Merchants exploit other inmates through manipulation in sharp trading of goods stolen from prison supplies or in trickery in gambling."

   Based on the above information, the inmate who beats other inmates so that they provide him with extra cigarettes and coffee is, most likely, a

   (A) tough.
   (B) gorilla.
   (C) merchant.
   (D) hipster.

2. A Corrections Officer may not smoke while on duty or in any nonsmoking areas of the correctional facility at any time. The Receiving Room is a nonsmoking area.

   Officer Jomes arrives at the facility 15 minutes before his shift begins. He visits the officer on duty in the Receiving Room and, while there, smokes two cigarettes. Officer Jomes's conduct is

   (A) proper, because no one in the Receiving Room objects to the cigarette smoke.
   (B) improper, because there is no smoking allowed in the Receiving Room at any time.
   (C) proper, because Officer Jomes is not yet on duty.
   (D) improper, because Officer Jomes should be more concerned about his health.

3. A Corrections Officer's badge is a proud possession. It identifies him or her as a trained professional on the prison staff. The badge is issued to the Corrections Officer but remains the property of the Corrections Department. The department requires that the Corrections Officer wear the badge over the left pocket whenever in uniform and that the Corrections Officer keep it within his or her possession at all times.

Corrections Officer Berkey is at home on his day off and is trying to get some well-deserved rest. His four-year-old son, Billy, is whining and begging his daddy to take him to the zoo. Finally, Corrections Officer Berkey hands his badge to Billy saying, "Go out and play Corrections Officer with your friends and leave me alone." Corrections Officer Berkey's action is

(A) proper; he needs his rest.
(B) improper; Billy is not wearing a uniform.
(C) proper; Billy is his own child and is under his control.
(D) improper; regulations require a Corrections Officer to physically possess the badge even when not wearing it.

4. The constitutionally guaranteed attorney-client privilege provides that the information a client gives to an attorney be kept in confidence. The attorney may advise the client and may prepare a defense based on this private information but must not disclose any of it to the court or to the public.

Attorney Kleiner has come to see Inmate Greene, who is awaiting trial in a matter alleging racial bias. Kleiner has a reputation of being a fiery defense attorney; some would even suggest that he engages in unethical tactics. As Kleiner and Greene converse, Corrections Officer Torto listens intently. When the attorney's visit is over, Torto prepares notes about Greene's admissions to Kleiner and Kleiner's defense strategies. Torto sends these notes to the prosecutor. Corrections Officer Torto's action is

(A) appropriate; justice is best served if the prosecution has all the facts.
(B) inappropriate; the attorney-client privilege guarantees privacy.
(C) appropriate; Kleiner may thereby be prevented from performing unethical acts.
(D) inappropriate; this information should be reserved for the judge and not passed to the prosecutor.

5. Any person over 18 may visit an inmate with the inmate's consent during normal visiting hours. Any person under 18 must be accompanied to the Visiting Room by an adult visitor. An inmate's lawyer may visit an inmate at certain times other than normal visiting hours.

The following visitors each come separately and at different times during normal visiting hours to see Inmate Blank: Mrs. Blank, the inmate's grandmother; Ms. Kelly, the inmate's lawyer; David Blank, the inmate's 16-year-old brother; and John Gallo, a 25-year-old former inmate. Inmate Blank consents to see each of them. Who should NOT be allowed into the Visiting Room?

(A) Mrs. Blank
(B) Ms. Kelly
(C) David Blank
(D) John Gallo

QUESTIONS 6 AND 7 ARE BASED ON THE FOLLOWING INFORMATION.

A Corrections Officer may be assigned to distribute packages and letters to inmates. The officer must inspect each package and, if the contents are acceptable, must deliver the package to the inmate within 48 hours after it has arrived at the facility. Letters may not be opened by the officer, and they must be delivered to the addressee within 24 hours after arrival. There is no limit to the number of letters an inmate may receive.

6. Six letters arrive for Inmate Randall on Monday afternoon. Officer Suarez gives three of the letters to Inmate Randall on Tuesday and gives the other three letters to Inmate Randall on Wednesday. The officer's action is

   (A) appropriate, because other inmates would become jealous if they saw Inmate Randall receive so many letters on the same day.

   (B) inappropriate, because the officer should have waited 48 hours before delivering any of the letters.

   (C) appropriate, because Officer Suarez needed time to open and review the contents of the letters to make sure they were acceptable.

   (D) inappropriate, because all six of the letters should have been delivered to the inmate within 24 hours after their arrival.

7. On Saturday a package arrives addressed to Inmate Shibutani. Corrections Officer Park opens the package and discovers that it contains socks, photos of the inmate's children, and a box of homemade fudge. On Sunday morning, Corrections Officer Park delivers the package to Inmate Shibutani. This action by the officer is

   (A) correct; there is no reason to withhold this acceptable package from the inmate.

   (B) incorrect; packages should be held for 48 hours.

   (C) correct; the fudge will melt if held in the mailroom.

   (D) incorrect; there should be no mail delivery on Sunday.

8. Under the Penal Law, a Corrections Officer is a peace officer. A peace officer is charged with keeping the peace whether officially on duty or not and whether in uniform or not. A peace officer must attempt to prevent crime from occurring, must attempt to stop crime in progress, and must attempt to assist crime victims.

   Corrections Officer Rice, who has completed his day's tour at the prison where he is employed, is on his way home. About 10 blocks from his home, he comes upon a woman screaming that her purse has just been snatched. Corrections Officer Rice begins to chase the perpetrator, who is still visible running up the street. The purse snatcher suddenly turns, shoots, and kills Officer Rice. Corrections Officer Rice's widow files to collect "death-in-the-line-of-duty" benefits. Mrs. Rice's request is

   (A) proper; Corrections Officer Rice was murdered in cold blood.

   (B) improper; Rice was off duty when he was killed.

   (C) proper; it is the duty of peace officers to assist victims of crimes in progress.

   (D) improper; Rice deliberately put himself in unnecessary danger.

9. A Corrections Officer may be required to accept sums of money for bail and to issue receipts for money received. The Corrections Officer must be both honest and extremely careful, because very large sums of money may be involved. A Corrections Officer who mishandles bail money may be subject to criminal charges and penalties.

Corrections Officer Pulaski has been in charge of bail monies at the correctional center for the past five years. During this time, Pulaski has received money and has issued receipts with no oversight. An audit has recently revealed a discrepancy of nearly a half million dollars. The superintendent of the facility has suspended Pulaski and has ordered a grand jury investigation. This action by the superintendent is

(A) proper; criminal behavior must be punished.
(B) improper; accidents can happen and carelessness is not a crime.
(C) proper; Pulaski is a likely suspect and a full investigation is called for.
(D) improper; since Pulaski issued receipts, he cannot be held responsible for the missing money.

10. The Commissioner of Corrections may permit any prisoner confined in a state prison, excepting one awaiting the sentence of death, to attend the funeral of his or her father, mother, child, brother, sister, husband, or wife, within the state, or to visit such relative during his or her illness if death is imminent. Any expenses incurred under these provisions, with respect to any prisoner, shall be deemed an expense of maintenance of the prison and be paid from monies available therefore; but the warden, if the rules and regulations of the Commissioner of Corrections shall so provide, may allow the prisoner or anyone in his behalf to reimburse the state for such expense.

Martha, who is serving a sentence for armed robbery, receives word that her mother, who has been undergoing treatment for cancer, has taken a sudden turn for the worse and is not expected to survive.

(A) Martha may visit her mother in the hospital.
(B) Martha may not visit her mother but may attend her funeral.
(C) Martha may visit her mother but may attend her mother's funeral only if she pays her own expenses.
(D) Martha may not visit her mother nor go to the funeral unless she can arrange to have her family pay her way.

11. The nature of correction work is such that security of the facility may be in jeopardy if even one post is not covered at all times. There can be no exceptions to this rule.

Corrections Officer Macmillan is scheduled to work a 7 a.m. to 3 p.m. shift. Macmillan arrived at her post promptly at 7 this morning. She is in the middle of root canal work and scheduled a dental appointment at 4 p.m. today. Her dentist's office is a 30-minute drive from the facility at which she works. Macmillan expects to be relieved at 3 p.m., but her relief does not appear, and she remains on her post until 3:30 p.m. At 3:30, when the relief still has not arrived, Macmillan leaves for her dental appointment. Officer Macmillan's action is

(A) correct; it is important for her health that she meet her dental appointment and not leave the root canal unfinished.

(B) incorrect; there are to be no exceptions to the full-coverage rule.

(C) correct; a half hour of voluntary overtime is already beyond the call of duty.

(D) incorrect; Macmillan should have told her supervisor why she was leaving.

12. Prison inmates who often have histories of short tempers have few avenues for venting frustrations and hostilities in prison. Since physical violence and destruction of property are not permitted, inmates tend to become verbally abusive. Corrections Officers are ready targets of verbal abuse. They must be somewhat thick-skinned and must not overreact to angry words.

Corrections Officer Fulco is escorting a group of inmates from the exercise yard back to their cell block on a glorious spring day. The inmates are reluctant to come inside and begin to stray from the line and to cajole Officer Fulco to extend their exercise time. Officer Fulco sharply demands their obedience, and an inmate turns, spits at her, and regales her with choice profanity about "you dumb women." Corrections Officer Fulco retorts, "Shut up, you dirty loser, and do as you're told." Officer Fulco's reaction is

(A) appropriate; one insult deserves another, and the inmates expect this type of behavior.

(B) inappropriate; Officer Fulco should recognize anger and frustration and not take the words personally.

(C) appropriate; Fulco's job is to get the inmates back to their cell block, and this method will be effective.

(D) inappropriate; inmates shower regularly, and to call them "dirty" is inaccurate.

13. Discipline must be maintained at all times, even when maintenance of order entails infringement of some prisoners' rights and entitlement.

One noontime in the dining hall, Inmate Vulgaris leans over and crumbles potato chips into Inmate Topekian's soda. Topekian promptly tosses the contents of the cup into Vulgaris's face. Inmate Davis joins the fray by throwing a chicken leg at Topekian. Then many inmates begin throwing food and pandemonium breaks loose. Corrections Officers Lynch and DaSilva promptly close the cafeteria line, send for assistance, and herd all the inmates back to their cells. This action by Corrections Officers Lynch and DaSilva is

(A) proper; if inmates were throwing food, they had obviously already had enough to eat.

(B) improper; prisoners must be fed three full meals a day.

(C) proper; this is a reasonable way to restore order.

(D) improper; the inmates still in line will later have it in for the officers for making them miss lunch.

practice test

QUESTIONS 14–16 ARE BASED ON THE FOLLOWING PASSAGE.

A person who intends to effect or facilitate the escape of a prisoner, whether the escape is effected or attempted or not, and who enters a prison, or conveys to a prisoner any information, or sends into a prison any disguise, instrument, weapon, or other thing, is guilty of felony if the prisoner is held upon a charge, arrest, commitment, or conviction for a felony. The person is guilty of a misdemeanor if the prisoner is held upon a charge, arrest, commitment, or conviction of a misdemeanor.

14. Johnny O. is serving time after conviction for the felony crime of armed robbery. Johnny's friend, Frank, devises an escape scheme and writes a letter to Johnny detailing the plans. Frank, without telling of the contents of the letter, asks Mary P. to deliver the letter to Johnny when she visits the prison to see her husband, Bob. The letter is intercepted by a Corrections Officer.

    (A) Frank and Mary are both guilty of felonies.
    (B) Frank is guilty of a felony; Mary is guilty of a misdemeanor.
    (C) Frank is guilty of a felony; Mary is not guilty.
    (D) Frank is guilty of a misdemeanor; Mary is not guilty.

15. On a visit to her boyfriend, Bill, who is awaiting trial in the county jail on a felony charge of grand larceny, Joan orally transmits to Bill instructions for fashioning a cutting tool from objects available to him in the jail. Bill follows these instructions, which had been the invention of Joan's brother Tom, creates the tool, and escapes.

    (A) Joan and Tom are both guilty of felonies.
    (B) Joan is guilty of a felony; Tom is guilty of a misdemeanor.
    (C) Joan is guilty of a felony; Tom is not guilty.
    (D) Neither Joan nor Tom is guilty.

16. While charming little Debbie, age 4, distracts a guard, Barbara manages to smuggle a gun to Jim, who is completing a sentence on a misdemeanor conviction. In the course of his escape, Jim shoots and severely injures a Corrections Officer.

    (A) Barbara is guilty of a felony; Debbie is guilty of a misdemeanor.
    (B) Barbara is guilty of a felony; Debbie is not guilty.
    (C) Barbara and Debbie are both guilty of misdemeanors.
    (D) Barbara is guilty of a misdemeanor; Debbie is not guilty.

17. A Corrections Officer is responsible for the health and welfare of the prisoners in his or her charge. Since the Corrections Officer is familiar with these inmates and their habits, it is his or her duty to notice changes in behavior that may indicate something is wrong.

    Inmate Mashke has always been an enthusiastic basketball player. At every opportunity, Mashke could be seen shooting for the net. For three days now Mashke has been sitting out of basketball scrimmage and has not practiced his set shots. Corrections Officer Garcia, who is regularly assigned to Mashke's group, asks Mashke why he is not playing. Mashke responds, "I just don't feel like it." On the fourth morning, Garcia summons Mashke and insists that he accompany Garcia to sick call to consult with the doctor. Officer Garcia's action is

    (A) proper; Mashke is developing a mental illness and should be treated at once.
    (B) improper; malingering prisoners should not be mollycoddled.
    (C) proper; a sudden change of energy level and interests should be investigated by a professional.
    (D) improper; the prison budget is limited, and medical attention should not be wasted on a prisoner who is not ill.

18. *Regulation:* Use the minimum necessary force to maintain order, but do not hesitate to use force to protect life.

Corrections Officer Braun comes upon a fight in progress in the kitchen. Two prisoners are grappling on the floor, pummeling each other with their fists, ringed by a group of cheering, goading fellow inmates. Officer Braun strides through the group and says, "Come on, break it up." The inmates continue fighting. Corrections Officer Braun then says, "If you don't stop, I'll have to shoot." When the fighting does not stop, Braun aims carefully at one prisoner's foot, fires, and wounds him. Corrections Officer Braun's action is

(A) proper; the fight had to be broken up.

(B) improper; life was not in danger, and less force could have stopped the fight.

(C) proper; a kitchen with its available knives and fire is a very dangerous location for a fight.

(D) improper; in such a dangerous situation, a Corrections Officer should shoot to kill.

19. Corrections Officer Wong is admitting Mary Adams, who is awaiting arraignment after having been picked up as a suspected burglar. Officer Wang asks Adams for her handbag. Adams replies, "I'll only be here for a couple of hours. My family will have me out in no time. Why go through all that paperwork?" Officer Wang agrees that the effort is unwarranted, takes no possessions from Adams, and does not bother to issue toilet supplies and bedding. Officer Wong's action is

(A) correct; it is not worthwhile to spend time taking inventory of possessions, nor is it cost effective to hand out supplies to an inmate who will not be there long enough to use them.

(B) incorrect; the prisoner might want to wash or take a nap while awaiting release.

(C) correct; Mary Adams has not been proven guilty so should not have her possessions impounded as if she were.

(D) incorrect; the prison rules apply to all prisoners.

QUESTIONS 19 AND 20 ARE BASED ON THE FOLLOWING INFORMATION.

Upon admission to a facility, all prisoners, regardless of status—awaiting trial, convicted and awaiting sentence, or awaiting transfer—must surrender wallets, belts, neckties, and shoelaces. The intake officer must record all items, including itemized contents of purses and wallets, on the daily manifest and must issue a receipt to the prisoner, keeping a duplicate receipt for the prisoner's file. All new prisoners must be given a towel, a bar of soap, a toothbrush, toothpaste, and one blanket.

20. Corrections Officer Sohan has just received Vincent Wyler, who was today convicted of a felonious crime and who will be sentenced in three weeks. Wyler was unable to post bond and has been imprisoned for some time. He has lost a good deal of weight while in prison and is in danger of losing his trousers without a belt. Wyler demonstrates his problem to Officer Sohan and asks if he may keep his belt to hold up his pants. Corrections Officer Sohan replies, "I'm sorry, but prison rules do not permit." Officer Sohan's action is

(A) appropriate; the rule does not specify any exceptions.

(B) inappropriate; prison decorum requires that all male prisoners wear trousers.

(C) appropriate; a prisoner who has lost weight in prison is a prime candidate for suicide.

(D) inappropriate; a little kindness is never out of order.

QUESTIONS 21–27 ARE BASED ON THE FOLLOWING CHART.

Schedule of Prisoners' Court Appearances						
Inmate	Date	Docket #	Charge	County	Court	Judge
Brock	4/12	612392	armed robbery	Kings	Criminal	Gabriel
Whinston	4/15	528789	embezzlement	Queens	Appeals	Cook
Sowders	4/15	139190	grand larceny	Prince	Supreme	Herndon
Torak	4/15	797591	vehicular homicide	Kings	Criminal	Gabriel
Laduca	4/26	427388	manslaughter two	Pawn	Superior	Molina
Persaud	5/2	437792	burglary	Prince	County	Schwartz
Crofton	5/3	821692	armed robbery	Rook	Criminal	Reilly
Hughes	5/7	668190	burglary	Queens	Appeals	Cook

21. The inmate who is scheduled to be in court on the busiest day is

(A) Herndon.

(B) Persaud.

(C) Sowders.

(D) Laduca.

22. The docket number for the case coming up in Superior Court is

(A) 437792.

(B) 472388.

(C) 139190.

(D) 427388.

23. Two prisoners who will be tried before the same judge are
    (A) Torak and Whinston.
    (B) Whinston and Hughes.
    (C) Gabriel and Reilly.
    (D) Brock and Hughes.

24. The prison is located in Rook County. Which inmate will NOT need to be transported across a county line for her scheduled court appearance?
    (A) Reilly
    (B) Rook
    (C) Laduca
    (D) Crofton

25. The judges who will sit on cases in which people were killed are
    (A) Molina and Gabriel.
    (B) Gabriel and Reilly.
    (C) Laduca and Torak.
    (D) Pawn and Rook.

26. The docket number of the burglary not yet up for appeal is
    (A) 668190.
    (B) 437729.
    (C) 437792.
    (D) 528789.

27. Which statement is most accurate with reference to the cases being tried on April 15?
    (A) The docket numbers all end with the same two digits.
    (B) Two of the crimes are strictly "money crimes."
    (C) The trial of Inmate Sowders will be in the Prince Court of Appeals.
    (D) Judge Schwartz will hear the case of Inmate Torak in Kings Criminal Court.

28. Arrest may be a frightening and humiliating experience, especially for young first offenders. Corrections Officers must be alert to signs of depression, such as withdrawal and lethargy, as well as to verbal threats of suicide.

    A 47-year-old suspect is brought in on a charge of exposing himself to little girls. He sits motionless on the bench, glassily staring ahead or at the floor, and responds in nearly whispered monosyllables when questioned. Corrections Officer Cheskis gets the suspect into a holding pen as quickly as possible, thinking, "This is a nice quiet one who will give me no trouble." Corrections Officer Cheskis then ignores the prisoner. Officer Cheskis's action is
    (A) correct; the suspect is not young.
    (B) incorrect; depressed suspects, especially those who are deeply embarrassed by their own behavior, should be watched for suicide.
    (C) correct; the suspect did not say that he was considering suicide.
    (D) incorrect; sex offenders always attempt suicide.

29. A Corrections Officer escorting a group of inmates from one location to another within the prison must always walk behind the last inmate. At no time should an inmate be permitted to be behind the escorting Corrections Officer.

    Corrections Officer Uyeda is escorting a group of inmates from their cell block to the recreation yard. As the group marches two by two down the corridor, Inmate Daley turns to Officer Uyeda and says, "I forgot my Frisbee. May I please go back for it?" Correction Officer Uyeda replies, "I'm sorry. You'll have to play with something else today and remember your Frisbee tomorrow." Officer Uyeda's response is
    (A) appropriate; a prisoner going back to his cell would break up the neat double-file line.
    (B) inappropriate; Frisbee is an approved activity and should not be forbidden.
    (C) appropriate; upon returning to the group, Daley would be behind Corrections Officer Uyeda.
    (D) inappropriate; a Corrections Officer should not refuse a reasonable request when it is so politely made.

30. All visitors to inmates must be checked electronically and visually before being admitted to the visiting area. This rule means that every visitor must pass through metal detectors, open all handbags and packages, and submit to a pat-down.

On a bitterly cold day, Mrs. Ramirez comes with her baby, Luisa, to visit her husband, Inmate Ramirez. Mrs. Ramirez carries the baby through the metal detectors and permits Corrections Officer Perry to search her handbag and the gift parcel she is bringing. Correction Officer Perry also pats down Mrs. Ramirez, but when he asks her to unwrap the baby from the blankets in which it is swaddled, she complains that it is too cold and the baby will get sick. Corrections Officer Perry waves Mrs. Ramirez into the visiting area. Corrections Officer Perry's action is

- **(A)** proper; a duty of a peace officer is to protect the health of the public.
- **(B)** improper; babies are notorious smugglers.
- **(C)** proper; Mrs. Ramirez was otherwise so cooperative that surely her concern for her baby's health is genuine.
- **(D)** improper; the rule applies to all visitors, and the baby is a visitor.

QUESTIONS 31 AND 32 ARE BASED ON THE FOLLOWING INFORMATION.

Subject to the availability of an escort, any prisoner may go to the prison library during an unscheduled period to research precedents to his or her own case and to prepare a defense. The Corrections Officer assigned as librarian may assist prisoners in locating appropriate materials and may instruct inmates in the use of the books and microfilm. The librarian/Corrections Officer may not suggest an actual defense, nor may the Corrections Officer assist in preparation of papers.

31. Inmate Lisa feels that her court-appointed attorney did not represent her case adequately and is planning to prepare her own appeal. She approaches the librarian, Corrections Officer Stavrou, and asks which volumes to consult with reference to illegal search and seizure and inadmissible evidence. Officer Stavrou replies, "I am not permitted to choose books for you." Corrections Officer Stavrou's response is

- **(A)** correct; choosing books would be helping with the defense.
- **(B)** incorrect; choosing books is assisting in locating appropriate materials.
- **(C)** correct; if Corrections Officer Stavrou does not know which books would be most helpful, he should not make any recommendation.
- **(D)** incorrect; Officer Stavrou should have suggested sources that deal with inadequate representation.

32. Corrections Officer Ford, who has been assigned to the prison library, notices that Inmate Eiss is struggling to prepare an appeal after conviction for state tax fraud. Officer Ford recognizes that Inmate Eiss firmly understands the law involved and the concepts necessary to his own defense, but Eiss is expressing himself poorly. Officer Ford sits down with Eiss and proceeds to rewrite large portions of a lengthy document supporting Eiss's position. Officer Ford's action is

(A) appropriate; Eiss knows exactly what he wants to say but needs help getting it on paper.

(B) inappropriate; a Corrections Officer is not permitted to assist in the preparation of appeal papers.

(C) appropriate; Eiss understands the law so well it is obvious he is innocent.

(D) inappropriate; other inmates will realize that Corrections Officer Ford is a good writer and will make too many demands on her time.

QUESTIONS 33–35 ARE BASED ON THE FOLLOWING PASSAGE.

A male between the ages of 16 and 30, convicted of a felony, who has not heretofore been convicted of a crime punishable by imprisonment in a state prison, may, in the discretion of the trial court, be sentenced to imprisonment in the state reformatory. Where a male person between the ages of 16 and 21 is convicted of a felony, or where the term of imprisonment of a male convict for a felony is fixed by the trial court at one year or less, the court may direct the convict to be imprisoned in a county penitentiary, instead of a state prison, or in the county jail located in the county where sentence is imposed.

33. Harry, age 32, has been convicted of a felony and has been sentenced to a term of 11 months.

(A) Harry must serve his term in a state prison.

(B) The court may sentence Harry to the state reformatory.

(C) Harry must serve his term in either the county penitentiary or the county jail.

(D) The court may direct that Harry serve at a state prison, the county penitentiary, or the county jail.

34. Mark, age 20, recently released from state prison after serving time for a felony committed when he was 16, has just been convicted of another felony.

(A) Mark must serve his new term in a state prison.

(B) Mark may not serve his term at the state reformatory.

(C) Mark must serve his term at the county penitentiary.

(D) Mark may serve his term in any one of the following: state penitentiary, county penitentiary, state reformatory, or county jail.

35. George, age 27, has just been convicted for his first crime and has been sentenced to a term of four to seven years.

(A) George must serve his term in a state prison.

(B) George may be sentenced to either state prison or the state reformatory.

(C) George may serve his time in a state prison or in the county penitentiary but not in the state reformatory.

(D) George may serve his sentence at a state prison or at the county jail of the county in which he is sentenced.

36. Inmates' families often travel great distances at personal expense and under conditions of physical hardship in order to visit with inmates. Correction Officers should, therefore, try to insure that visits are satisfying and productive for both inmate and visitor, while maintaining all prison rules and regulations.

Inmate Thompkins's husband has traveled six hours by bus to visit with his wife at the women's prison. Mr. Thompkins enters the visiting area, which is posted with "No Smoking" signs, and lights up a cigarette. Corrections Officer Bradley approaches Mr. Thompkins and says, "Smoking is not permitted here. Please put out your cigarette or I will have to ask you to leave." Corrections Officer Bradley's action is

(A) appropriate; only people with legitimate business at the prison are permitted to smoke there.

(B) inappropriate; Mr. Thompkins is disobeying the rule and should be ejected at once.

(C) appropriate; Officer Bradley is doing his best to permit the visit to proceed and yet to have the rules obeyed.

(D) inappropriate; after Mr. Thompkins's long trip, the cigarette will relax him and will make the visit more productive and satisfying.

QUESTIONS 37 AND 38 ARE BASED ON THE FOLLOWING INFORMATION.

Between the hours of 9 p.m. and 6 a.m., all prisoners must be securely locked into their cells. Life-threatening emergencies such as sudden acute illness of an inmate or fire in the facility constitute legitimate reasons for suspension of this rule.

37. At 9:25 p.m., Corrections Officer Mohan receives a telephone call from Veronica Lake, attorney for Inmate Robert Kim. Ms. Lake has an important matter that she would like to discuss with her client before his court appearance, which is scheduled for 10 a.m. tomorrow, and asks that he be brought to the telephone. Corrections Officer Mohan tells Ms. Lake that it is past lockup time and Inmate Kim must remain in his cell. Officer Mohan's action is

(A) correct; need for attorney–client communication is not a life-threatening situation.

(B) incorrect; Inmate Kim may be facing the death penalty if his attorney does not have the information to represent him properly.

(C) correct; all requests for attorney–client contact outside of visiting hours must be made in writing.

(D) incorrect; the attorney–client privilege, since it is constitutionally guaranteed, overrides prison rules.

38. At 1:15 a.m. a small fire, probably electrical in origin, breaks out in the guard tower at the southwest corner of the prison yard. Upon learning of this fire, the Corrections Officers on duty in cell block B in the northeast wing of the prison rouse all the inmates and march them two by two into the recreation yard. This action by the Corrections Officers is

(A) appropriate; fire is a life-threatening situation.

(B) inappropriate; the inmates will be in the way of the firefighters if they are in the yard.

(C) appropriate; two by two is an orderly manner by which to move inmates and prevent panic.

(D) inappropriate; a small fire in the southwest guard tower does not threaten the lives of inmates in a northeast cell block.

39. Corrections Officers must scrupulously avoid favoritism or even the appearance of favoritism among inmates.

Inmate Zenkel has thick, waist-length, flaming red hair. Zenkel requests Corrections Officer Plunkett to issue him an extra towel for drying his hair. Corrections Officer Plunkett denies this request. Officer Plunkett's refusal is

(A) proper; men in prison should not have long hair.

(B) improper; if Zenkel's hair is not dried properly, he may catch cold and in turn infect other inmates.

(C) proper; giving an extra towel to Zenkel might be interpreted as favoritism by other inmates.

(D) improper; Zenkel is likely to lodge a discrimination complaint.

40. Inmates are entitled to prompt, appropriate medical care for all legitimate illnesses or injuries. A Corrections Officer is responsible for securing medical care for inmates who require it but may deny care to an inmate who is obviously faking it. A Corrections Officer must be wary of denying care without just cause.

Inmate Torbert approaches Corrections Officer Popovich and complains of a severe toothache. Torbert demands to be taken to the dentist at once. Officer Popovich knows that Torbert has a full set of dentures. Nevertheless, Popovich arranges for a visit to the dentist within the hour. Officer Popovich's action is

(A) appropriate; Popovich is not a dentist, and the mouth pain could come from a source other than teeth.

(B) inappropriate; it is impossible to have a toothache with no teeth.

(C) appropriate; inmates may be tempted to withhold reporting illnesses if they expect to be ridiculed.

(D) inappropriate; clearly Torbert is trying to get out of the day's assignments.

QUESTIONS 41–48 ARE BASED ON THE FOLLOWING CHART. "IN" REFERS TO MOVEMENT INTO THE NAMED LOCATION; "OUT" REFERS TO MOVEMENT OUT OF THAT LOCATION. NOTE: PRISONERS DO NOT NECESSARILY RETURN TO THEIR CELLS BETWEEN ACTIVITIES.

Wednesday Morning Prisoner Movement							
Location	# of inmates at 7 a.m.	movement	8 a.m.	9 a.m.	10 a.m.	11 a.m.	noon
Cell block A	52	in	7	24	46	22	13
		out	28	31	20	37	23
Cell block B	60	in	5	15	35	25	21
		out	32	40	21	39	35
Cell block C	74	in	4	28	28	36	30
		out	30	52	47	28	40
Receiving Room	12	in	21	17	8	10	4
		out	12	15	9	21	9
In Court or In Transit	0	leave	20	0	0	0	13
		return	0	0	0	0	7
Sick Call	0	in	21	3	1	7	2
		out	0	16	2	7	5
Hospital (off premises)	9	in	0	3	0	2	0
		out	4	1	0	1	0
Recreation Yard	0	in	0	80	80	80	0
		out	0	0	80	80	80
Wood Shop	0	in	28	30	34	34	0
		out	0	28	30	34	34
Kitchen	0	in	16	48	48	62	0
		out	0	16	48	48	62
Released or Transferred	0	out only	5	3	12	8	0

41. At which hour could the greatest number of inmates be found in their cells?
    (A) 7 a.m.
    (B) 9 a.m.
    (C) 11 a.m.
    (D) 12 a.m.

42. How many new inmates entered the prison this morning?
    (A) 44
    (B) 60
    (C) 72
    (D) 77

43. How many inmates were off the premises at noon?
    (A) 26
    (B) 34
    (C) 54
    (D) 62

44. At which hour were the fewest inmates working in the kitchen?
    (A) 9
    (B) 10
    (C) 11
    (D) 12

45. How many prisoners could be found in Cell block A at 10 a.m.?

(A) 50
(B) 65
(C) 77
(D) 129

46. How many prisoners spent more than one-half day in court?

(A) 6
(B) 13
(C) 20
(D) 27

47. Approximately what percent of the on-premises inmates participated in recreational activities this morning?

(A) 65%
(B) 75%
(C) 82%
(D) 100%

48. How many prisoners were moved out of their cells at the hour at which the greatest number were moved from their cells?

(A) 98
(B) 104
(C) 123
(D) 132

49. The parole board carefully looks over a prisoner's file when considering that prisoner for parole. Since the file is crucial to the board's decision, it is very important that all notations in the file be clear and complete.

At 3:12 p.m. on Thursday, June 11, Corrections Officer Bodenheim observes Inmate Carlucci taking a swift kick at Inmate Otten's left shin. Bodenheim then observes Inmate Otten giving Inmate Carlucci a hard punch to the right jaw that sends Carlucci heavily to the ground. Correction Officer Bodenheim writes in Carlucci's file: "Thursday, June 11, 3:12 p.m.: Carlucci kicked Inmate Otten." He writes in Otten's file: "Thursday, June 11, 3:12 p.m.: Otten punched Inmate Carlucci in the jaw and knocked him down." These notations are

(A) appropriate; they tell what each inmate did.
(B) inappropriate; Otten's file should include the provocation for his behavior.
(C) appropriate; the notations carefully detail date and time.
(D) inappropriate; the notation in Carlucci's file should specify that Carlucci kicked Otten's left shin.

50. 1 p.m. and 1 a.m. are official inmate-counting times. At the 1 p.m. count, each inmate must stand inside his or her cell at the front gate and must respond with his or her name when addressed by the Corrections Officer. At the 1 a.m. count, the Corrections Officer must be satisfied that the inmate is in the cell. If the Correction Officer cannot see the inmate's face or if the Corrections Officer cannot visibly see that the inmate is breathing or cannot hear sleep sounds from the inmate, the officer must enter the cell to be certain that the inmate is in the bed.

Corrections Officer Holier is making the 1 p.m. inmate count. She arrives at the cell of Inmate Petroski and finds the inmate lying face down on the cot. Holier says, "Petroski, stand up and be counted." The inmate replies, "Go away, I'm too tired to get up." Officer Holier sharply repeats, "Get up right now," and remains in front of Inmate Petroski's cell. Officer Holier's action is

(A) correct; the rules require inmates to stand at the 1 p.m. check.
(B) incorrect; there is no question as to the presence or the identity of the inmate.
(C) correct; punishment of inmates requires that they not be allowed to lie down when tired.
(D) incorrect; Holier should go into the cell to check on Petroski's breathing.

QUESTIONS 51 AND 52 ARE BASED ON THE FOLLOWING INFORMATION.

Sick call is a favorite diversion of inmates. If permitted, some inmates would demand daily medical care. A Corrections Officer must use some personal judgment in weeding out chronic complainers from the truly ill. Medical care must not be denied when justified.

51. While making a routine cell check, Correction Officer Djerf smells vomit and sees Inmate Constantine doubled over the lavatory. Constantine appears to be very pale and shaky. Djerf says, "Come on, Constantine, let's go see the nurse." Inmate Constantine replies, "No, no, I'll be okay. I just have an upset stomach." Djerf persists and forcibly escorts Constantine to sick call. Djerf's action is

    (A) proper; the smell will soon make other inmates ill.
    (B) improper; the inmate has not asked to go to sick call.
    (C) proper; all apparently ill inmates should receive medical evaluation and care.
    (D) improper; Constantine probably forced himself to vomit to get attention.

52. Inmate Wright was received on the cell block only yesterday. At the medical check upon intake, Wright received a clean bill of health. This morning Wright is refusing to go to his first scheduled activity, claiming he has a migraine headache. Corrections Officer Paik says, "The doctor said you were healthy just yesterday. We don't allow stayabeds here. Up and out." Officer Paik's action is

    (A) correct; Wright is not sick.
    (B) incorrect; Wright has not been in the prison long enough to establish a reputation for begging off work detail.
    (C) correct; Wright's medical report says nothing about migraines.
    (D) incorrect; Wright has a headache and should be allowed to lie down.

53. All packages addressed to inmates must be opened and inspected for contraband before delivery to the inmates. If a Corrections Officer discovers an item of contraband in a package, the entire contents of the package must be withheld. The contents of the package must be itemized on an inventory list in triplicate, and copies of the inventory must be delivered to the inmate, placed in the inmate's file, and kept with the prison records.

    A package arrives at the prison addressed to Inmate Eberle. Corrections Officer Ficklen opens the package and shakes each item enclosed. As Ficklen flips through the pages of a crossword puzzle book, a small note containing details of an escape plan falls out. Officer Ficklen makes out a list in triplicate of the contents of the package, including on the list the crossword puzzle book and the escape plan. Ficklen gives a copy of the list and the items of clothing from the package to Inmate Eberle, withholding the escape plan and the crossword puzzle book. Corrections Officer Ficklen's action is

    (A) appropriate; Ficklen made a complete inventory list in triplicate and gave a copy to the inmate.
    (B) inappropriate; the crossword puzzle book was harmless and should have been given to the inmate.
    (C) appropriate; the clothing in the package was badly needed and was totally unrelated to the contraband.
    (D) inappropriate; Ficklen should have confiscated all of the contents of the package.

THE FOUR PARAGRAPHS BELOW ARE DESCRIPTIONS OF FOUR PERSONALITY TYPES OFTEN ATTRIBUTED TO YOUTHFUL OFFENDERS. USE THESE DESCRIPTIONS TO ANSWER QUESTIONS 54–59.

"Personality W"

These offenders are lazy and show a general lack of interest in most things around them. Their actions are childish, and often we would consider them as helpless. They are weak and, although they lose their tempers, they are not violent. Frequently they seem preoccupied and may give the impression of being "out of it."

"Personality X"

Offenders in this class feel very guilty and genuinely sorry for their actions, but they are quite likely to repeat the same thing tomorrow. Despite being very selective about their friendships, they usually are willing to talk about their problems. These individuals frequently have nervous or anxious ways. They may impress you as feeling sad or unhappy much of the time.

"Personality Y"

This type of offender is very hostile and aggressive, showing little, if any, concern for the welfare of others. These people have a strong need to create excitement since, for them, things quickly get too boring. Attempts to control them verbally are not very effective. They are frequently both verbally and physically aggressive. Without qualms, they will lie and manipulate others for their own gain.

"Personality Z"

These individuals have usually been involved in gang activities and demonstrate a high degree of loyalty to that peer group. They are relatively unconcerned about adults because their pleasure is obtained by going along with their friends. Except for their delinquent acts, these people appear quite normal. They are able to get along reasonably well in correctional institutions but generally revert to their prior behavior after release.

54. A counselor described a young offender, Jack K., as follows: "Was nervous during our talk, bit his nails, looked sad and worried, although attentive. Last week he told me he felt 'real bad' about handing in his work report late, and I could see that he did. But the very next day, he was late again with his report." These comments best fit the description of which personality?
   (A) W
   (B) X
   (C) Y
   (D) Z

55. A counselor described a young offender, Edward F., as follows: "Prefers the company of his former gang members. This is his second time at the institution. He probably won't be able to steer clear of involvement when he gets out again. Gets along with fellow offenders, appears normal, but won't talk about his problems." These comments most nearly fit the description of which personality?
   (A) W
   (B) X
   (C) Y
   (D) Z

56. A counselor described a young offender, Arthur B., as follows: "Seems to be melancholy for long periods of time. Regrets deeply that he hurt another youngster rather badly in a gang fight before being sentenced. Has only one or two friends." These comments most nearly fit the description of which personality?

(A) W
(B) X
(C) Y
(D) Z

57. A counselor described a young offender, George H., as follows: "Didn't seem to care when I suggested that he didn't show enough interest in our activities. When in the shops he tends to stand off on one side, thinking instead of actively working. He's got a temper but doesn't start fights." These comments most nearly fit the description of which personality?

(A) W
(B) X
(C) Y
(D) Z

58. A counselor described a young offender, Charles D., as follows: "He is ready to argue at the slightest provocation. Once when he beat another youth he said he was not sorry for what he did, and he did exactly the same thing the next day, watching almost maliciously for my reaction. He seems to really want only his own way." These comments most nearly fit the description of which personality?

(A) W
(B) X
(C) Y
(D) Z

59. A counselor described a young offender, Larry M., as follows: "Admitted that he had been bullying some younger residents for 'kicks,' then told me to mind my own business. Kept interrupting me and continued to do so even when I asked him to stop." These comments most nearly fit the description of which personality?

(A) W
(B) X
(C) Y
(D) Z

60. If a prisoner has committed a serious infraction of prison rules, the prisoner may be disciplined by being placed in solitary confinement. A prisoner in solitary confinement receives two meals a day taken alone in the cell, is permitted one-half hour of daily exercise alone in a small yard, may receive two letters a week, and is denied visitors. However, a prisoner in solitary may consult with his or her attorney between the hours of 2 p.m. and 4 p.m. each day.

Inmate Sawyer has served one week of a two-week confinement in solitary. Sawyer's wife and two small children arrive at the prison to visit Inmate Sawyer. Corrections Officer Finn informs Mrs. Sawyer that Inmate Sawyer is in solitary and cannot have visitors. Corrections Officer Finn then informs Sawyer that his family has come to visit but that he cannot see them. Sawyer requests an emergency meeting with his attorney. Attorney Thatcher arrives at 2:15 p.m. and asks to take Inmate Sawyer's wife and children in with him to see Sawyer. Corrections Officer Finn permits Attorney Thatcher to bring the children but bars Mrs. Sawyer. Officer Finn's action is

(A) correct; children are not considered prohibited visitors.

(B) incorrect; attorneys and visitors are not permitted at the same time.

(C) correct; the attorney-client privilege allows attorneys to bring to prisoners whatever or whomever they please.

(D) incorrect; solitary confinement is a punishment, and part of that punishment is denial of visitors except for the attorney.

QUESTIONS 61 AND 62 ARE BASED ON THE FOLLOWING INFORMATION.

Physical restraint of prisoners' bodies should be held to a minimum. However, physical restraints in the form of handcuffs and leg irons are required whenever prisoners are being transferred from an institution to any other place. Physical restraints should also be used when a prisoner's behavior threatens the life or safety of any human being.

61. Inmates Tinker and Evers are both scheduled to appear for trial in the same courthouse on the same day. Corrections Officer Chance handcuffs both Tinker and Evers and clamps a set of leg irons onto Tinker's right leg and Evers's left. This action by Officer Chance is

(A) appropriate; the prisoners cannot run away when shackled together.

(B) inappropriate; prisoners are no threat to life or safety when riding the bus.

(C) appropriate; handcuffs constitute good weapons for beating each other over the head.

(D) inappropriate; the rule requires a minimum of restraint, which implies that either handcuffs or leg irons should be adequate.

62. Corrections Officer Kaplan, on routine patrol in the cell block, comes upon Inmate Serran thrashing wildly on the floor of his two-inmate cell, banging his head and flailing his arms and legs. Kaplan immediately calls for assistance, and Officer Buffamonte joins her with a straitjacket. Together they restrain Serran and transport him to the infirmary. This action by Corrections Officer Kaplan is

(A) correct; the inmate might have seriously injured Officer Kaplan.

(B) incorrect; the inmate was in no way a threat to the life or safety of his cellmate.

(C) correct; the inmate might have hurt himself badly if allowed to continue.

(D) incorrect; the inmate should have been handcuffed at once.

63. A Corrections Officer being called to a disciplinary hearing on any charges is entitled to request the personnel office to produce all documents that the Corrections Officer feels could bolster his or her defense.

Corrections Officer Blakelee's new supervisor has placed charges alleging that Blakelee has reported late on two occasions within the supervisor's three-week tenure. Blakelee's attorney requests Blakelee's attendance records for all seven years of her employment at this prison and copies of all performance reviews. Corrections Officer Arthur of the prison personnel office readily produces the attendance records for all seven years but releases only two years' performance reviews. This action by Corrections Officer Arthur is

(A) appropriate; performance reviews are irrelevant to a charge of lateness.

(B) inappropriate; Blakelee is entitled to any documents that she feels will be helpful.

(C) appropriate; if Blakelee persists in being late, she should be disciplined.

(D) inappropriate; two years' worth of attendance records would be adequate.

64. Prisoners facing the death penalty are entitled to a last meal of their choice. The request for the last meal is to be honored, no matter how bizarre.

Inmate O'Day has been convicted of the sex murder of a child and has received the death penalty. All appeals have been exhausted, and execution has been scheduled for midnight. The priest has come for O'Day's final confession, and O'Day has requested that his last meal be strictly Kosher. Corrections Officer Assalty laughs at this request and suggests that O'Day would be better off with corned beef and cabbage. Officer Assalty's action is

(A) appropriate; O'Day is Catholic, and there is no reason for the prison to go to the trouble of bringing in a Kosher meal.

(B) inappropriate; O'Day should be permitted to try every possible way to save his soul.

(C) appropriate; an Irishman should be sent off with an Irish dinner.

(D) inappropriate; for the last meal, the prisoner has free choice.

65. A men's prison is a very macho environment. Any appearance of effeminate behavior on the part of an inmate is likely to subject that inmate to harassment. Overt homosexual behavior may pose a real danger to the safety of homosexual inmates. Corrections Officers must be alert to the possibility of antagonism toward homosexuals and must defuse dangerous encounters.

Inmate White is a slightly built individual who tends to swing his hips when he walks and who avoids groups of inmates who brag about their sexual prowess. For the most part, other inmates have ignored White in the three months he has been in the cell block. Last week Inmate Ford was transferred into the cell block. Ford has no effeminate mannerisms, but he has clearly been attracted to White, and the feeling seems to be mutual. Of course the other inmates have noticed, and all Corrections Officers are on edge. In the exercise yard, Ford sidles up to White and puts his arm around him. Corrections Officer Collins bellows, "Hey, you two, stop smooching." Officer Collins's action is

(A) appropriate; homosexual acts are permitted only in private.

(B) inappropriate; the officer is calling all the inmates' attention to the couple.

(C) appropriate; Collins is warning them to stop before they get hurt.

(D) inappropriate; a Corrections Officer should not interfere in inmates' private lives.

**FOR QUESTIONS 66–70, MARK
(A) IF ONLY THE FIRST SENTENCE IS GRAMMATICALLY CORRECT.
(B) IF ONLY THE SECOND SENTENCE IS GRAMMATICALLY CORRECT.
(C) IF BOTH SENTENCES ARE GRAMMATICALLY CORRECT.
(D) IF NEITHER SENTENCE IS GRAMMATICALLY CORRECT.**

66. **(1)** Once the count has begun, there were no interruptions.
　　(2) Some things must be decided between the Corrections Officers of the institution themselves.

67. **(1)** There appears to be conditions that encourage accidents in this prison.
　　(2) When the inmate first come up to the institution, he was in an emotionally disturbed state and required constant supervision.

68. **(1)** It is a good rule for we Corrections Officers to follow.
　　(2) The change in the rules had a good effect on the morale of the inmates.

69. **(1)** There are a bed and a washstand in every cell.
　　(2) I feel bad because Inmate Scott never has visitors.

70. **(1)** Good morale in a prison is when there are no fights taking place.
　　(2) By 8 a.m. every inmate must straighten up his cell.

71. Needless to say, prison inmates are not permitted to possess weapons at any time. To be certain that there are no concealed weapons in the cells, Corrections Officers must periodically inspect all cells.

At 9 a.m. on Monday, Corrections Officer Blumner announces to the inmates of Cell block D, "We will be doing a weapons check in the cells Tuesday at noon." This action is

(A) proper; inmates will take the weapons out of the cells.

(B) improper; the search should not be limited to the cells.

(C) proper; inmates should be warned when their privacy will be invaded.

(D) improper; more weapons will be confiscated if inmates are not warned to hide them.

72. Prison inmates can be ingenious at fashioning weapons from eating utensils. At the end of the meal, the inmates bus their trays one at a time, and the Corrections Officer who receives the trays counts all items on each one. When all the trays have been bused, the Corrections Officer counts all cutlery before inmates are dismissed from the dining hall.

At the end of breakfast, Corrections Officer Vorperian counts the cutlery and finds she is one spoon short. She counts all the inmates in the room, then recounts the spoons. One spoon still appears to be missing. Vorperian announces that no one will leave the room until all the spoons are accounted for. Corrections Officers then approach the inmates one by one in an attempt to secure the spoon. The action taken by Officer Vorperian is

(A) appropriate; no cutlery may leave the dining hall.

(B) inappropriate; a spoon is not a dangerous weapon.

(C) appropriate; the spoon is government property and appears to have been stolen.

(D) inappropriate; Vorperian should have trusted the other Corrections Officers to have collected all of the cutlery from the trays.

73. Rehabilitation of offenders is a major function of the prison system. Rehabilitation involves changing attitudes, training in vocational skills, and basic education. Rehabilitation programs tend to be expensive, but they keep inmates productively occupied and may save the public money in the long run.

Inmate Mullins, who is facing the death penalty, asks to enroll in a GED preparatory course in order to earn a high school equivalency diploma. Corrections Officer Milowe grants this request and assigns Inmate Mullins to a regularly scheduled class. This action by Officer Milowe is

(A) appropriate; Mullins will never make anything of himself without a high school diploma.

(B) inappropriate; Mullins is about to die and will have no use for a high school diploma.

(C) appropriate; Mullins may learn something useful and will keep busy.

(D) inappropriate; limited funds should not be wasted in educating inmates who have no use for rehabilitation.

QUESTIONS 74 AND 75 ARE BASED ON THE FOLLOWING PASSAGE.

Criminal acts are classified according to several standards. One is whether the crime is major or minor. A major offense, such as murder, would be labeled a felony, whereas a minor offense, such as reckless driving, would be considered a misdemeanor. Another standard of classification is the specific kind of crime committed. Examples are burglary and robbery, which are terms often used incorrectly by individuals who are not aware of the actual difference as defined by law. A person who breaks into a building to commit a theft or other major crime is guilty of burglary, while robbery is the felonious taking of an individual's property from his person or in his immediate presence by the use of violence or threat. Other common criminal acts with distinct legal definitions are larceny and assault. The unlawful taking of another's property without his consent and with the intent of depriving him belongs to the first classification, while a violent attack on someone or an unlawful threat or attempt to do physical harm belongs to the second category.

74. A young woman was threatened at knife point by a criminal who demanded that she give him her pocketbook and gold watch. The woman screamed and the criminal, frightened, ran off without taking anything. According to the information in the passage, the crime committed was

(A) assault.

(B) robbery.

(C) larceny.

(D) burglary.

75. A man who has been asleep on a bus awakes to find that $350 in cash has been taken from him. According to the passage, he was subjected to

(A) robbery.

(B) burglary.

(C) larceny.

(D) assault.

76. On a regularly scheduled basis, all inmates are required to attend lectures presented by outside speakers. These lectures are intended to assist with transition back to society and to address such diverse subjects as planning and sticking to a budget, job hunting, and landlord–tenant relations.

    This week's lecture presented by a public health physician is to be on AIDS prevention and will include a slide presentation of clinical diagrams. Inmate Osborne approaches Corrections Officer Nunno and asks to be excused from the AIDS lecture saying, "I have a queasy stomach, and besides, my religion doesn't allow me to look at dirty pictures." Corrections Officer Nunno denies the request and requires Inmate Osborne to attend the lecture. Officer Nunno's action is

(A) proper; this sounds like a lame excuse.

(B) improper; freedom of religion is not suspended in prison.

(C) proper; this is a required lecture on an important health topic.

(D) improper; pornography has no place in prison.

77. In order to maintain discipline, a Corrections Officer must make it clear that he or she is in charge at all times. Corrections Officers must not permit inmates to order them around in any way. On the other hand, a Corrections Officer's effectiveness is enhanced by firm, polite leadership.

    It is 2 a.m. and Corrections Officer Karsky is on a catwalk doing regular rounds, keys jangling loudly as he walks. Inmate Connolly shouts from his cell, "Hey, cut the noise and let a guy sleep." Officer Karsky says, "Sorry," and pockets the keys. Officer Karsky's action is

(A) appropriate; common courtesy is never out of order.

(B) inappropriate; inmates will lose respect if they find that they can get their way so easily.

(C) appropriate; if the Corrections Officer is noisy he may miss the sounds of a prison break in progress.

(D) inappropriate; inmates should be kept aware of the officer's presence at all times, and jangling keys make a good reminder.

QUESTIONS 78–80 ARE BASED ON THE FOLLOWING INFORMATION.

A large proportion of the people who are behind bars are not convicted criminals but people who have been arrested and are being held until their trial in court. Experts have often pointed out that this detention system does not operate fairly. For instance, a person who can afford to pay bail usually will not get locked up. The theory of the bail system is that the person will make sure to show up in court when he is supposed to, since he knows that otherwise he will forfeit his bail—he will lose the money he put up. Sometimes a person who can show that he or she is a stable citizen with a job and a family will be released on "personal recognizance" (without bail). The result is that the well-to-do, the employed, and the family person can often avoid the detention system. The people who do wind up in detention tend to be the poor, the unemployed, the single, and the young.

78. Bartels and Murillo are picked up as they run from a bank carrying sacks of money, and both are charged with armed robbery. Bail is set. Bartels is able to raise bail and is released. Murillo is unable to raise bail and is held in detention. This result is

- **(A)** fair; a person who is able to raise bail obviously must be innocent.
- **(B)** unfair; it has no relation to guilt or innocence.
- **(C)** fair; the law should be tougher on poor people than on the rich.
- **(D)** unfair; the robbers deserve equal punishment.

79. Marlene Rogers, a divorcee with two sons ages 8 and 10, is charged with prostitution. Rogers is a homeowner and is regularly employed as a bookkeeper at a business in the community. Rogers is released on "personal recognizance." This means that

- **(A)** the judge knows Rogers well.
- **(B)** Rogers does not have to show up for trial.
- **(C)** Rogers has no record of previous convictions.
- **(D)** Rogers does not need to put up bail.

80. Barney Tripp, an unemployed, single, homeless 19-year-old, is in detention awaiting trial on a misdemeanor charge. He complains bitterly to Corrections Officer Lucas that he is an innocent victim of the system and is being treated as a common criminal. Corrections Officer Lucas responds, "If you are in jail, then jail is where you belong." Officer Lucas' statement is

- **(A)** correct; the American system of justice means justice for all.
- **(B)** incorrect; there are some innocent people who are in jail awaiting trial.
- **(C)** correct; everyone who cannot raise bail must belong in jail.
- **(D)** incorrect; Tripp should have been released on personal recognizance.

QUESTIONS 81–87 ARE BASED ON THE INFORMATION IN THE PASSAGE AND THE TABLE ON THE NEXT PAGE.

Coordination of operations within the entire prison system entails encoding each prison inmate along a number of dimensions and entering the code into the mainframe computer at central corrections headquarters. Each inmate on intake is assigned a 10-digit number. The first four digits identify the inmate by name. Digits five and six refer to the county of jurisdiction. Digits seven and eight designate the offense for which the inmate was convicted. The last two digits identify the institution in which the inmate is first incarcerated. Subsequent institutional transfers are indicated by adding a hyphen and additional digits after the tenth digit.

Identification Codes					
County	2nd to Last Pair	Conviction	Next to Last Pair	Institution	Last Pair
Ames	20	Armed Robbery	07	Allenby Prison	38
Cork	41	Burglary	76	Bates Hospital	13
Kent	62	Grand Larceny	43	Crofton Prison	29
Lime	03	Manslaughter One	92	Harrod Juvenile Facility	66
Tara	55	Murder Three	25	Prouse Prison	74
Wall	18	Rape	11	Tarton Correctional Institute	81

Inmates Currently Being Tracked	
Burns	4273034381
Chen	6842180738
Diorio	8256627666
Fenton	7311181129
Flood	6100209238
Greenberg	3987624329
Herrmann	2361182513-38
Howe	8663551138
Jones	0909417681
O'Malley	9805201138
Rivera	5683181166
Williams	5386037681

81. The county in which the greatest number of violent criminals was convicted is
    (A) Wall.
    (B) Ames.
    (C) Tara.
    (D) Lime.

82. The inmate who is serving a sentence on conviction for murder is
    (A) Jones.
    (B) Bums.
    (C) Herrmann.
    (D) Greenberg.

83. The inmate who was convicted for armed robbery was sent to
    (A) Bates Hospital.
    (B) Allenby Prison.
    (C) Croften Prison.
    (D) Tarton Correctional Institute.

84. Inmate 8663
    (A) is under age 18.
    (B) has spent time in the hospital.
    (C) is serving a sentence for armed robbery.
    (D) is in Allenby Prison.

85. Of the following inmates, the youngest is probably
    (A) 5386.
    (B) 5683.
    (C) 9805.
    (D) 0909.

86. If upon appeal Inmate Chen's conviction is overturned, but Chen is tried and convicted on a new charge so that her new number is 6842187638, the new conviction will be on a charge of
    (A) grand larceny.
    (B) armed robbery.
    (C) burglary.
    (D) manslaughter one.

87. The facility to which violent criminals do NOT seem to be assigned is
    (A) Tarton Correctional Institute.
    (B) Bates Hospital.
    (C) Crofton Prison.
    (D) Harrod Juvenile Facility.

88. Corrections Officers are required to uphold the Constitution. The Constitution provides that convicted felons be deprived of the right to vote in federal elections.

    Inmate Rushneck, who is currently undergoing trial on a charge of homicide, has sent for an absentee ballot for the presidential election. Corrections Officer Semmes refuses to deliver the ballot to Rushneck. Officer Semmes's action is

    (A) appropriate; Rushneck is being tried on a felony charge.
    (B) inappropriate; Rushneck has not been convicted of anything.
    (C) appropriate; Rushneck's voting might interfere with the trial.
    (D) inappropriate; Rushneck might be innocent.

89. The privacy of the confessional extends to clergy-inmate communications within the prison walls. While a clergyman should counsel and encourage an inmate to tell the whole story to the authorities, the clergyman is under no obligation to divulge any information.

    Paul Jernigan, in detention pending trial, asks to see a priest. Jernigan gives the priest information that could affect the outcome of the trial, and the priest urges Jernigan to volunteer this information to the prosecutor. Jernigan tells the priest that he will have to think about it. As the priest leaves, Corrections Officer Potamkin asks, "Did he confess? What did he tell you?" The priest declines to give any information to Potamkin. Potamkin angrily tells the priest, "You are obstructing justice. Because of you a guilty person may go free and an innocent person may be punished. It is your duty as a priest to protect the innocent and to see that justice is done." This action by Corrections Officer Potamkin is

    (A) appropriate; the suspect should not be permitted to protect someone else by taking the rap himself.
    (B) inappropriate; the Correction Officer has no proof that the suspect gave incriminating information.
    (C) appropriate; much taxpayer money will be saved if the suspect pleads guilty and thereby avoids a costly trial.
    (D) inappropriate; the priest has a right to remain silent.

90. Inmates assigned to maximum security facilities are considered the most desperate individuals and are deemed extremely dangerous to each other, to prison personnel, and to society at large. These prisoners must be controlled with extra surveillance. Any reasonable means must be used to prevent these prisoners from escaping.

    Corrections Officer Urinyi, standing guard at 4 a.m. in a watch tower at the corner of the prison compound, senses activity below. Looking down, Officer Urinyi sees that two inmates have tunneled beneath the wall and are inching their way on their bellies towards the woods beyond the open space. Officer Urinyi recognizes the inmates as Hammer and Gruber. She takes careful aim and shoots first the forward escapee and then the one closer to the prison walls. Officer Urinyi then sounds a general alarm. This action by Corrections Officer Urinyi is

    (A) correct; she has effectively foiled the escape.
    (B) incorrect; the escapees are flat on their bellies and pose no danger to anyone.
    (C) correct; Urinyi recognizes the prisoners and knows that they are dangerous criminals.
    (D) incorrect; the alarm will alert other inmates to the existence of the escape tunnel.

91. Under no circumstances may drugs be used in the prison. If an inmate is found with drugs in his or her possession, the drugs must be confiscated and the inmate must be disciplined. Any person attempting to bring drugs into a prison is guilty of a misdemeanor, even if the quantity of drugs is within the legal limit for individual possession.

Betsy Barker has come to the prison to visit her best friend, Inmate Troy. At the entry to the prison, Corrections Officer Fagoo searches Barker's pocketbook. In the pocketbook Officer Fagoo sees an open package of cigarettes. Fagoo takes the package of cigarettes from the pocketbook and sniffs them, detecting an odor of marijuana. Fagoo confiscates the cigarettes and arrests Betsy Barker. This action by Corrections Officer Fagoo is

(A) proper; Barker is smuggling drugs into the prison.

(B) improper; the cigarettes are Barker's personal property.

(C) proper; anyone bringing drugs into the prison is guilty of a crime.

(D) improper; the officer should have held the cigarettes for Barker while Barker visited her friend.

QUESTIONS 92–95 ARE BASED ON THE FOLLOWING PASSAGE.

The success or failure of a criminal prosecution usually depends upon the evidence presented to the court. Evidence may be divided into three major classifications: direct evidence, circumstantial evidence, and real evidence. Evidence must also be admissible, that is, material and relevant. An eyewitness account of a criminal act is direct evidence. Where an eyewitness does not have immediate experience, but reasonably infers what happened, circumstantial evidence is offered. Real evidence comprises objects introduced at a trial to prove or disprove a fact. For example, a gun, fingerprints, or bloodstains are real evidence. Real evidence may be direct or circumstantial. Evidence is immaterial if it is unimportant to the trial. For example, if someone is being tried for larceny of a crate of oranges, it is immaterial that the oranges were yellow in color. Evidence is irrelevant or immaterial if it does not prove the truth of a fact at issue. For example, if a murder had been committed with a bow and arrow, it is irrelevant to show that the defendant was well-acquainted with firearms.

92. Jones and Smith go into a room together and close the door. Richards stands outside the door and sees Jones and Smith go in. A shot is heard and Smith rushes out with a smoking gun in his hand. Richards rushes into the room and finds Jones lying on the floor, dead. Richards did not see Smith fire the shot. At Smith's trial for murdering Jones, Richards tells the court what he saw and heard. Richards's story is

(A) inadmissible evidence.

(B) real evidence.

(C) irrelevant evidence.

(D) circumstantial evidence.

93. In Smith's trial for murdering Jones, Smith's attorney could prove that Smith was an excellent student of history in high school. Such evidence would most likely be classified as

(A) real and material.

(B) direct and relevant.

(C) immaterial and irrelevant.

(D) circumstantial and admissible.

94. As Smith's trial for murdering Jones proceeds, the prosecutor proves that Smith owned the gun that killed Jones. Of the following, such evidence is most likely

(A) direct.

(B) inadmissible.

(C) irrelevant.

(D) material.

95. As Smith's trial for murdering Jones continues, the prosecutor introduces a surprise witness, Rogers. Rogers says that from an apartment across the street he looked into the window of the room where Jones and Smith were and saw Smith point a gun at Jones and shoot him, after which Jones fell to the floor and Smith rushed out of the room. Rogers's story is best described as

(A) real and circumstantial evidence.

(B) direct and relevant evidence.

(C) circumstantial and admissible evidence.

(D) relevant and real evidence.

96. The goal of imprisonment is to release a rehabilitated individual to society. Rehabilitation includes modification of attitudes and behavior and preparation for earning a livelihood. The educational programs in the prison include academic and vocational programs. Inmates who are considered unsuited to the programs they have chosen may be denied access.

Inmate Sarahn is serving a six-year sentence for assault with a deadly weapon. Two years remain to his term. Sarahn's service in this prison has been marked by his short temper and his frequent involvement in fights. Sarahn has expressed a desire to learn to be a barber and would like to join the class that is taught in the prison. Corrections Officer Teplitski refuses to admit Sarahn to the class. Officer Teplitski's action is

(A) appropriate; a violent individual should not be offered easy access to scissors and razors.

(B) inappropriate; the classroom is the ideal place to teach proper use of tools and instruments.

(C) appropriate; not enough time remains in Sarahn's term for proper training.

(D) inappropriate; Sarahn should be permitted to learn a trade so that he need not resort to crime to earn a living.

97. Corrections Officers must maintain complete and accurate files on all inmates. Recordkeeping includes entering all noticeable behavior by an inmate, both exceptionally good behavior and violations of rules. The record should include the date and nature of the behavior, circumstances under which the behavior was observed, and action taken—whether praise or discipline was offered.

Inmate Gallagher, who has generally been an unremarkable prisoner, approaches Corrections Officer Crown with a request to make telephone calls beyond the permitted number. When Corrections Officer Crown hesitates to grant this favor, Gallagher holds out two $10 bills to Crown. Crown refuses to take the money and denies Gallagher permission to make the excess phone calls. Gallagher returns to assigned activities, and Crown ignores the incident. This action by Crown is

(A) proper; a Corrections Officer should never accept bribes.

(B) improper; the phone calls must have been very important to Gallagher.

(C) proper; permitting an inmate to make calls in excess of the rules is worth more than $20.

(D) improper; Officer Crown should have recorded the attempted bribe in Gallagher's file.

98. Corrections Officers are subject to stress and danger in their daily work and so develop a strong sense of internal loyalty and camaraderie with one another. Corrections Officers will readily spring to the defense of their colleagues and, of course, expect the same in return. At the same time, Corrections Officers are peace officers and are sworn to uphold the law.

Corrections Officer Floyd has become aware that a cook and three Corrections Officers have been smuggling cocaine into the prison and selling it to inmates at great profit to themselves. Two of the Corrections Officers involved are very good friends of

Floyd. Floyd observes the smuggling operation and is certain that his assessment of what is going on is correct. Corrections Officer Floyd then reports this activity to his supervisor. This action by Officer Floyd is

(A) appropriate; if his friends had any loyalty to Floyd, they would have cut him in.

(B) inappropriate; Floyd should have reported only the cook and not his fellow officers.

(C) appropriate; illegal activity must be stopped by the authorities.

(D) inappropriate; other Correction Officers in the prison will lose respect for Floyd if he betrays the wrongdoers.

99. Once convicted and imprisoned, an inmate forfeits a variety of rights and privileges, chief among them his or her personal liberty. However, all inmates retain certain basic human and civil rights that may be suspended only when safety demands.

Inmates Ng and Ie are both serving long terms in a maximum security facility. The prison service of both inmates has been unremarkable; neither has been involved in any incident worthy of notice or discipline. Both inmates happen to be conversant in the same foreign language and spend a great deal of time speaking to one another in this language, which is unintelligible to everyone on the prison staff. Corrections Officer Perry orders Ng and Ie to speak only English. When they continue to communicate in their own tongue, Perry punishes each with four days in solitary confinement. This action by Officer Perry is

(A) appropriate; the inmates could have been plotting an uprising.

(B) inappropriate; the inmates gave no indication that they were endangering anyone's safety.

(C) appropriate; the inmates were denying the Corrections Officer's civil rights.

(D) inappropriate; freedom of speech must never be curtailed in any way.

100. Every prisoner has the right to participate in preparation of his or her own appeal. The prison library is well stocked with law books appropriate for prisoners' use, and the Corrections Officer who serves as librarian is familiar with various sources. The library space is small, so that supervision does not require assignment of too many Corrections Officers. Because of space restrictions, only prisoners actively pursuing appeal are permitted use of the library.

Inmate Mariani requests permission to use the prison library during a period in which he was scheduled to be in the gym. In the library Mariani chooses a book at random, opens it on the table before him, and proceeds to write personal letters. The librarian, Corrections Officer Kane, looks over Mariani's shoulder, sends for an escort, and ejects Mariani from the library. This action by Officer Kane is

(A) appropriate; the purpose of the library is to prepare appeals.

(B) inappropriate; Mariani was not using books needed by anyone else.

(C) appropriate; inmates are not permitted to use the library to shirk their other assignments.

(D) inappropriate; Officer Kane should have helped Mariani find the best books to prepare his appeal.

ANSWER KEY AND EXPLANATIONS

1. B	21. C	41. A	61. A	81. A
2. B	22. D	42. C	62. C	82. C
3. D	23. B	43. D	63. B	83. B
4. B	24. D	44. D	64. D	84. D
5. C	25. A	45. A	65. B	85. B
6. D	26. C	46. B	66. A	86. C
7. A	27. B	47. D	67. D	87. A
8. C	28. B	48. C	68. B	88. B
9. C	29. C	49. B	69. C	89. D
10. A	30. D	50. A	70. B	90. A
11. B	31. B	51. C	71. D	91. C
12. B	32. B	52. B	72. A	92. D
13. C	33. D	53. D	73. C	93. C
14. C	34. B	54. B	74. A	94. D
15. A	35. B	55. D	75. C	95. B
16. D	36. C	56. B	76. C	96. A
17. C	37. A	57. A	77. A	97. D
18. B	38. D	58. C	78. B	98. C
19. D	39. C	59. C	79. D	99. B
20. A	40. A	60. D	80. B	100. A

1. **The correct answer is (B).** Beating other inmates to extract cigarettes and coffee from them is using violence to intimidate and to gain favors, behavior typical of the gorilla.

2. **The correct answer is (B).** The Receiving Room is a nonsmoking area. The fact that Jomes is not on duty is irrelevant.

3. **The correct answer is (D).** The rule clearly says "Hold on to the badge." The badge is the property of the Corrections Department, and Berkey does not have the discretion to let his child play with and possibly lose or break it.

4. **The correct answer is (B).** The attorney–client privilege is inviolate. Anything one says to the other is strictly between the two. The Correction Officer has no right to listen in. If the officer inadvertently overhears anything, he or she has no right to pass it on.

5. **The correct answer is (C).** David Blank is under age 18 and may be admitted as a visitor only if accompanied by an adult.

6. **The correct answer is (D).** The regulation is that all letters must be delivered within 24 hours and that letters should not be opened by Corrections Officers. There is no limit to the number of letters that may be delivered.

7. **The correct answer is (A).** The contents of the package are harmless. The regulation permits that packages may be held 48 hours if necessary; it does not require the delay. Sunday is just another workday in the prison; prisoners may have their mail.

8. **The correct answer is (C).** Under the Penal Law, a peace officer is on duty at all times, even when not officially on duty at his or her regular job. Rice was acting properly as a peace officer and so was killed in the line of duty. (Remember that even if you personally disagree, you must answer solely on the basis of the information given.)

9. **The correct answer is (C).** There certainly is reason to suspect Pulaski, and investigation is the proper route to take. He cannot be charged and punished simply on the basis of suspicion.

10. **The correct answer is (A).** Death appears to be imminent for Martha's mother, and Martha may visit her in the hospital. It appears from the passage that Martha may go to the funeral as well and that the state will incur the costs, though family reimbursement is welcome.

11. **The correct answer is (B).** There can be no exceptions to the full-coverage rule. This is a matter of safety for Corrections Officers and inmates.

12. **The correct answer is (B).** A Corrections Officer should never stoop to the behavior or the language of the inmates. The Corrections Officer is a professional and must serve as a role model. A Correction Officer who cannot stand insults should not be in this business.

13. **The correct answer is (C).** The action seems destined to restore order by eliminating opportunity for further food fights. No one will suffer from missing one meal.

14. **The correct answer is (C).** Frank was attempting to help a convicted felon to escape, so Frank is guilty of a felony. Mary was an innocent courier; she did not intend to help Johnny to escape, so, within the scope of the passage, she is not guilty.

15. **The correct answer is (A).** The prisoner being assisted to escape is being held on a felony charge; therefore, those who assist in his escape are guilty of felonies. Although all of the assistance is given orally, it is obviously useful. Both Joan and Tom are parties to Bill's escape.

16. **The correct answer is (D).** Debbie is a very young child, far too young to be charged with criminal intent; she is innocent. Since Jim was serving a sentence on a misdemeanor conviction, Barbara is guilty only of a misdemeanor. Jim, on the other hand, is now in serious trouble. The next person who tries to help Jim escape will be guilty of a felony.

17. **The correct answer is (C).** Garcia is alert and sensitive but is not qualified to diagnose Mashke's problem. Insisting on taking the inmate for medical evaluation is a very appropriate action.

18. **The correct answer is (B).** A fist fight on the floor does not represent a life-threatening situation. The officer used excessive force.

19. **The correct answer is (D).** The prison rules apply equally to all prisoners, whether convicted or not.

20. **The correct answer is (A).** The rule lists the items that must be confiscated, and belts are clearly among the items. The reason that inmates may not keep their belts is clearly suicide related, but considering Wyler a suicide candidate is assuming too much. The answer to the question is directly tied to the stated rule. The intake officer could solve the inmate's problem by issuing him trousers in a smaller size.

21. **The correct answer is (C).** The busiest day, with three prisoners scheduled to appear in court, is April 15. Sowders is scheduled for that date.

22. **The correct answer is (D).** This case is that of Laduca, who is up for manslaughter two.

23. **The correct answer is (B).** Whinston and Hughes will both be tried before Judge Cook.

24. **The correct answer is (D).** Crofton will be tried in Criminal Court in Rook County.

25. **The correct answer is (A).** Judge Molina will sit on the case of Laduca, who is charged with manslaughter two; Judge Gabriel will sit on the case of Torak, who is charged with vehicular homicide.

26. **The correct answer is (C).** The burglary trial of Persaud is docketed as 437792 in Prince County Court. The other burglary trial, that of Hughes and docketed as 668190, will be in Queens Appeals Court.

27. **The correct answer is (B).** Embezzlement and grand larceny both involve stealing money from unsuspecting victims. The other choices are all incorrect because the docket numbers of the three cases on April 15 end with different digits. Sowders will be tried in Prince Supreme Court; and Judge Gabriel will sit on the trial of Torak.

28. **The correct answer is (B).** The suspect's behavior is consistent with depression, especially in light of the charge against him. While young offenders may be more prone to suicide, suicide watch must not be limited to them.

29. **The correct answer is (C).** A Corrections Officer cannot observe in front and behind at the same time. The rule is clear. The officer's response, "I'm sorry," is a recognition of the polite "May I please . . ."

30. **The correct answer is (D).** The reason for this rule is obvious. Babies themselves are not smugglers, but their wrappings provide an excellent hiding place for contraband being smuggled by adults.

31. **The correct answer is (B).** Helping to choose books to support the inmate's own plan of defense is precisely the function of the librarian. Choice (D), suggesting an alternate defense, would be out of order.

32. **The correct answer is (B).** The rule clearly states that the officer may not help with the preparation of papers—even if making no suggestions.

33. **The correct answer is (D).** Harry is too old to be sent to the state reformatory, but since his term is for only 11 months, he may be sent to county penitentiary, to county jail, or to state prison.

34. **The correct answer is (B).** Mark, as a second offender, cannot serve his term in the state reformatory. Even though Mark's sentence is for a term well in excess of one year, he may serve his time at the county penitentiary or at the county jail because he is between the ages of 16 and 21. Mark may, of course, be sent to a state prison.

35. **The correct answer is (B).** As a first offender between the ages of 16 and 30, George may be sent to the state reformatory. State prison is also an option. George's term is too long for a man his age to serve at the county penitentiary or the county jail.

36. **The correct answer is (C).** Never assume literacy. The visitor may not be aware of the smoking prohibition or may have just lit up unconsciously. The officer is correct in informing the visitor of the rule and in requesting compliance. After that long trip, the visitor is unlikely to risk ejection.

37. **The correct answer is (A).** Choice (B) makes assumptions far beyond the given facts. The facts present no legitimate reason for suspension of the prison rules. The conference can wait until morning.

38. **The correct answer is (D).** This is common sense in light of the facts.

39. **The correct answer is (C).** Even if the request seems quite reasonable, complying with it could give the appearance of favoritism.

40. **The correct answer is (A).** While this may well be a case of malingering, the officer has no way of knowing for sure. Let the dentist decide.

41. **The correct answer is (A).** You do not need to do any calculations to answer this question. At the start of the day all inmates except the few in the Receiving Room or at the hospital are in their cells.

42. **The correct answer is (C).** Add up all the inmates who passed through the Receiving Room this morning: $12 + 21 + 17 + 8 + 10 + 4 = 72$.

43. **The correct answer is (D).** Prisoners who are off premises are at court, are in the hospital, or have been released or transferred elsewhere. In turn: 33 prisoners went to court in two groups and only 7 have returned, so there are $33 - 7 = 26$ prisoners at court. There were 9 prisoners in the hospital at the start of the day, and 5 more have gone there; meanwhile, 6 have returned, so, $(9 + 5) - 6 = 14 - 6 = 8$ are in the hospital at noon.
Add up the releases: $5 + 3 + 12 + 8 = 28$.
$26 + 8 + 28 = 62$ prisoners are off premises at noon.

44. The correct answer is (D). At noon, 62 inmates left the kitchen and none entered; therefore, no inmates were working in the kitchen at noon.

45. The correct answer is (A). Add those inmates moved in at 8, 9, and 10 to the number of inmates already in Cell block A at the start of the day. Subtract from that total the number moved out in the same hours: $(52 + 7 + 24 + 46) - (28 + 31 + 20) = 129 - 79 = 50$.

46. The correct answer is (B). Of the 20 inmates who left for court at 8 a.m., only 7 returned at noon; 13 remained for more than a half day.

47. The correct answer is (D). $80 \times 3 = 240$ inmates who participated in recreation. The total prison population was roughly 258 prisoners: 52 in Cell Block A + 60 in Cell Block B + 74 in Cell Block C + 72 new inmates admitted during the day = 258. The number of inmates off premises varied during the morning, but clearly almost all of the inmates who were on premises took recreation, in other words, just about 100%.

48. The correct answer is (C). At 9 a.m., 31 inmates were moved from Cell Block A, 40 were moved from Cell Block B, and 52 were moved out of Cell Block C, for a total of 123 inmates moved. To be certain that this is the greatest number of inmates moved out of their cell blocks at any hour, you must do the arithmetic for each hour. Thus, the movement out of cells at 8 a.m. was $28 + 32 + 30 = 90$; at 10 a.m. it was $20 + 21 + 47 = 88$; at 11 a.m. it was $37 + 39 + 28 = 104$; and at noon it was $23 + 35 + 40 = 98$.

49. The correct answer is (B). Carlucci's kicking was the provocation and the punch by Otten was retaliatory. The incomplete entry might lead the parole board to conclude that Otten was aggressive and thereby dangerous. Otten may have overreacted, but the record should clearly describe the known reasons for actions.

50. The correct answer is (A). This is prison and rules must be obeyed. This is the 1 p.m. check, not the 1 a.m. check, so the officer does not need to enter the cell. The inmate's identity is not in question, but the inmate must obey the rules.

51. The correct answer is (C). The inmate certainly appears to be ill, and the officer is correctly insisting that he receive medical care.

52. The correct answer is (B). Migraine headaches come on suddenly. A person who did not have a migraine headache yesterday could certainly have one today. If the inmate had a long history of feigning illness in prison, the officer might be justified in discounting the claim. However, this is a new inmate, so the Corrections Officer should take the inmate's word and let him go to sick call.

53. The correct answer is (D). The rule says that all contents of a package containing contraband must be held, regardless of the nature of the noncontraband contents that are present.

54. The correct answer is (B). Jack K. is a typical "X," nervous and truly sorry for his shortcoming but unable to change his habits.

55. The correct answer is (D). Edward F. is a "Z." He gets along in prison and gets along with other inmates, but he keeps coming back.

56. The correct answer is (B). Arthur B., another "X," seems unhappy much of the time and, because he is selective, has few friends.

57. The correct answer is (A). George H. shows the lack of interest in activities or events that is typical of the "W."

58. The correct answer is (C). "Y" is hostile and aggressive and gets pleasure from having others notice these aspects of his behavior. Charles D. fits this pattern.

59. The correct answer is (C). Larry M. is another hostile and aggressive "Y."

60. The correct answer is (D). Part of a prisoner's punishment in solitary is denial of visitors. Of course children are visitors; choice (A) is ridiculous. The attorney's privilege applies to the right to consult and the right to confidentiality of communication. The attorney does not have the right to contravene prison rules.

61. **The correct answer is (A).** The rule says ". . . handcuffs and leg irons . . . whenever being transferred."

62. **The correct answer is (C).** The inmate is a human being and must be restrained from doing damage to himself. The Corrections Officer correctly considers the welfare of the inmate as well as that of other inmates and Corrections Officers.

63. **The correct answer is (B).** If the officer or the officer's attorney feels that the documents would be helpful to the defense, the documents should be provided.

64. **The correct answer is (D).** The request may seem strange, but the prisoner is entitled to the last meal of his choice.

65. **The correct answer is (B).** More than inappropriate, this behavior is foolhardy. Rather than defusing a problem, the officer is needlessly drawing attention to it. This situation must be handled very quietly and delicately, attracting as little inmate attention as possible.

66. **The correct answer is (A).** Sentence 2 is incorrect because *between* should be used only when there are two; undoubtedly there are far more than two Corrections Officers at the institution, so the proper word is *among.*

67. **The correct answer is (D).** Sentence 1 is incorrect because subject and verb do not agree in number. *Conditions,* the subject of the sentence, is plural, so the verb *appear* must also be plural. Sentence 2 is incorrect because the verb must be in the past tense, *came.*

68. **The correct answer is (B).** Sentence 1 is incorrect because the preposition *for* must take the objective case (*us*). If you leave the Corrections Officers out of the sentence, you can see that "It is a good rule for us to follow."

69. **The correct answer is (C).** Both of these sentences are correct. In sentence 1, *bed and washstand* constitutes a plural subject that takes the plural verb *are.* In sentence 2, it is correct to feel bad when you are sorry. To feel badly refers to the sense of touch.

70. **The correct answer is (B).** Sentence 1 is incorrect because a *when* clause cannot serve to define a noun. The sentence would be better recast, "Good morale *exists* in a prison when there are no fights taking place."

71. **The correct answer is (D).** The element of surprise is very important in a weapons search. Giving the inmates the opportunity to hide their weapons outside the cells is, in effect, allowing them to keep the weapons.

72. **The correct answer is (A).** Vorperian is in charge, and she is correct in not allowing any cutlery to leave the dining hall. Desperate prisoners might very well modify a spoon to be used as a weapon or use it for digging.

73. **The correct answer is (C).** Laws change and sentences can be reversed. Rehabilitation is a worthwhile goal. Even if Mullins never has use for the high school diploma, the time spent studying is time that he is not creating any problems in the institution.

74. **The correct answer is (A).** An unlawful threat or attempt to do physical harm, even if unsuccessful, constitutes assault.

75. **The correct answer is (C).** Larceny is the taking of another's property. It differs from robbery because violence is not involved.

76. **The correct answer is (C).** Attendance at the lecture is required and is intended as a benefit to the inmates. Clinical diagrams are not "dirty pictures," so dictates of the inmate's religion have no bearing on lecture attendance.

77. **The correct answer is (A).** Requesting quiet at 2 a.m. is not an unreasonable demand. There is no harm in the officer's compliance. In fact, the inmates are more likely to respect him for his humanity.

78. **The correct answer is (B).** The law is not always fair. Sometimes expediency must rule. Presumably Murillo does not qualify for release on his own recognizance, so, in the absence of bail (which he could not afford to forfeit), he must be held to assure his appearance at trial. Choice (D) is the wrong answer because detention pending trial does not constitute punishment. Neither suspect deserves any punishment until trial and conviction.

79. **The correct answer is (D).** It is assumed that Rogers, with her roots in the community, will appear on schedule for trial. The court feels it does not need to hold bail to guarantee her appearance.

80. **The correct answer is (B).** Some of the people being held in jail pending trial will be acquitted of the crimes of which they are accused. Tripp may, indeed, be innocent. However, Tripp does not qualify for release on personal recognizance.

81. **The correct answer is (A).** Inmates from Wall County were convicted for an armed robbery, a murder, and two rapes. From Ames County there was one rape and one manslaughter. In Tara County there was one rape conviction. The convictions from Lime County were for nonviolent crimes, grand larceny and burglary.

82. **The correct answer is (C).** Herrmann, 2361182513-38, with the code 25, is serving a sentence for murder in the third degree.

83. **The correct answer is (B).** Chen, 6842180738, who is serving a sentence for armed robbery, code 07, is serving at Allenby Prison, code 38.

84. **The correct answer is (D).** Howe, 8663551138, has been assigned to Allenby Prison, code 38.

85. **The correct answer is (B).** Of the inmates listed, only Rivera, 5683181166, has been assigned to Harrod Juvenile Facility, code 66.

86. **The correct answer is (C).** If Chen's number were to change to 6842187638, she would be serving on conviction for burglary, code 76. Her current number, 6842180738, indicates that the original conviction was on a charge of armed robbery, code 07.

87. **The correct answer is (A).** Of the facilities listed, only Tarton Correctional Institute, code 81, has received no prisoners convicted of violent crimes. Prisoners sent to Tarton have been convicted of grand larceny and burglary. The other facilities appear to receive prisoners convicted of both violent and nonviolent crimes.

88. **The correct answer is (B).** Only convicted felons are to be deprived of the franchise. Since the trial is still in progress, Rushneck has not been convicted and is entitled to vote. Choice (D) is not the right answer because innocence or guilt is irrelevant to the loss of the vote; conviction is what governs.

89. **The correct answer is (D).** As a clergyman, the priest has the right to maintain the suspect's information in confidence. Choice (B) may be making a correct statement, but it is not based solely on the information presented.

90. **The correct answer is (A).** Absolutely, the prisoners must not be allowed to escape. Prompt action is essential; an alarm might present an opportunity to escape.

91. **The correct answer is (C).** This is good work by Fagoo. Barker is bringing marijuana into the prison, a prohibited act. Even if Baker was simply carrying her own supply for later use outside the prison, by carrying it in she became a lawbreaker.

92. **The correct answer is (D).** Richards was not an actual eyewitness to the shooting, so his testimony cannot be considered direct evidence, but what he did hear and see before and after the shooting constitutes circumstantial evidence.

93. **The correct answer is (C).** Smith's academic record has absolutely nothing to do with his guilt or innocence in this murder case.

94. **The correct answer is (D).** Smith's ownership of the murder weapon is very important evidence in this trial.

95. **The correct answer is (B).** The testimony of an eyewitness is direct evidence; if Rogers actually witnessed the murder, his testimony is certainly relevant.

96. **The correct answer is (A).** Safety considerations within the prison take precedence over the inmate's desire to learn a trade. If the inmate is still violent after four years in prison, his behavior has not been modified. It would be most inappropriate to put potentially deadly weapons into his hands.

97. **The correct answer is (D).** To the extent that the officer refused to accept the bribe and denied the favor to the inmate, the action was correct. Had there been only the request (without the attempted bribe), the incident could have gone unrecorded. However, attempted bribery is clearly outside of acceptable behavior by inmates. As such, the Corrections Officer should have recorded the behavior in the inmate's file.

98. **The correct answer is (C).** Illegal drugs, smuggling, and profiteering by prison staff are all not permitted. Officer Floyd is absolutely correct in reporting this activity to the supervisor. In fact, the duty to report illegal activity transcends duty of loyalty to one's fellow officers.

99. **The correct answer is (B).** Officer Perry may feel uncomfortable when the inmates converse and he cannot understand a word, but the inmates have a right to talk to one another. In the absence of any behavior that might lead to suspicion of illegal planning, the Corrections Officer cannot prohibit free conversation or punish the inmates.

100. **The correct answer is (A).** The inmate is using his free time, not avoiding assigned tasks; but he is not using the library for its intended purpose. His actions show that Mariani has come to write letters, not to research an appeal. Thus, the Correction Officer is appropriately ejecting Mariani so as to leave space for inmates who have legitimate library business.

ANSWER SHEET PRACTICE TEST 5

1. Ⓐ Ⓑ Ⓒ Ⓓ	18. Ⓐ Ⓑ Ⓒ Ⓓ	35. Ⓐ Ⓑ Ⓒ Ⓓ	52. Ⓐ Ⓑ Ⓒ Ⓓ	69. Ⓐ Ⓑ Ⓒ Ⓓ
2. Ⓐ Ⓑ Ⓒ Ⓓ	19. Ⓐ Ⓑ Ⓒ Ⓓ	36. Ⓐ Ⓑ Ⓒ Ⓓ	53. Ⓐ Ⓑ Ⓒ Ⓓ	70. Ⓐ Ⓑ Ⓒ Ⓓ
3. Ⓐ Ⓑ Ⓒ Ⓓ	20. Ⓐ Ⓑ Ⓒ Ⓓ	37. Ⓐ Ⓑ Ⓒ Ⓓ	54. Ⓐ Ⓑ Ⓒ Ⓓ	71. Ⓐ Ⓑ Ⓒ Ⓓ
4. Ⓐ Ⓑ Ⓒ Ⓓ	21. Ⓐ Ⓑ Ⓒ Ⓓ	38. Ⓐ Ⓑ Ⓒ Ⓓ	55. Ⓐ Ⓑ Ⓒ Ⓓ	72. Ⓐ Ⓑ Ⓒ Ⓓ
5. Ⓐ Ⓑ Ⓒ Ⓓ	22. Ⓐ Ⓑ Ⓒ Ⓓ	39. Ⓐ Ⓑ Ⓒ Ⓓ	56. Ⓐ Ⓑ Ⓒ Ⓓ	73. Ⓐ Ⓑ Ⓒ Ⓓ
6. Ⓐ Ⓑ Ⓒ Ⓓ	23. Ⓐ Ⓑ Ⓒ Ⓓ	40. Ⓐ Ⓑ Ⓒ Ⓓ	57. Ⓐ Ⓑ Ⓒ Ⓓ	74. Ⓐ Ⓑ Ⓒ Ⓓ
7. Ⓐ Ⓑ Ⓒ Ⓓ	24. Ⓐ Ⓑ Ⓒ Ⓓ	41. Ⓐ Ⓑ Ⓒ Ⓓ	58. Ⓐ Ⓑ Ⓒ Ⓓ	75. Ⓐ Ⓑ Ⓒ Ⓓ
8. Ⓐ Ⓑ Ⓒ Ⓓ	25. Ⓐ Ⓑ Ⓒ Ⓓ	42. Ⓐ Ⓑ Ⓒ Ⓓ	59. Ⓐ Ⓑ Ⓒ Ⓓ	76. Ⓐ Ⓑ Ⓒ Ⓓ
9. Ⓐ Ⓑ Ⓒ Ⓓ	26. Ⓐ Ⓑ Ⓒ Ⓓ	43. Ⓐ Ⓑ Ⓒ Ⓓ	60. Ⓐ Ⓑ Ⓒ Ⓓ	77. Ⓐ Ⓑ Ⓒ Ⓓ
10. Ⓐ Ⓑ Ⓒ Ⓓ	27. Ⓐ Ⓑ Ⓒ Ⓓ	44. Ⓐ Ⓑ Ⓒ Ⓓ	61. Ⓐ Ⓑ Ⓒ Ⓓ	78. Ⓐ Ⓑ Ⓒ Ⓓ
11. Ⓐ Ⓑ Ⓒ Ⓓ	28. Ⓐ Ⓑ Ⓒ Ⓓ	45. Ⓐ Ⓑ Ⓒ Ⓓ	62. Ⓐ Ⓑ Ⓒ Ⓓ	79. Ⓐ Ⓑ Ⓒ Ⓓ
12. Ⓐ Ⓑ Ⓒ Ⓓ	29. Ⓐ Ⓑ Ⓒ Ⓓ	46. Ⓐ Ⓑ Ⓒ Ⓓ	63. Ⓐ Ⓑ Ⓒ Ⓓ	80. Ⓐ Ⓑ Ⓒ Ⓓ
13. Ⓐ Ⓑ Ⓒ Ⓓ	30. Ⓐ Ⓑ Ⓒ Ⓓ	47. Ⓐ Ⓑ Ⓒ Ⓓ	64. Ⓐ Ⓑ Ⓒ Ⓓ	81. Ⓐ Ⓑ Ⓒ Ⓓ
14. Ⓐ Ⓑ Ⓒ Ⓓ	31. Ⓐ Ⓑ Ⓒ Ⓓ	48. Ⓐ Ⓑ Ⓒ Ⓓ	65. Ⓐ Ⓑ Ⓒ Ⓓ	82. Ⓐ Ⓑ Ⓒ Ⓓ
15. Ⓐ Ⓑ Ⓒ Ⓓ	32. Ⓐ Ⓑ Ⓒ Ⓓ	49. Ⓐ Ⓑ Ⓒ Ⓓ	66. Ⓐ Ⓑ Ⓒ Ⓓ	83. Ⓐ Ⓑ Ⓒ Ⓓ
16. Ⓐ Ⓑ Ⓒ Ⓓ	33. Ⓐ Ⓑ Ⓒ Ⓓ	50. Ⓐ Ⓑ Ⓒ Ⓓ	67. Ⓐ Ⓑ Ⓒ Ⓓ	84. Ⓐ Ⓑ Ⓒ Ⓓ
17. Ⓐ Ⓑ Ⓒ Ⓓ	34. Ⓐ Ⓑ Ⓒ Ⓓ	51. Ⓐ Ⓑ Ⓒ Ⓓ	68. Ⓐ Ⓑ Ⓒ Ⓓ	85. Ⓐ Ⓑ Ⓒ Ⓓ

answer sheet

Practice Test 5

85 QUESTIONS • 3 HOURS

Directions: You will be given 10 minutes to study the three pictures that follow and to try to remember as many details as you can. You may not take any notes during this time. Then answer the questions that follow.

Contents of a Woman's Handbag

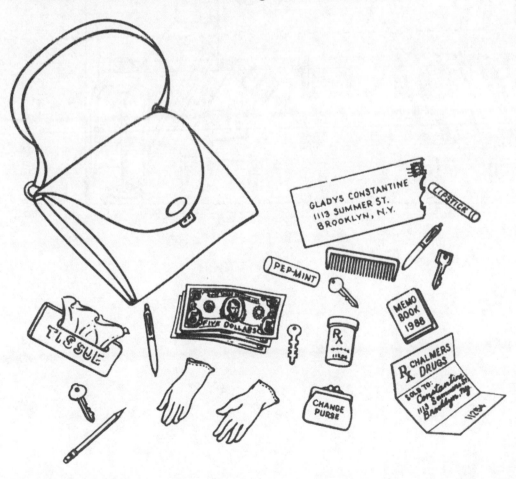

203

The Waiting Room

Contents of a Male Suspect's Pockets

QUESTIONS 1–6 ARE BASED ON THE PICTURE "CONTENTS OF A WOMAN'S HANDBAG."

1. Where does Gladys Constantine live?
   - **(A)** Chalmers Street in Manhattan
   - **(B)** Summer Street in Manhattan
   - **(C)** Summer Street in Brooklyn
   - **(D)** Chalmers Street in Brooklyn

2. How many keys were in the handbag?
   - **(A)** 2
   - **(B)** 3
   - **(C)** 4
   - **(D)** 5

3. How much money was in the handbag?
   - **(A)** Exactly five dollars
   - **(B)** More than five dollars
   - **(C)** Exactly ten dollars
   - **(D)** Less than one dollar

4. The sales slip found in the handbag shows the purchase of which of the following?
   - **(A)** The handbag
   - **(B)** Lipstick
   - **(C)** Tissues
   - **(D)** Prescription medicine

5. Among the items in the handbag were
   - **(A)** a pair of gloves.
   - **(B)** two right gloves.
   - **(C)** two left gloves.
   - **(D)** three gloves.

6. Which of the following items was NOT in the handbag?
   - **(A)** A comb
   - **(B)** A mirror
   - **(C)** A packet of tissues
   - **(D)** A pencil

7. "Full completion of the sentence means that the final limit of the penalty imposed by the court has been reached and there is no longer any legal authority over the offender in connection with that particular offense." According to this statement, where there is full completion of the sentence,

(A) no further punishment or restraint can be imposed by the government for the offense in question.

(B) the court has given the maximum penalty permitted under the law and society can no longer impose any legal restrictions on the offender.

(C) the full limit of the penalty permitted by law for the offense has not been imposed by the court.

(D) there is no longer any legal authority over the former offender.

8. "Under the state-use system of prison labor, the state conducts a business of manufacture but the use or sale of the goods is limited to the institution where manufactured or to other state institutions and agencies." According to this statement, under the state-use system of prison labor, the

(A) goods manufactured can be used only by state prisons.

(B) products of inmate labor cannot be sold on the open market.

(C) state competes with private industry in the manufacture of all those articles that are needed to operate a penal institution.

(D) variety of articles manufactured is limited to those that can be used in the institution where they are made.

9. "The distinction in the criminal law of the United States between a misdemeanant and a felon was that the former received a sentence of a year or over." Of the following, the most accurate conclusion based on this statement is that under the criminal law of the United States

(A) a felony was considered a more serious crime than a misdemeanor.

(B) all crimes were classified as misdemeanors or felonies.

(C) all persons accused of felonies received sentences of more than a year.

(D) some misdemeanants received the same prison sentence as some felons.

10. "Paroles may be granted by the board of managers at any time, and prisoners are referred to the board for parole consideration whenever the warden and the classification committee believe they have received the maximum benefit from institutional treatment and training and the conditions in the community are relatively favorable." Of the following, the most accurate conclusion based on this statement is that

(A) a parole, to be valid, must be approved by the classification committee and the board of managers.

(B) during periods of economic depression very few paroles are granted, because employment conditions in the community are not favorable.

(C) prisoners become eligible for parole upon completion of the required minimum part of their sentence provided their conduct in prison has been satisfactory.

(D) prisoners who have not yet benefited from the institutional treatment program are not likely to be referred for parole consideration.

11. "No other apex of prison life has invaded the public interest as frequently as the matter of punishment." According to this statement, it is most reasonable to assume that the

 (A) extent of public interest in all prison matters is very great.
 (B) punishment is not the only aspect of prison life in which the public has been interested.
 (C) punishment of any prison inmate will be criticized by the public whenever it is brought to light.
 (D) study of the punishment of prison inmates is not any easy task.

12. "The old prison is gradually being changed into something that might diagnose and treat the prisoners rather than punish them." According to this statement,

 (A) diagnosis and treatment will succeed whenever punishment fails.
 (B) the objectives and methods of the prison are being modified.
 (C) the old prison and the new have very little in common.
 (D) where diagnosis and treatment fail, punishment must be tried.

QUESTIONS 13–18 ARE BASED ON THE PICTURE "THE WAITING ROOM."

13. A desk is shown in the drawing. Which of the following is on the desk?

 (A) A plant
 (B) A telephone
 (C) An in-out file
 (D) An "information" sign

14. On which floor is the waiting area?

 (A) Basement
 (B) Main floor
 (C) Second floor
 (D) Third floor

15. The door immediately to the right of the desk as you see it is the door to

 (A) the personnel office.
 (B) the elevator.
 (C) another corridor.
 (D) the stairs.

16. Among the magazines on the tables in the waiting area are

 (A) *Time* and *Newsweek*.
 (B) *Reader's Digest* and *TV Guide*.
 (C) *New York* and *Reader's Digest*.
 (D) *Time* and *TV Guide*.

17. One door is partly open. This is the door to

 (A) the director's office.
 (B) the personnel manager's office.
 (C) the stairs.
 (D) an unmarked office.

18. Which of the following statements about the picture is NOT correct?

 (A) There is an ashtray on one table.
 (B) There are no people in the room.
 (C) There is an EXIT sign above the door to the stairs.
 (D) The director is in Room 2B.

19. "Physical and mental health are essential to the peace officer." According to this statement, the peace officer must be

 (A) as wise as he or she is strong.
 (B) smarter than most people.
 (C) sound in mind and body.
 (D) stronger than the average criminal.

20. "Teamwork is the basis of successful law enforcement." The factor stressed by this statement is

 (A) cooperation.
 (B) determination.
 (C) initiative.
 (D) pride.

practice test

21. "Legal procedure is a means, not an end. Its function is merely to accomplish the enforcement of legal rights. A litigant has no vested interest in the observance of the rules of procedure as such. All that he should be entitled to demand is that he be given an opportunity for a fair and impartial trial of his case. He should not be permitted to invoke the aid of technical rules merely to embarrass his adversary." According to this paragraph, it is most correct to state that

(A) observance of the rules of procedure guarantees a fair trial.
(B) embarrassment of an adversary through technical rules does not make for a fair trial.
(C) a litigant is not interested in the observance of rules of procedure.
(D) technical rules must not be used in a trial.

22. "One theory states that all criminal behavior is taught by a process of communication within small intimate groups. An individual engages in criminal behavior if the number of criminal patterns which he has acquired exceeds the number of noncriminal patterns." This statement indicates that criminal behavior is

(A) learned.
(B) instinctive.
(C) hereditary.
(D) reprehensible.

23. "The law enforcement staff of today requires training and mental qualities of a high order. The poorly or partially prepared staff member lowers the standard of work, retards his or her own earning power, and fails in a career meant to provide a livelihood and social improvement." According to this statement,

(A) an inefficient member of a law enforcement staff will still earn a good livelihood.
(B) law enforcement officers move in good social circles.
(C) many people fail in law enforcement careers.
(D) persons of training and ability are essential to a law enforcement staff.

24. "In this state, no crime can occur unless there is a written law forbidding the act or the omission in question, and even though an act may not be exactly in harmony with public policy, such act is not a crime unless it is expressly forbidden by legislative enactment." According to this statement,

(A) a crime is committed with reference to a particular law.
(B) acts not in harmony with public policy should be forbidden by law.
(C) noncriminal activity will promote public welfare.
(D) legislative enactments frequently forbid actions in harmony with public policy.

QUESTIONS 25–30 ARE BASED ON THE PHOTOGRAPH "CONTENTS OF A MALE SUSPECT'S POCKETS."

25. The suspect had a slip in his pocket showing an appointment at an outpatient clinic on

(A) February 9, 1988.
(B) September 2, 1988.
(C) February 19, 1988.
(D) September 12, 1988.

26. The transistor radio that was found on the suspect was made by
(A) RCA.
(B) GE.
(C) Sony.
(D) Zenith.

27. What was the total value of the coins found in the suspect's pockets?
(A) 56¢
(B) 77¢
(C) $1.05
(D) $1.26

28. All EXCEPT one of the following were found in the suspect's pockets. Which was NOT found?
(A) A ticket stub
(B) A comb
(C) A subway token
(D) A pen

29. Which statement about the contents of the suspect's pockets is correct?
(A) There are three dollar bills.
(B) There are two keys.
(C) The subway tokens have holes in their centers.
(D) There is an earpiece for listening to the radio.

30. The pockets of the suspect contained more of one kind of coin than of any other denomination. The most frequently occurring coin is a
(A) penny.
(B) nickel.
(C) dime.
(D) quarter.

31. "The unrestricted sale of firearms is one of the main causes of our shameful crime record." According to this statement, one of the causes of our crime record is the
(A) development of firepower.
(B) ease of securing weapons.
(C) increased skill in using guns.
(D) scientific perfection of firearms.

32. "Every person must be informed of the reason for his arrest unless he is arrested in the actual commission of a crime. Sufficient force to effect the arrest may be used, but the courts frown on brutal methods." According to this statement, a person does not have to be informed of the reason for his arrest if
(A) brutal force was not used in effecting it.
(B) the courts will later turn the defendant loose.
(C) the person arrested knows force will be used if necessary.
(D) the reason for it is clearly evident from the circumstances.

33. "An important duty of a court attendant is to keep order in the court." On the basis of this statement, it probably is true that
(A) it is more important for a court attendant to be strong than it is for him or her to be smart.
(B) people involved in court trials are noisy if not kept in check.
(C) not every duty of a court attendant is important.
(D) the maintenance of order is important for the proper conduct of court business.

34. "Ideally, a correctional system should include several types of institutions to provide different degrees of custody." On the basis of this statement, one could most reasonably say that
(A) as the number of institutions in a correctional system increases, the efficiency of the system increases.
(B) the difference in degree of custody for the inmate depends on the types of institutions in a correctional system.
(C) the greater the variety of institutions, the stricter the degree of custody that can be maintained.
(D) the same type of correctional institution is not desirable for the custody of all prisoners.

35. "The enforced idleness of a large percentage of adult men and women in our prisons is one of the direct causes of the tensions that burst forth in riot and disorder." On the basis of this statement, a good reason why inmates should perform daily work of some kind is that

  (A) better morale and discipline can bc maintained when inmates are kept busy.
  (B) daily work is an effective way of punishing inmates for the crimes they have committed.
  (C) law-abiding citizens must work; therefore, labor should also be required of inmates.
  (D) products of inmates' labor will in part pay the cost of their maintenance.

36. "With industry invading rural areas, the use of the automobile, and the speed of modern communications and transportation, the problems of neglect and delinquency are no longer peculiar to cities but are an established feature of everyday life." This statement implies most directly that

  (A) delinquents are moving from cities to rural areas.
  (B) delinquency and neglect are found in rural areas.
  (C) delinquency is not as much of a problem in rural areas as in cities.
  (D) rural areas now surpass cities in industry.

37. "Young men from minority groups, if unable to find employment, become discouraged and feel that life is hopeless because of their economic position and may finally resort to any means of supplying their wants." The most reasonable of the following conclusions that may be drawn from this statement only is that

  (A) discouragement sometimes leads to crime.
  (B) in general, young men from minority groups are criminals.
  (C) unemployment turns young men from crime.
  (D) young men from minority groups are seldom employed.

38. "To prevent crime, we must deal with the possible criminal long before he reaches the prison. Our aim should be not merely to reform the lawbreakers but to strike at the roots of crime: neglectful parents, bad companions, unsatisfactory homes, selfishness, disregard for the rights of others, and bad social conditions." This statement recommends

  (A) abolition of prisons.
  (B) better reformatories.
  (C) compulsory education.
  (D) general social reform.

39. "There is evidence that shows that comic books that glorify the criminal and criminal acts have a distinct influence in producing young criminals." According to this statement,

  (A) comic books affect the development of criminal careers.
  (B) comic books specialize in reporting criminal acts.
  (C) young criminals read comic books exclusively.
  (D) young criminals should not be permitted to read comic books.

40. Suppose a study shows that juvenile delinquents are equal in intelligence but three school grades behind juvenile nondelinquents. On the basis of this information only, it is most reasonable to say that
   (A) a delinquent usually progresses to the educational limit set by his or her intelligence.
   (B) educational achievement depends on intelligence only.
   (C) educational achievement is closely associated with delinquency.
   (D) lack of intelligence is closely associated with delinquency.

41. "There is no proof today that the experience of a prison sentence makes a better citizen of an adult. On the contrary, there seems to be some evidence that the experience is an unwholesome one that frequently confirms the criminality of the inmate." From this paragraph only, it may be best concluded that
   (A) prison sentences tend to punish rather than rehabilitate.
   (B) all criminals should be given prison sentences.
   (C) we should abandon our penal institutions.
   (D) penal institutions are effective in rehabilitating criminals.

42. "Many children who are exposed to contacts and experiences of a delinquent nature become educated and trained in crime in the course of participating in the daily life of the neighborhood." From this statement only, we may reasonably conclude that
   (A) delinquency passes from parent to child.
   (B) neighborhood influences are usually bad.
   (C) schools are training grounds for delinquents.
   (D) None of the above conclusions is reasonable.

43. "Old age insurance, for whose benefits city employees are now eligible, is one feature of the Social Security Act that is wholly administered by the federal government." On the basis of this statement only, it may reasonably be inferred that
   (A) all retired city employees are now drawing old age insurance.
   (B) all city employees favor becoming eligible for old age insurance.
   (C) the city has no part in administering Social Security old-age insurance.
   (D) only the federal government administers the Social Security Act.

44. "A peace officer's revolver is a defensive, and not offensive, weapon." On the basis of this statement only, a peace officer should best draw his or her revolver to
   (A) fire at an unarmed burglar.
   (B) force a suspect to confess.
   (C) frighten a juvenile delinquent.
   (D) protect his or her own life.

45. "First-aid by the Corrections Officer is sometimes defined as the bridge between the accident and the doctor. It is the immediate and temporary treatment given in cases of accident or sudden illness before professional medical service can be obtained." This statement means most nearly that the Corrections Officer administers first-aid
   (A) when proper medical attention is not immediately available.
   (B) to avoid accidents due to sudden illness.
   (C) by providing professional medical services.
   (D) to avoid the necessity for summoning a doctor.

YOU WILL BE GIVEN 10 MINUTES TO STUDY THE PICTURES THAT FOLLOW AND TO TRY TO REMEMBER AS MANY DETAILS AS YOU CAN. YOU MAY NOT TAKE ANY NOTES DURING THIS TIME. THEN ANSWER THE QUESTIONS THAT FOLLOW.

At the Bank

Meeting of the Board

practice test

Study Group

QUESTIONS 46–52 ARE BASED ON THE PICTURE "AT THE BANK."

46. The teller is
- **(A)** wearing a striped tie.
- **(B)** wearing glasses.
- **(C)** making change.
- **(D)** left-handed.

47. On the ledge in front of the teller is a(n)
- **(A)** calendar.
- **(B)** ashtray.
- **(C)** bank book.
- **(D)** pen holder.

48. The woman in the striped dress is
- **(A)** carrying a handbag.
- **(B)** wearing a pendant.
- **(C)** holding gloves.
- **(D)** third in line.

49. The man wearing a hat is also
- **(A)** handing money to the teller.
- **(B)** wearing a bow tie.
- **(C)** talking to another man in the line.
- **(D)** smoking a pipe.

50. All of the following statements about the picture are true EXCEPT:
- **(A)** There are three people in line.
- **(B)** The man with the hat is wearing glasses.
- **(C)** The last man in line has dark hair.
- **(D)** There is no money in view.

51. The time of day is
- **(A)** early morning.
- **(B)** lunchtime.
- **(C)** mid-afternoon.
- **(D)** late afternoon.

52. The teller's name is
- **(A)** R. Smith.
- **(B)** T. Jones.
- **(C)** T. Smith.
- **(D)** R. Jones.

QUESTIONS 53 AND 54 ARE BASED ON THE FOLLOWING PASSAGE.

There are at least two main difficulties in the field of criminology. The first difficulty is the conflict between the objectivity needed for science and the ideology of reformers. While social concern was the mainspring of criminology from its beginning, applied criminology, a relatively new branch of the field, tries to bring about changes in both the offender and society itself to deal with the problems of crime. The second difficulty involves the criminologist's own feelings in responses and patterns that must be subjected to objective analysis. No scientist in any field can afford to let his personal values or the moral code of the times affect his search for truth.

53. According to the passage, the aim of applied criminology is to
- **(A)** improve the attitudes of those dealing with the problems of crime.
- **(B)** develop better conditions throughout the penal system.
- **(C)** bring about changes in both the offender and society.
- **(D)** eliminate the conflict between reformist feeling and scientific objectivity.

54. It is indicated in the passage that one of the difficulties in the study of criminology is
- **(A)** the tendency of individual criminologists to allow their opinions on morality to influence their scientific judgment.
- **(B)** an inability on the part of the offender to change his views about society.
- **(C)** duplication of the services offered criminals by the criminologists.
- **(D)** conflict among penologists as to the allocation of funds available for prison reform.

QUESTIONS 55-57 ARE BASED ON THE FOLLOWING PASSAGE.

At the receiving institutions, newly committed inmates are confined to a separate wing or building for a definite period of time, usually one month. This quarantine period is partly to afford a convenient opportunity for case study without interrupting prison routine. It is during this period that the various examinations and interviews are carried on. The period also permits close observation, by picked officers, of personality traits and habits, relations to other inmates, and reaction to discipline. It prevents the social contamination that results from placing offenders by guesswork into situations where they may be injured or may cause injury to other inmates.

55. According to the passage, the quarantine period
- **(A)** begins after the medical examinations have been completed.
- **(B)** is used to study how the inmate behaves.
- **(C)** is used only if the disease is contagious.
- **(D)** is of different lengths for different inmates.

56. According to the passage, if there were no quarantine period, the study of the new inmate would probably
- **(A)** not be possible.
- **(B)** interfere with other prison operations.
- **(C)** not get the full cooperation of all concerned.
- **(D)** require extra help.

57. According to the passage, an undesirable result that is avoided by keeping new inmates in a separate wing or building is
- **(A)** the bad influence of other inmates.
- **(B)** poor discipline.
- **(C)** overcrowding in the institution.
- **(D)** the bad influence of unqualified officers.

QUESTIONS 58–63 ARE BASED ON THE PICTURE "MEETING OF THE BOARD."

58. How many of the men at the table have glasses?
- **(A)** 1
- **(B)** 2
- **(C)** 3
- **(D)** 4

59. How many of the men are wearing dark suits?
- **(A)** 1
- **(B)** 2
- **(C)** 3
- **(D)** 4

60. Which of the following items is NOT shown on the table?
- **(A)** A file box
- **(B)** A water pitcher
- **(C)** An ashtray
- **(D)** A glass of water

61. The man at the head of the table is
- **(A)** pointing to the map.
- **(B)** reading the papers in front of him.
- **(C)** looking at a man on his right.
- **(D)** looking at a man on his left.

62. All of the following statements are true EXCEPT:
- **(A)** There are seven men at the table.
- **(B)** The map is directly behind the man at the head of the table.
- **(C)** The man who is speaking has a glass of water in front of him.
- **(D)** One of the men is holding a pipe.

63. The man with the mustache is
- **(A)** holding a pencil.
- **(B)** wearing a striped tie.
- **(C)** bald.
- **(D)** wearing a dark suit.

QUESTIONS 64-66 ARE BASED ON THE FOLLOWING PASSAGE.

The final step in an accident investigation is the making out of the report. In the case of a traffic accident, the officer should go right from the scene to his office to write up his report. However, if a person was injured in the accident and taken to a hospital, the officer should visit him there before going to his office to prepare his report. This personal visit to the injured person does not mean that the officer must make a physical examination; but he should make an effort to obtain a statement from the injured person or persons. If this is not possible, information should be obtained from the attending physician as to the extent of the injury. In any event, without fail, the name of the physician should be secured and the report should state the name of the physician and the fact that he told the officer that, at a certain stated time on a certain stated date, the injuries were of such and such a nature. If the injured person dies before the officer arrives at the hospital, it may be necessary to take the responsible person into custody at once.

64. When a person has been injured in a traffic accident, the one of the following actions that it is necessary for the officer to take in connection with the accident report is to

(A) prepare the report immediately after the accident, and then go to the hospital to speak to the victim.

(B) do his utmost to verify the victim's story prior to preparing the report of the incident.

(C) be sure to include the victim's statement in the report in every case.

(D) try to get the victim's version of the accident prior to preparing the report.

65. When one of the persons injured in a motor vehicle accident dies, the above passage provides that the officer

(A) must immediately take the responsible person into custody, if the injured person is already dead when the officer appears at the scene of the accident.

(B) must either arrest the responsible person or get a statement from him, if the injured person dies after arrival at the hospital.

(C) may have to immediately arrest the responsible person, if the injured person dies in the hospital prior to the officer's arrival there.

(D) may refrain from arresting the responsible person, but only if the responsible person is also seriously injured.

66. When someone has been injured in a collision between two automobiles and is given medical treatment shortly thereafter by a physician, the one of the following actions that the officer must take with regard to the physician is to

(A) obtain his name and his diagnosis of the injuries, regardless of the place where treatment was given.

(B) obtain his approval of the portion of the report relating to the injured person and the treatment given him prior to and after his arrival at the hospital.

(C) obtain his name, his opinion of the extent of the person's injuries, and his signed statement of the treatment he gave the injured person.

(D) set a certain stated time on a certain stated date for interviewing him, unless he is an attending physician in a hospital.

QUESTIONS 67–69 ARE BASED ON THE FOLLOWING PASSAGE.

After examining a document and comparing the characters with specimens of other handwritings, the laboratory technician may conclude that a certain individual definitely did write the questioned document. This opinion could be based on a large number of similar, as well as a small number of dissimilar but explainable, characteristics. On the other hand, if the laboratory technician concludes that the person in question did not write the questioned document, such an opinion could be based on the large number of characteristics that are dissimilar, or even on a small number that are dissimilar provided that these are of overriding significance, and despite the presence of explainable similarities. The laboratory expert is not always able to give a positive opinion. He may state that a certain individual probably did or did not write the questioned document. Such an opinion is usually the result of insufficient material, either in the questioned document or in the specimens submitted for comparison. Finally, the expert may be unable to come to any conclusion at all because of insufficient material submitted for comparison or because of improper specimens.

67. When a handwriting expert compares the handwriting on two separate documents and decides that they were written by the same person, her conclusions are generally based on the fact that
    (A) a large number of characteristics in both documents are dissimilar, but the few similar characteristics are more important.
    (B) all the characteristics are alike in both documents.
    (C) similar characteristics need to be explained as to the cause for their similarity.
    (D) most of the characteristics in both documents are alike and their few differences are readily explainable.

68. If a laboratory technician carefully examines a handwritten threatening letter and compares it with specimens of handwriting made by a suspect, she would be most likely to decide that the suspect did not write the threatening letter when the handwriting specimens and the letter have
    (A) a small number of dissimilarities.
    (B) a small number of dissimilar but explainable characteristics.
    (C) important dissimilarities despite the fact that these may be few.
    (D) some similar characteristics that are easily imitated or disguised.

69. There are instances when even a trained handwriting expert cannot decide definitely whether or not a certain document and a set of handwriting specimens were written by the same person. This inability to make a positive decision generally arises in situations where
    (A) only one document of considerable length is available for comparison with a sufficient supply of handwriting specimens.
    (B) the limited nature of the handwriting specimens submitted restricts their comparability with the questioned document.
    (C) the dissimilarities are not explainable.
    (D) the document submitted for comparison does not include all the characteristics included in the handwriting specimens.

QUESTIONS 70–75 ARE BASED ON THE PICTURE "STUDY GROUP."

70. How many people are in this picture?
    (A) 5
    (B) 6
    (C) 7
    (D) 8

71. The person wearing boots
    (A) is lying down.
    (B) has blond hair.
    (C) has a mustache.
    (D) is smoking a cigarette.

72. The person wearing a print blouse
    (A) is commanding the attention of the rest of the group.
    (B) is also wearing a leather jacket.
    (C) wears glasses.
    (D) None of these.

73. The man who is wearing long sleeves
    (A) is raising one hand for attention.
    (B) is leaning on his right elbow.
    (C) is leaning on his left elbow.
    (D) is typing on a laptop computer.

74. The man with the ponytail
   (A) is looking at his watch.
   (B) is holding a folder.
   (C) is speaking.
   (D) Cannot tell from this picture.

75. The majority of people in this picture are seated on
   (A) a sofa.
   (B) folding chairs.
   (C) the bare floor.
   (D) thick carpeting.

QUESTIONS 76–79 ARE BASED ON THE FOLLOWING PASSAGE.

Crime and the Criminal

Criminology is more than the study of one type of prohibited behavior called crime; it is also the study of the individual who engages in this behavior—the criminal. This criminal must, in a court of law, be proved guilty of the offense with which he is charged and then convicted. As for the subject of crime, since the police are the first to learn of the commission of a crime, they are the source of the best, if still imperfect, data on crime. After the crime becomes known to the police, the next stage consists of the detection and apprehension of the suspected criminal through informers, fingerprints, modus operandi files, or the use of devices like the polygraph (lie detector). The appearance of the accused before the magistrate and the matter of bail come next. Surprisingly, many people think that bail payment is required as proof of a person's honesty, or as a test of a person's interest in his case. The sole function of bail, however, is to guarantee the appearance of the defendant at the time of his trial.

Not all individuals who engage in criminal actions are considered by the law to be criminals. For example, some of these individuals are adjudged insane. Unfortunately, insanity is not the same as psychosis: the latter is a medical concept, while the former is a legal term. The famous Durham Rule, now the law for federal jurisdictions, holds that if the crime is the product of a mental disease, the individual is insane.

76. Which of the following is closest in meaning to the definition of criminology given in the passage? Criminology is the study of
   (A) the behavior known as crime.
   (B) the criminals who commit crimes.
   (C) courts of law.
   (D) crime and criminals.

77. According to this passage, the only purpose of bail is to
   (A) serve as evidence of a person's financial reliability.
   (B) test a person's honesty.
   (C) make sure that the arrested person will show up for his or her trial.
   (D) find out if a person thinks his or her case is serious.

78. According to the passage, "psychosis" is
   (A) a medical concept.
   (B) a legal term.
   (C) a diagnostic term.
   (D) the same as insanity.

79. The "Durham Rule" referred to in the passage states that
   (A) insane individuals will commit more crimes than will sane people.
   (B) certain crimes are so strange that they must have been committed by someone insane.
   (C) if an insane person commits a crime, he or she will be freed under the law.
   (D) a person committing a crime as a result of a mental illness is insane.

QUESTIONS 80-82 ARE BASED ON THE FOLLOWING PASSAGE.

Group counseling may contain potentialities of an extraordinary character for the philosophy and especially the management and operation of the adult correctional institution. Primarily the change may be based upon the valued and respected participation of the rank-and-file of employees in the treatment program. Group counseling provides new treatment functions for correctional workers. The older, more conventional duties and activities of correctional officers, teachers, maintenance foremen and other employees, which they currently perform, may be fortified and improved by their participation in group counseling. Psychologists, psychiatrists, and classification officers may also need to revise their attitudes toward others on the staff and toward their own procedures in treating inmates to accord with the new type of treatment program that may evolve if group counseling were to become accepted practice in the prison. The primary locale of the psychological treatment program may move from the clinical center to all places in the institution where inmates are in contact with employees. The thoughtful guidance and steering of the program, figuratively its pilot-house, may still be the clinical center. The actual points of contact of the treatment program will, however, be wherever inmates are in personal relationship, no matter how superficial, with employees of the prison.

80. According to the passage, a basic change that may be brought about by the introduction of a group counseling program into an adult correctional institution would be that the
(A) educational standards for correctional employees would be raised.
(B) management of the institution would have to be selected primarily on the basis of ability to understand and apply the counseling program.
(C) conventional duties of correctional employees would assume less importance.
(D) rank-and-file employees would play an important part in the treatment program for inmates.

81. According to the passage, the one of the following that is NOT mentioned specifically as a change that may be required by or result from the introduction of group counseling in an adult correctional institution is a change in the
(A) attitude of the institution's classification officers toward their own procedures in treating inmates.
(B) attitude of the institution's psychologist toward Corrections Officers.
(C) place where the treatment program is planned and from which it is directed.
(D) principal place where the psychological treatment program makes actual contact with the inmates.

82. According to the passage, under a program of counseling in an adult correctional institution, treatment of inmates takes place
(A) as soon as they are admitted to the prison.
(B) chiefly in the clinical center.
(C) mainly where inmates are in continuing close and personal relationships with the technical staff.
(D) wherever inmates come in contact with prison employees.

QUESTIONS 83–85 ARE BASED ON THE FOLLOWING PASSAGE.

As a secondary aspect of this revolutionary change in outlook resulting from the introduction of group counseling into the adult correctional institution, there must evolve a new type of prison employee, the true correctional or treatment worker. The top management will have to reorient their attitudes toward subordinate employees, respecting and accepting them as equal participants in the work of the institution. Rank may no longer be the measure of value in the inmate treatment program. Instead, the employee will be valuable whatever his location in the prison hierarchy or administrative plan in terms of his capacity to relate himself constructively to inmates as one human being to another. In group counseling, all employees must consider it their primary task to provide a wholesome environment for personality growth for inmates in work crews, cell blocks, clerical pools, or classrooms. The above does not mean that custodial care and precautions regarding the prevention of disorders or escapes are cast aside or discarded by prison workers. On the contrary, the staff will be more acutely aware of the cost to the inmates of such infractions of institutional rules. Gradually, it is hoped, these instances of uncontrolled responses to overpowering feelings by inmates will become much less frequent in the treatment institution. In general, men in group counseling provide considerably fewer disciplinary infractions when compared with a control group of those still on a waiting list to enter group counseling, and especially fewer than those who do not choose to participate. It is optimistically anticipated that some day people in prison may have the same attitudes toward the staff, the same security in expecting treatment as do patients in a good general hospital.

83. According to the passage, under a program of group counseling in an adult correctional institution, that employee will be most valuable in the inmate treatment program who

(A) can establish a constructive relationship of one human being to another between himself and the inmate.

(B) gets management to accept him as an equal participant in the work of the institution.

(C) is in contact with the inmate on work crews, cell blocks, clerical pools, or classrooms.

(D) provides the inmate with a proper home environment for wholesome personality growth.

84. According to the passage, the group counseling method of inmate treatment in an adult correctional institution should cause prison employees to

(A) be more acutely aware of the cost of maintaining strict prison discipline.

(B) discard old and outmoded notions of custodial care and the prevention of disorders and escapes.

(C) neglect this aspect of prison work unless proper safeguards are established.

(D) realize more deeply the harmful effect on the inmate of breaches of discipline.

85. According to the passage, a result that is expected from the group counseling method of inmate treatment in an adult correctional institution is

(A) a greater desire on the part of potential delinquents to enter the correctional institution for the purpose of securing treatment.

(B) a large reduction in the number of infractions of institutional rules by inmates.

(C) a steady decrease in the crime rate.

(D) the introduction of hospital methods of organization and operation into the correctional institution.

ANSWER KEY AND EXPLANATIONS

1. C	18. A	35. A	52. D	69. B
2. C	19. C	36. B	53. C	70. A
3. B	20. A	37. A	54. A	71. B
4. D	21. B	38. D	55. B	72. A
5. A	22. A	39. A	56. B	73. D
6. B	23. D	40. C	57. A	74. B
7. A	24. A	41. A	58. C	75. A
8. B	25. A	42. D	59. D	76. D
9. A	26. C	43. C	60. B	77. C
10. D	27. D	44. D	61. D	78. A
11. B	28. D	45. A	62. D	79. D
12. B	29. B	46. B	63. A	80. D
13. D	30. C	47. D	64. D	81. C
14. C	31. B	48. B	65. C	82. D
15. B	32. D	49. D	66. A	83. A
16. D	33. D	50. B	67. D	84. D
17. B	34. D	51. B	68. C	85. B

1-6. **If you missed any of these questions, look back at the pictures and observe more closely.**

7. The correct answer is (A). When the sentence has been completed, the offender is no longer under the authority of the state *for that particular offense* and is not subject to any further restraint or punishment in connection with that offense.

8. The correct answer is (B). If the use or sale of prison-made items is limited to the institution where manufactured or to other state institutions and agencies, these items cannot be sold on the open market.

9. The correct answer is (A). The statement makes it clear that the classification of crimes is based upon the length of sentence and that there is no overlap. Obviously, the more serious crime draws the longer sentence. Choice (B) introduces a subject not covered in the statement. If you chose choice (C), reread the quotation more carefully.

10. The correct answer is (D). Prisoners must have benefited from their treatment and training; in other words, they must be deemed "rehabilitated" before being considered for parole. This is the only condition mentioned in the statement. Serving a minimum part of the sentence and good behavior are important factors in the granting of parole, but questions must be answered on the basis of the statement alone.

11. The correct answer is (B). No other aspect of prison life has interested the public as much as punishment, but the public is interested in other aspects.

12. The correct answer is (B). The word "changed" in the quotation is the key to the answer.

13-18. **If you missed any of these questions, look back at the pictures and observe more closely.**

19. The correct answer is (C). Physical and mental health refers to body and mind.

20. The correct answer is (A). Teamwork is cooperation.

21. The correct answer is (B). The last sentence makes this statement.

22. The correct answer is (A). The statement is telling us that criminal behavior is learned from one's friends.

23. The correct answer is (D). The first sentence makes this point. The remainder of the passage amplifies the statement.

24. **The correct answer is (A).** The definition of a crime is that it is an act or an omission that is forbidden by law.

25-30. **If you missed any of these questions, look back at the pictures and observe more closely.**

31. **The correct answer is (B).** An unrestricted sale of firearms leads to the ease of securing weapons.

32. **The correct answer is (D).** If a person is arrested during the commission of a crime, the reason for his or her arrest is so obvious that the person need not be told why he or she is being arrested.

33. **The correct answer is (D).** If a duty of the court officer is to keep order in the court, then maintenance of order is important for conduct of court business.

34. **The correct answer is (D).** All prisoners do not need the same type of custody, so a correctional system should provide several different types of institutions to serve the variety of needs.

35. **The correct answer is (A).** Busy inmates are less likely to be bored and will have less time to cause trouble. The other choices may or may not be true, but they have absolutely nothing to do with the statement.

36. **The correct answer is (B).** All the statement says is that delinquency and neglect are found everywhere, in rural areas as well as in the city. Transportation, communication, and industry are the means by which delinquency is transmitted, not the delinquents themselves.

37. **The correct answer is (A).** Unemployment leads to hopelessness and discouragement, leading in turn to crime to satisfy needs.

38. **The correct answer is (D).** The list of roots of crime constitutes areas in which social reform is needed.

39. **The correct answer is (A).** Comic books that glamorize crime can influence young people towards a life of crime.

40. **The correct answer is (C).** The statement correlates poor academic achievement with delinquency, specifically stating that delinquents, despite their equal intelligence with nondelinquents, are behind in school.

41. **The correct answer is (A).** If a person comes out of prison no better a citizen than when he or she entered, the prison has not rehabilitated, but it most certainly has still punished that person. The statement refers only to adults, so the conclusion of choice (C) is unwarranted.

42. **The correct answer is (D).** Every child is exposed to many influences, so choice (A) is incorrect. Schools and neighborhoods are the training grounds and daily experiences of children, but most children do not become delinquents, so most of these influences are not bad.

43. **The correct answer is (C).** If old age insurance is wholly administered by the federal government, the city has no part in its administration. Choice (D) is incorrect because old age insurance is only one feature of the Social Security Act administered by the federal government; other features of the act may well be administered by other authorities.

44. **The correct answer is (D).** A defensive weapon is used for self-protection.

45. **The correct answer is (A).** First-aid is emergency, temporary treatment until the doctor arrives.

46-52. **If you missed any of these questions, look back at the pictures and observe more closely.**

53. **The correct answer is (C).** See the third sentence.

54. **The correct answer is (A).** Scientific objectivity requires that personal values and judgments not enter into observation and analysis.

55. **The correct answer is (B).** Observation of personality traits and habits, of relations to other inmates, and of reaction to discipline is study of behavior.

56. **The correct answer is (B).** The quarantine allows for this observation to occur outside of prison routine so as not to interfere with other prison operations.

57. **The correct answer is (A).** Keeping new inmates separate and out of situations in which they may be injured implies that other inmates might injure them, either physically or by influencing them to behave in ways that would immediately create a bad prison record.

58-63. **If you missed any of these questions, look back at the pictures and observe more closely.**

64. **The correct answer is (D).** Prior to writing the report, the officer should try to obtain a statement from the injured person or persons; that is, the officer should try to get the victim's version of the accident.

65. **The correct answer is (C).** See the last sentence.

66. **The correct answer is (A).** This answer is made very clear in the next-to-last sentence.

67. **The correct answer is (D).** See the second sentence.

68. **The correct answer is (C).** The third sentence explains the significance of dissimilarities.

69. **The correct answer is (B).** Any one of the answers might be correct, but the answer based on the passage is found in the last sentence.

70-75. **If you missed any of these questions, look back at the picture and observe more closely.**

76. **The correct answer is (D).** The definition is given in the first sentence of the paragraph.

77. **The correct answer is (C).** The answer is in the last sentence of the first paragraph.

78. **The correct answer is (A).** *Psychosis* is a medical concept; *insanity* is a legal term.

79. **The correct answer is (D).** See the last sentence of the second paragraph.

80. **The correct answer is (D).** The whole point of the group counseling program is that all employees of the prison will be involved in the treatment and rehabilitation of inmates.

81. **The correct answer is (C).** The passage specifically states that the "pilot-house," the place in which the program is planned and from which it is directed, would not be changed.

82. **The correct answer is (D).** Since everyone working in the institution is involved in the counseling program, treatment takes place wherever there is contact between inmates and prison employees.

83. **The correct answer is (A).** The employee most valuable to the treatment process is the employee who is most able to develop human, one-to-one relationships with inmates, regardless of the employee's position in the institution.

84. **The correct answer is (D).** Because of their personal interest in inmates as human beings, the staff will be concerned with setbacks to growth and eventual freedom created by discipline infractions.

85. **The correct answer is (B).** A result, shown by some studies, is that inmates in the group counseling program will not create as many disciplinary breaches as those not in such a program.

ANSWER SHEET PRACTICE TEST 6: PROMOTION EXAM

1. Ⓐ Ⓑ Ⓒ Ⓓ	21. Ⓐ Ⓑ Ⓒ Ⓓ	41. Ⓐ Ⓑ Ⓒ Ⓓ	61. Ⓐ Ⓑ Ⓒ Ⓓ	81. Ⓐ Ⓑ Ⓒ Ⓓ
2. Ⓐ Ⓑ Ⓒ Ⓓ	22. Ⓐ Ⓑ Ⓒ Ⓓ	42. Ⓐ Ⓑ Ⓒ Ⓓ	62. Ⓐ Ⓑ Ⓒ Ⓓ	82. Ⓐ Ⓑ Ⓒ Ⓓ
3. Ⓐ Ⓑ Ⓒ Ⓓ	23. Ⓐ Ⓑ Ⓒ Ⓓ	43. Ⓐ Ⓑ Ⓒ Ⓓ	63. Ⓐ Ⓑ Ⓒ Ⓓ	83. Ⓐ Ⓑ Ⓒ Ⓓ
4. Ⓐ Ⓑ Ⓒ Ⓓ	24. Ⓐ Ⓑ Ⓒ Ⓓ	44. Ⓐ Ⓑ Ⓒ Ⓓ	64. Ⓐ Ⓑ Ⓒ Ⓓ	84. Ⓐ Ⓑ Ⓒ Ⓓ
5. Ⓐ Ⓑ Ⓒ Ⓓ	25. Ⓐ Ⓑ Ⓒ Ⓓ	45. Ⓐ Ⓑ Ⓒ Ⓓ	65. Ⓐ Ⓑ Ⓒ Ⓓ	85. Ⓐ Ⓑ Ⓒ Ⓓ
6. Ⓐ Ⓑ Ⓒ Ⓓ	26. Ⓐ Ⓑ Ⓒ Ⓓ	46. Ⓐ Ⓑ Ⓒ Ⓓ	66. Ⓐ Ⓑ Ⓒ Ⓓ	86. Ⓐ Ⓑ Ⓒ Ⓓ
7. Ⓐ Ⓑ Ⓒ Ⓓ	27. Ⓐ Ⓑ Ⓒ Ⓓ	47. Ⓐ Ⓑ Ⓒ Ⓓ	67. Ⓐ Ⓑ Ⓒ Ⓓ	87. Ⓐ Ⓑ Ⓒ Ⓓ
8. Ⓐ Ⓑ Ⓒ Ⓓ	28. Ⓐ Ⓑ Ⓒ Ⓓ	48. Ⓐ Ⓑ Ⓒ Ⓓ	68. Ⓐ Ⓑ Ⓒ Ⓓ	88. Ⓐ Ⓑ Ⓒ Ⓓ
9. Ⓐ Ⓑ Ⓒ Ⓓ	29. Ⓐ Ⓑ Ⓒ Ⓓ	49. Ⓐ Ⓑ Ⓒ Ⓓ	69. Ⓐ Ⓑ Ⓒ Ⓓ	89. Ⓐ Ⓑ Ⓒ Ⓓ
10. Ⓐ Ⓑ Ⓒ Ⓓ	30. Ⓐ Ⓑ Ⓒ Ⓓ	50. Ⓐ Ⓑ Ⓒ Ⓓ	70. Ⓐ Ⓑ Ⓒ Ⓓ	90. Ⓐ Ⓑ Ⓒ Ⓓ
11. Ⓐ Ⓑ Ⓒ Ⓓ	31. Ⓐ Ⓑ Ⓒ Ⓓ	51. Ⓐ Ⓑ Ⓒ Ⓓ	71. Ⓐ Ⓑ Ⓒ Ⓓ	91. Ⓐ Ⓑ Ⓒ Ⓓ
12. Ⓐ Ⓑ Ⓒ Ⓓ	32. Ⓐ Ⓑ Ⓒ Ⓓ	52. Ⓐ Ⓑ Ⓒ Ⓓ	72. Ⓐ Ⓑ Ⓒ Ⓓ	92. Ⓐ Ⓑ Ⓒ Ⓓ
13. Ⓐ Ⓑ Ⓒ Ⓓ	33. Ⓐ Ⓑ Ⓒ Ⓓ	53. Ⓐ Ⓑ Ⓒ Ⓓ	73. Ⓐ Ⓑ Ⓒ Ⓓ	93. Ⓐ Ⓑ Ⓒ Ⓓ
14. Ⓐ Ⓑ Ⓒ Ⓓ	34. Ⓐ Ⓑ Ⓒ Ⓓ	54. Ⓐ Ⓑ Ⓒ Ⓓ	74. Ⓐ Ⓑ Ⓒ Ⓓ	94. Ⓐ Ⓑ Ⓒ Ⓓ
15. Ⓐ Ⓑ Ⓒ Ⓓ	35. Ⓐ Ⓑ Ⓒ Ⓓ	55. Ⓐ Ⓑ Ⓒ Ⓓ	75. Ⓐ Ⓑ Ⓒ Ⓓ	95. Ⓐ Ⓑ Ⓒ Ⓓ
16. Ⓐ Ⓑ Ⓒ Ⓓ	36. Ⓐ Ⓑ Ⓒ Ⓓ	56. Ⓐ Ⓑ Ⓒ Ⓓ	76. Ⓐ Ⓑ Ⓒ Ⓓ	96. Ⓐ Ⓑ Ⓒ Ⓓ
17. Ⓐ Ⓑ Ⓒ Ⓓ	37. Ⓐ Ⓑ Ⓒ Ⓓ	57. Ⓐ Ⓑ Ⓒ Ⓓ	77. Ⓐ Ⓑ Ⓒ Ⓓ	97. Ⓐ Ⓑ Ⓒ Ⓓ
18. Ⓐ Ⓑ Ⓒ Ⓓ	38. Ⓐ Ⓑ Ⓒ Ⓓ	58. Ⓐ Ⓑ Ⓒ Ⓓ	78. Ⓐ Ⓑ Ⓒ Ⓓ	98. Ⓐ Ⓑ Ⓒ Ⓓ
19. Ⓐ Ⓑ Ⓒ Ⓓ	39. Ⓐ Ⓑ Ⓒ Ⓓ	59. Ⓐ Ⓑ Ⓒ Ⓓ	79. Ⓐ Ⓑ Ⓒ Ⓓ	99. Ⓐ Ⓑ Ⓒ Ⓓ
20. Ⓐ Ⓑ Ⓒ Ⓓ	40. Ⓐ Ⓑ Ⓒ Ⓓ	60. Ⓐ Ⓑ Ⓒ Ⓓ	80. Ⓐ Ⓑ Ⓒ Ⓓ	100. Ⓐ Ⓑ Ⓒ Ⓓ

answer sheet

Practice Test 6: Promotion Exam

100 QUESTIONS • 3 HOURS 30 MINUTES

Directions: Each question has four suggested answers. Decide which one is the best answer.

1. The fundamental responsibility of prison management is the
   (A) secure custody and control of prisoners.
   (B) development of work programs for prisoners.
   (C) training of prisoners.
   (D) classification of prisoners.

2. The basic function of a correctional institution is
   (A) to operate at maximum efficiency.
   (B) to make certain every department understands that teamwork is vital and that all departments are important.
   (C) the protection of society and the rehabilitation of inmates.
   (D) the recognition that correctional institutions face more difficult problems than at any other time in our history.

3. Strict limitation and control of telephone calls made by inmates of a correctional institution is
   (A) desirable; it is a necessary security precaution.
   (B) undesirable; it causes a loss of incentive for good behavior.
   (C) desirable; the number of available telephones is limited.
   (D) undesirable; it destroys morale.

4. Of the following, the main purpose of the tool shadow board is to
   (A) enable employees to locate needed tools quickly.
   (B) indicate when a tool is missing.
   (C) provide a central place for storage of tools.
   (D) reduce accidents by storing tools in a safe place.

5. A Corrections Officer in a court pen searches police cases delivered there for temporary detention before he or she assumes custody of these prisoners. The prisoners are later taken before a judge. For the Corrections Officer to search the prisoners again when they are returned to the pen is

   (A) foolish, because the prisoners have not been out of the building and have been under surveillance at all times.
   (B) sensible, because the prisoners may have acquired contraband when they were out of the pen.
   (C) foolish, because the prisoners were thoroughly searched the first time.
   (D) sensible, because prisoners in court pens should be searched regularly several times each day.

6. A Corrections Officer patrolling a cell block at night sees an inmate writhing on the floor in apparent pain. In this situation, the Corrections Officer should

   (A) bear in mind that the inmate may be feigning and take necessary precautions.
   (B) enter the cell immediately to get the inmate back on the bed and give first-aid.
   (C) notify the officer in command of the tour right away.
   (D) summon a doctor immediately and wait for him or her to arrive.

7. Correctional institutions where there is good morale generally have fewer escapes and escape attempts than those where morale is poor. Morale can be controlled by the manner in which the institution is administered. Of the following, the most important element in the control of morale is

   (A) elimination of mail censorship.
   (B) improvements in prison sanitation.
   (C) liberal visiting provisions with emphasis on open visits.
   (D) well-trained and capable prison personnel.

8. Decision making can be defined as the

   (A) delegation of authority and responsibility to persons capable of performing their assigned duties with moderate or little supervision.
   (B) imposition of a supervisor's decision upon a work group.
   (C) technique of selecting the course of action with the most desired consequences and the least undesired or unexpected consequences.
   (D) process principally concerned with improvement of procedures.

9. "The form that a riot takes determines what measure will be used to suppress it. New forms of rebellion will require good judgment and great restraint by staff since a standard revolutionary technique is to provoke authorities into overreacting." Of the statements below, the one that follows best from this passage is that

(A) most riot situations can be readily controlled when personnel are adequately trained.

(B) a large percentage of offenders ordinarily take part in serious riots and therefore immediate suppression is sometimes difficult.

(C) control must be regained very quickly in situations where power has already been assumed by inmates.

(D) it is wise to make an estimate of the situation during riots before determining a course of action.

10. If one of the Corrections Officers you supervise does an exceptionally fine piece of work, it is usually best to

(A) say nothing to him lest he become conceited.

(B) tell him that none of his coworkers could have done as well.

(C) explain how the work could have been even better so that he will not become complacent.

(D) praise him for the work he has done so that he knows his efforts are appreciated.

11. Of the following, the most serious problem facing a captain when supervising new Corrections Officers is that, for the most part, these officers

(A) are afraid to face up to the responsibilities of their position.

(B) are overconfident and have a "know-it-all" attitude.

(C) have accepted this employment only as a stopgap until they find other work.

(D) have had no extensive formal training in this field of work.

12. It has been suggested that the in-service training of employees in the correctional field should continue from the time they start until the time they leave the department. Of the following, the chief justification for such a continuous program of in-service training is that

(A) a person's capacity for learning increases with age.

(B) because of a natural tendency to forget what one has learned and not put into practice, training must be repeated at regular intervals.

(C) employees are usually capable of further development on the job during the entire period of their employment.

(D) for learning to be effective, successive stages in the learning process must be correlated and coordinated.

13. When explaining to a subordinate the importance of the tier officer's initial contact with a new admission, the captain should stress most the
    (A) constructive influence this initial contact can have on the inmate's future adjustment to confinement.
    (B) desirability of getting the inmate to talk freely and without interruption.
    (C) harmful effect on the inmate's morale of a business-like approach to conducting this initial interview.
    (D) value of this initial interview to impress the inmate with the fact that violations of the rules will not be tolerated.

14. When explaining to a Corrections Officer why an unvaried routine in the conduct of tier post inspections is not desirable, a captain should stress most the fact that
    (A) a method of work that may be entirely acceptable in one situation generally proves to be unacceptable when transferred without modification to another.
    (B) inmates seeking to violate the institution's rules study the officer's habits so that they can time their activities to forestall detection.
    (C) it is important to have a clear understanding of the purposes of tier post inspection in order to be able to carry it out efficiently and intelligently.
    (D) the discovery of contraband is not the sole purpose of a tier post inspection.

15. A captain instructed subordinates that at all times the tier officer going off duty was to notify the on-coming officer of any inmate who should be particularly watched. The captain's instructions were
    (A) good, because the on-coming officer will not be surprised if a particular inmate behaves strangely.
    (B) poor, because alertness and initiative on the part of the on-coming officer may be reduced.
    (C) good, because the on-coming officer will benefit from the experiences and observations of the off-going officer.
    (D) poor, because all inmates should be given careful custody and close supervision.

16. "A cautious and observant officer seldom becomes involved in litigation initiated by an inmate who is injured during confinement on a tier." This statement is most probably based on the principle that such an officer will
    (A) avoid and prevent situations that might cause injury to an inmate.
    (B) avoid any and all disputes with inmates.
    (C) be able to persuade the inmate that litigation is not justified.
    (D) make sure that any injury to an inmate is the result of the inmate's own negligence.

17. A captain is summoned by a Corrections Officer to the cell of a newly committed inmate who has been taken suddenly ill. After observing the inmate, the captain thinks that the inmate's condition is due to nervous excitement resulting from commitment to the institution. The captain should

    (A) speak quietly to the inmate until a normal condition is restored.
    (B) give the inmate a mild sedative.
    (C) make the inmate comfortable and instruct the officer to keep a close watch.
    (D) secure medical assistance for the inmate.

18. "From the standpoint of custody, the first concern of the Corrections Officer in the court pen should be to lock the inmate in the pen as soon as possible." Of the following, the chief justification for this statement is the fact that the officer

    (A) can more easily take an accurate count of inmates confined in the pen.
    (B) may be the only obstacle between the inmate and escape.
    (C) can then give undivided attention to other important duties.
    (D) does not know how soon the inmate will have to be produced in court again.

19. When a Corrections Officer asks a certain captain's advice about handling specific work problems, the captain occasionally responds by first asking the Corrections Officer what he or she thinks should be done. This practice by the captain is generally

    (A) bad, since subordinates may be discouraged from asking questions in the future.
    (B) good, since it motivates subordinates to think about possible solutions.
    (C) bad, since Corrections Officers will question the motives of the captain.
    (D) good, since poorly thought-out action can lead to undesirable results.

20. Of the following, the best technique for a captain to use in training Corrections Officers is to

    (A) encourage them to ask questions at all times.
    (B) change their assignments frequently.
    (C) teach them how to analyze important facts in order to make their own decisions.
    (D) teach them how to evaluate inmate morale.

21. Captain A, just before instructing a Corrections Officer how to correctly search a cell for contraband, explained to the officer why it was important to follow the correct procedure. The captain's action was

    (A) good; a procedure is less likely to be forgotten if its purpose is understood.
    (B) poor; since the importance of searching for contraband is obvious, the explanation is a waste of time.
    (C) good; repetition is an effective aid in learning an operation.
    (D) poor; such an explanation distracts the Corrections Officer from the main points in the instruction.

22. If a Corrections Officer wants to talk to the captain about a personal problem, the captain should
    (A) be willing to discuss the matter with the officer.
    (B) refer the officer to the assistant deputy in order to keep the captain-Corrections Officer relationship impersonal.
    (C) tell the officer to discuss the matter with another Corrections Officer with whom he or she is friendly.
    (D) tell the officer that personal problems should not be discussed on the job.

23. Assume you are a corrections captain. Another captain has been newly assigned to your institution. For you to tell this new captain the strengths and weaknesses of some of the Corrections Officers he or she will supervise is
    (A) bad; bias will be introduced unknowingly into the work situation.
    (B) good; the new captain will be able to make various assignments of officers more intelligently.
    (C) bad; it will delay the new captain's adjustment to new responsibilities.
    (D) good; the abilities of a Corrections Officer change from day to day due to various factors.

24. The term "malingerer" is most correctly applied to an inmate who
    (A) bears an officer a grudge for a long time.
    (B) is a habitual liar.
    (C) pretends to be ill in order to avoid working.
    (D) takes a long time to recover from an illness.

25. "The person who makes an ideal inmate in the penitentiary frequently does not make an ideal parolee when released." Of the following, the best justification for this statement is that
    (A) adjustment to prison life is, in many respects, more complex than adjustment to civilian life.
    (B) high moral standards tend to remain well established once they have been developed.
    (C) prison-wise inmates are often on their best behavior while they remain in prison.
    (D) prison constitutes an acid test, and no person is ordinarily paroled unless he or she passes this test.

26. A representative group of young criminals in a certain state were found to be normal in intelligence, but 86% had been held back one to six grades in school. Of the following, the best inference from these data is that
    (A) lack of intelligence is closely associated with delinquency.
    (B) criminals should be removed from the school system as soon as possible.
    (C) educational maladjustments are closely associated with delinquency.
    (D) the usual rate at which criminals progress educationally represents the limit of their learning powers.

27. "One can only see what one observes, and one observes only things that are already in the mind." Of the following, the chief implication of this statement for the corrections captain is that
    (A) observation, to be effective, should be directed and conscious.
    (B) all aspects of a situation, unless the corrections captain exercises caution, are likely to strike him or her with equal forcefulness.
    (C) memory is essentially perception one step removed from observation.
    (D) observation should be essentially indirect if it is to be accurate.

28. "A promise to a subordinate is more important in a system of discipline than a promise to a superior." Of the following, the best justification for this statement is that
    (A) subordinates are generally in no position to make promises to superiors.
    (B) there is no obligation to make promises to subordinates.
    (C) discipline cannot be maintained if promises are broken.
    (D) discipline rests essentially on the respect of subordinates for their superior.

29. Suppose you are a captain. A Corrections Officer under your supervision submits a written recommendation concerning administrative procedure. You believe that the objective is worthwhile but that certain precautions are necessary. Of the following, the best action for you to take is to
    (A) submit the Corrections Officer's memorandum to the warden along with a statement of your own opinion.
    (B) submit the Corrections Officer's memorandum to the warden without additional comment.
    (C) advise the Corrections Officer to submit the memorandum to the warden directly.
    (D) advise the Corrections Officer to withdraw the memorandum.

30. "When assigned to duty in a large mess hall during inmate mess, it is important for officers to station themselves in such a way that they can see and be seen by their superior at all times." This statement is justified mainly because the
    (A) inmates will not attempt to create any disturbance when they see that the officers and their superior are in ready communication with each other.
    (B) officers will be able to show their superior that they are performing their jobs properly.
    (C) officers will be able to tell if the superior has left the mess hall.
    (D) superior might suddenly need to transmit an order to them quickly by means of a signal.

31. It has been recommended that the workweek of inmates employed in a program of prison industries be the same as the workweek for similar employment in private industry. From the standpoint of the major objectives of a prison industries program, the adoption of this recommendation is desirable mainly because
    (A) it will make possible the inclusion of a wider variety of employment in the prison industries program.
    (B) it will tend to make the deterrent objective of imprisonment more effective.
    (C) the rehabilitative process will be aided if conditions of work approach those in real life.
    (D) the prison industries will then be more profitable to operate since production will be greater.

32. Which one of the following is an important rule in carrying out an institutional program of inmate activities and privileges?
    (A) Do not curtail or revoke any inmate activity or privilege after it has been instituted.
    (B) Do not give privileges to one inmate that cannot be earned in the proper way by any other inmate.
    (C) Do not make any activity or privilege too pleasurable for the inmate.
    (D) Do not use the program to help maintain discipline.

33. Of the following, the most important reason why psychiatric social workers have difficulty achieving success in prisons is that
    (A) psychiatry and social work are not exact sciences.
    (B) neither inmates nor correctional officials are in sympathy with their work.
    (C) no precise goals have been established to guide them in their work.
    (D) they must tackle cases with which other treatment services have previously failed.

34. "Contraband" in a correctional institution is best defined as any article
    (A) that has been smuggled into the prison by an inmate.
    (B) that may be classified as a drug or alcoholic beverage.
    (C) the presence of which within the prison may jeopardize its safety and good order.
    (D) that may be sold or exchanged by an inmate for personal favors from the uniformed staff or other inmates.

35. A Corrections Officer under your supervision regularly submits considerably more infraction reports against inmates than other officers with similar posts. Of the following, the most desirable action for you to take is to
    (A) direct this officer to be fairer toward the inmates.
    (B) give this officer additional training in order to strengthen his or her disciplinary control over the inmates.
    (C) reprimand this officer for his or her poor control over the inmates.
    (D) take no special action, since in any such ranking there must always be one officer at the top and one at the bottom.

36. An officer under your supervision reports that he suspects a certain inmate of suicidal tendencies. Of the following, the best action for you to take first is to
    (A) have the officer prepare a report to forward to your superior.
    (B) rearrange the inmate's program so that he is always in the company of another inmate.
    (C) talk to the inmate and keep him under observation for a while in order to verify the accuracy of the officer's suspicions.
    (D) transfer the inmate to another cell where he may be kept under constant observation.

37. A captain sees a Corrections Officer deny an inmate's request to go to the medical clinic. This inmate has made similar requests in the past without cause and appears to have nothing the matter with her now. The captain should evaluate the officer's action as

(A) unsound, because if the inmate is really sick, the denial of the request may have serious consequences.

(B) unsound, because an officer should never be influenced by an inmate's previous record.

(C) sound, because if the inmate is really sick she will let the officer know it soon enough.

(D) sound, because it takes into account the inmate's previous record.

38. On a tour of the posts, you observe that in a cell block supervised by a new officer, the lineup of inmates is proceeding in a slow and disorderly manner. In this situation, it is most desirable that you, as captain,

(A) call the officer's attention to the fact that the lineup is not proceeding properly and then continue with your tour of posts.

(B) issue a mild reprimand and take personal command of the lineup in order to prevent further confusion.

(C) make a mental note of the situation and discuss the proper way of conducting a lineup at the next conference with your officer.

(D) take the officer aside and instruct him or her in the immediate action to take in order to correct this situation.

39. Suppose that on organized searches for contraband, more contraband is usually found on the post of one officer under your command than on the post of any other. The one of the following most likely to be an important contributing factor to the situation is the

(A) amount of time this officer has devoted to the study of the rule book.

(B) amount of training you have given your staff in the detection and control of contraband.

(C) special problems inherent in the type of post commanded by this officer.

(D) thoroughness with which the different types of posts are searched.

40. Suppose that a captain is required to review disciplinary reports against inmates prepared by Corrections Officers before forwarding them to the disciplinary officer. Of the following, the report the captain should return to a Corrections Officer for rewriting is one that

(A) fails to employ a high standard of written English.

(B) fails to recommend an appropriate punishment.

(C) is incomplete as to main details.

(D) relates to more than one inmate.

41. Suppose an inmate has made an unjustified complaint about you to your superior officer. The best of the following plans for you to follow is to

(A) make that inmate work harder and treat him roughly.

(B) see that the inmate gets all the dirty, disagreeable jobs.

(C) spread the word among the other inmates that the inmate is a "stool pigeon."

(D) go to your superior officer and tell him the truth.

42. A Corrections Officer assigned to some clerical duties accidentally destroys an important document that was to be presented in court as evidence in a few days. The best action for him to take first in this situation is to

(A) suggest that the case be postponed until more evidence can be obtained.

(B) immediately contact the person from whom the document was obtained and request another copy.

(C) say nothing at this time, but admit the destruction of the document if asked for it by his superior.

(D) notify his superior of the destruction of the document.

43. Assume you are a captain. A newly appointed Corrections Officer asks you what action she should take if, when patrolling a cell block at night, she notices that a prisoner has suddenly been taken violently ill. Of the following, the best advice for you to give this Corrections Officer is that she should

(A) open the cell immediately and apply first-aid as soon as possible.

(B) summon another guard before opening the cell.

(C) open the cell immediately, examine the inmate quickly, and summon a doctor if the illness seems real.

(D) carefully check on the circumstances of the case before opening the cell.

44. Suppose a Corrections Officer coming on duty reports to you that a prisoner is missing from the cell block. Of the following, the best reason for sounding an alarm immediately, even before checking the officer's count, is that

(A) the inmate may still be on the prison grounds.

(B) the escaped prisoner may have had an accomplice.

(C) there is no indication how long the inmate may have been missing from his cell.

(D) responsibility for the escape should be fixed immediately.

QUESTIONS 45–47 ARE BASED ON THE FOLLOWING EXAMPLE OF A CORRECTION OFFICER'S REPORT. THE REPORT CONSISTS OF SIXTEEN NUMBERED SENTENCES, SOME OF WHICH ARE NOT CONSISTENT WITH THE PRINCIPLES OF GOOD REPORT WRITING IN CORRECTIONAL MATTER.

(1) On January 5, I was assigned as the "A" officer on the third floor of Institution Y during the 12 midnight to 8 a.m. tour of duty. **(2)** At about 1:30 a.m. on said date, I heard a cry for help coming from the lower "A" section of the floor. **(3)** I immediately ran into the section and found inmate John Doe in cell number 5 holding up inmate Robert James who was hanging from the light fixture of the cell by a bedsheet. **(4)** One end of the bedsheet was tied to the outer frame of the light fixture, and the other end was tied around the neck of inmate James. **(5)** I immediately ran to the telephone to notify the control room and ask for assistance. **(6)** While waiting for assistance, I notified Corrections Officer Harold Smith who was assigned as the "B" officer on the floor and instructed inmate Doe to keep holding the hanging inmate in an upward position. **(7)** Corrections Officer Thomas Jones arrived at the scene together with Dr. Walker Frazer who was the physician on duty in the institution at the time. **(8)** Corrections Officer Smith and I then ran to cell number 5 while Corrections Officer Jones operated the "A" section locking mechanism to open the door to cell number 5. **(9)** When the cell door was opened, I, together with Corrections Officer Smith and

Dr. Frazer, entered the cell where I cut the bedsheet with my pen knife to let the hanging inmate down. **(10)** I found no suicide note in the cell. **(11)** Dr. Frazer ordered the inmate to be placed on the floor outside of the cell so that he could inject emergency medication into the inmate's chest and administer artificial respiration. **(12)** Both Corrections Officer Smith and I assisted in administering artificial respiration under the physician's supervision. **(13)** After the administration of artificial respiration for a period of approximately one-half hour, Dr. Frazer pronounced inmate James dead. **(14)** The dead inmate's cell partner, inmate John Doe, stated that he awoke from his sleep and saw his cell partner hanging from the ceiling with a sheet tied around his neck. **(15)** There were no pictures anywhere in the cell which would give information as to the deceased's family ties. **(16)** It is believed that inmate James committed suicide because of his concern about the sentence he would receive when he appeared in court for sentencing on January 6.

45. A good report should be arranged in logical order. Which of the following sentences does NOT appear in proper sequence?

(A) Sentence 2
(B) Sentence 10
(C) Sentence 3
(D) Sentence 13

46. Only material relevant to the main thought of a report should be included. Which of the following sentences contains material that is *least* relevant to this report?

(A) Sentence 2
(B) Sentence 11
(C) Sentence 14
(D) Sentence 15

47. Good reports should contain accurate statements based upon definite information. Which of the following sentences contains material that is NOT based on definite information?

(A) Sentence 5
(B) Sentence 6
(C) Sentence 9
(D) Sentence 16

48. Assume that you are a captain. An inmate comes to you with a request arising out of a grievance that he believes to be legitimate. You can see that the inmate is making a request that is important to him. You consider the inmate's request carefully and decide that you cannot grant it. It is best for you to

(A) give the inmate a firm "no" answer and your reason for doing so.
(B) grant the inmate's request because of its importance, but point out to him that there were very good reasons for not granting the request.
(C) tell the inmate that his request is an important one and you will let him know in the not-too-distant future whether the request can be granted.
(D) tell the inmate that there are two sides to granting his request and that you will ask the deputy warden to frame a written response to the inmate.

49. To schedule an official count at or near the time of officer shift changes is usually found to be a

(A) bad practice, since officers coming on duty resent being held up while a previous shift makes its count.
(B) good practice, since a large number of officers will be on hand if discrepancies in the count are found.
(C) bad practice, since officers responsible for the count are too easily distracted.
(D) good practice, since accuracy in the count is assured and interference with inmate activities is avoided.

50. The three major ideologies affecting law enforcement and court and correctional activities are the punitive, therapeutic, and preventive ideologies. Of the following, the most correct statement is that the
   (A) therapeutic ideology rather than the punitive or preventive ideology is recognized as offering the ultimate promise for reducing crime.
   (B) preventive ideology seeks to promote development of a healthy personality by means of immediate and drastic social changes so that criminals will engage in socially approved conduct.
   (C) therapeutic ideology considers the criminal to be a victim of defective personality conditioning and, consequently, generally seeks a lifetime clinical treatment approach by specially trained psychiatrists.
   (D) punitive ideology has as its major objective the protection of society, and severe punishment is viewed as useful in reforming criminals.

51. Increases in recidivist rates can result from
   (A) more liberal enforcement of parole supervision.
   (B) increased use of probation by the courts.
   (C) stricter enforcement of probation supervision.
   (D) more liberal law enforcement.

52. If a Corrections Officer were to attend a preparatory class on supervisory techniques, he or she would most likely be instructed that a good supervisor is one who
   (A) believes in strong and centralized administrative control.
   (B) is extremely ambitious.
   (C) maintains a favorable attitude toward those he or she encounters.
   (D) maintains his or her own method of handling problems.

53. Of the following, the most important consideration for recommending a promotion to captain should be the Corrections Officer's
   (A) capacity to take disciplinary action.
   (B) ability to control inmate movement.
   (C) detailed knowledge of departmental rules and regulations.
   (D) seniority.

54. A Corrections Officer under your supervision as captain attempts to conceal the fact that he or she has made an error. You should proceed on the assumption that
   (A) evasion may well be overlooked if the error occurred in a matter of no great importance.
   (B) a desire for concealment indicates an antisocial attitude.
   (C) the Corrections Officer was ignorant of proper procedures and that the matter should be dropped.
   (D) the evasion indicates something wrong in the fundamental relationship between the Corrections Officer and his or her captain.

55. If a corrections captain is to be an effective leader of those under her, she must

(A) utilize whatever motives she is able to discern in the officers working under her.

(B) develop the assets of the officers and encourage them to work for the good of the organization as a whole.

(C) avoid the use of regular conferences lest her officers be deprived of initiative.

(D) outline repeatedly and in great detail the work to be performed by each member of the group.

56. Inmates generally find their place within some group in the institution. A certain Corrections Officer makes it a practice to find out as much as he can about such groups and the reasons for changes in their composition. The Corrections Officer's practice in this regard is

(A) bad; a Corrections Officer who develops a reputation for not minding his own business will be taken hostage in the event of a disturbance.

(B) bad; within institutional rules, an inmate has as much right to a personal social life as anyone else.

(C) good; institutional security may depend upon such observations.

(D) good; most inmates are appreciative when Corrections Officers show a personal interest in their activities.

57. "It is generally accepted in the correctional field that society is best protected when a very high percentage of all releases are by parole." This is true primarily because

(A) it costs much less to handle inmates on parole than to incarcerate them.

(B) the "bad risks" who need it most will be under supervision after release.

(C) indeterminate sentences give correctional administrators maximum flexibility.

(D) determining what constitutes success or failure on parole is relatively easy.

58. Which of the following statements concerning riots and disturbances in correctional institutions is correct?

(A) A system that provides for informal communications between staff and inmates is the best way to prevent riots and disturbances.

(B) Research studies have identified a set of causes that always precipitates a riot.

(C) Sudden or unexpected changes in institutional routines or policies may result in a major disturbance.

(D) The best way to prevent riots is to have an effective informant system.

59. Penologists generally agree that the way a custodial prison maintains stability within its walls is

(A) through the granting of privileges.

(B) through the exercise of total power by guards.

(C) by treating all inmates alike in order to destroy the influence of inmate leaders.

(D) by dealing with leaders chosen by the inmates.

60. "It must be ironic to a prisoner to recall that society spared no expense to afford him three, four, or five trials and appeals at enormous cost but then proceeds to forget his plight." This statement implies that

(A) more money should be spent for the treatment of prisoners and less for the adjudication of criminal cases.

(B) substantial sums of money are justifiably required to ensure that the innocent are not wrongly convicted.

(C) less money should be spent on the judicial process, since it has not helped to reduce the rate of recidivism.

(D) more money should be spent for a prisoner's treatment in order to be consistent with the investment in convicting him or her.

61. "Extra security precautions are generally advisable in the supervision of prisoners at mess." This is so mainly because

(A) different classes of inmates mingle together freely at mess

(B) large numbers of prisoners are concentrated together in one place

(C) prisoners are usually dissatisfied with institution food

(D) prison riots may begin anywhere

62. In a certain correctional institution, a captain discharging an inmate asked the latter some personal questions, such as "Where do your parents live?" "What is your mother's name?" etc. The purpose of asking these questions was probably to

(A) check the accuracy of the information on the discharge papers.

(B) motivate the inmate to renew family ties.

(C) prevent a substitution of inmates.

(D) show an interest in the inmate's welfare.

63. Suppose that a study of prison inmates shows that the rate of recidivism increases as the number of offenses increases. That is, 10% of first offenders become second offenders, 30% of second offenders become third offenders, 70% of third offenders become fourth offenders, etc. If the findings of this study are valid, then it is most reasonable to assume that

(A) environment plays a minor role in the predisposition towards criminal behavior.

(B) exposure to prison life inevitably leads to the commission of further crimes.

(C) first offenders represent the most fruitful field for intensive rehabilitation efforts.

(D) it would be desirable to house together offenders who have committed the same number of offenses.

64. "Since inmate programs of work, recreation, vocational training, etc., have not been effective in reducing crime or the rate of recidivism, they should be abandoned." A basic weakness of this criticism is that it fails to take into account that these programs

(A) are also needed to keep inmates occupied.

(B) are not intended to achieve the purposes stated.

(C) cannot influence the majority of criminals since they are not apprehended.

(D) have been tried for only a very short time.

65. Of the following, the best reason for using tear gas in the event of a serious disturbance in a correctional institution is that it

(A) permanently disables the ringleaders.

(B) teaches the inmates that disturbances will not be permitted.

(C) effectively curbs the disturbance without harm to the inmates.

(D) is what the public expects in a case of disturbance in a correctional institution.

66. Suppose that you are a corrections captain, and a newly appointed Corrections Officer reports to you for duty. Of the following, the best procedure for you to follow to assure his rapid orientation to his work is to

(A) ask him to briefly survey his qualifications for the job.

(B) observe him carefully as he performs the routine aspects of his duties.

(C) make a careful study of his work record previous to his coming to the Department.

(D) review with him the important elements of the job he will be required to perform.

67. A captain notices that one Corrections Officer does not get along well with the other officers. Of the following, the best thing for the captain to do in such a situation is to

(A) make an effort to learn the reason for the difficulty in order to resolve the problem.

(B) overlook the matter, since the work will probably be unaffected.

(C) prepare a report of the situation to a superior officer and be guided by the latter's decision.

(D) tell all the officers they must work together harmoniously or risk disciplinary action.

68. The practice of admitting a new prisoner to the institution without a complete strip shakedown is

(A) desirable only if the officer delivering the prisoner gives written assurance that the prisoner has been frisked and is free of contraband.

(B) not desirable under any circumstances.

(C) desirable only if the prisoner has been brought directly from another institution.

(D) not desirable except with material witnesses.

69. "A captain should patrol at irregular and unexpected times throughout his or her tour." This method of patrol is preferable to patrols at scheduled times mainly because

(A) the captain has greater flexibility in scheduling the day's activities.

(B) patrols will not be forgotten or reduced if they become habitual.

(C) officers on post know that the captain will be around to inspect their work.

(D) it gives a truer picture of actual conditions on the different posts.

70. Of the following vocational training courses suitable for a women's institution, the one that has more value than the others because of its effect on institutional morale is a course in

(A) beauty culture.

(B) homemaking.

(C) practical nursing.

(D) child care.

71. Of the following, the best method for enforcing discipline among inmates of a penal institution is

(A) reclassification of the offending inmates.

(B) transfer or reassignment.

(C) deprivation of privileges.

(D) use of duress or compulsion.

72. In the institutions of the Department of Corrections, special security procedures are observed with an inmate sentenced to death or to a long term in a state prison. Such special procedures are advisable mainly because
    (A) the department is only temporarily responsible for someone who is actually a prisoner of the State.
    (B) friends and accomplices on the outside may attempt to free such an inmate by force.
    (C) isolation of such an inmate from the rest of the prison population is not practicable.
    (D) the severity of the sentence may impel such an inmate to commit a desperate act.

73. Assume that a new warden has been placed in charge of an institution. He is faced with the problem of deciding how strict or how relaxed discipline should be. It would be better for him to begin by setting standards of discipline that are
    (A) relaxed rather than strict, because discipline should bear a direct relationship to the kind of violations committed and to the manner of their being committed.
    (B) relaxed rather than strict, since the goodwill of correctional personnel is a primary consideration.
    (C) strict rather than relaxed, because it is easier to relax discipline than to tighten it.
    (D) strict rather than relaxed, since both inmates and Corrections Officers usually devise all manner of stratagems to see how far a new warden can be pushed.

74. The principle of administration that states that the responsibility of higher authority for the acts of subordinates must be absolute means that
    (A) each superior officer is held responsible for all the acts of his or her subordinates.
    (B) each subordinate is held responsible for his or her own acts.
    (C) the chief executive alone is not responsible for the acts of his or her subordinates.
    (D) coordinate officers are responsible for the acts of one another.

75. The principal argument against the heavy weighting of seniority in a correction department promotion examination is that the seniority credits
    (A) tend to give credit for age.
    (B) create ill will among employees with shorter seniority.
    (C) violate the spirit of career service.
    (D) offer no positive assurance of competency.

76. In planning courses for a Corrections Officers' training program, it is most important to make the content of each lesson capable of being
    (A) taught in one class meeting.
    (B) connected to something the trainee already knows and can do.
    (C) spread over a number of class meetings.
    (D) fully learned by the trainees as something entirely new.

77. There is strong disagreement among correctional administrators concerning the use of inmate councils. The most feasible approach concerning the use of inmate councils is generally the
    - **(A)** elimination of inmate advisory groups, since membership in such a group gives the inmate an opportunity to exploit other inmates.
    - **(B)** formation of inmate advisory groups to deal with particular problems, with such groups dissolving as soon as the problems are resolved.
    - **(C)** popular election by inmates of an inmate advisory group to meet at frequent periodic intervals.
    - **(D)** taking of formal surveys by supervisory correction personnel to determine inmate attitudes.

78. A major point of emphasis in the instruction of a Corrections Officer concerns security and the causes of breach of security. Experience has shown that most escapes are traceable directly to
    - **(A)** relatives who smuggle escape instruments to inmates.
    - **(B)** officers who smuggle contraband to inmates.
    - **(C)** the haphazard handling of keys and tools.
    - **(D)** the lack of knowledge among inmates as to the possible consequences of escape.

79. "A good correctional program should be carried out in such a way that problem cases are revealed long before they reach a critical state." A Corrections Officer could best help carry out such a program by
    - **(A)** consulting with superiors as to the type of disciplinary action to be taken with problem cases.
    - **(B)** learning to recognize the signs of trouble and how to deal with them.
    - **(C)** preparing a good case against the inmates in the event a disciplinary hearing is held
    - **(D)** getting the help of other Corrections Officers in dealing with critical situations

80. Assume that as a Corrections Captain you are assigned to conduct a refresher training course for Corrections Officers. Of the following, the best reason for employing group discussion rather than routine lecture methods is that
    - **(A)** learning is more efficient when officers participate actively in the process.
    - **(B)** the scope of a training course can be laid out more precisely when one person is responsible for the course.
    - **(C)** the more experienced the officers, the more likely they will benefit from a lecture course.
    - **(D)** less time has to be devoted to a course that has a well-defined purpose.

81. "The competent Corrections Captain attempts to develop respect rather than fear on the part of the officers under his or her supervision." Of the following, the chief justification for this statement is that
    (A) experience has demonstrated that negative incentives are more effective than positive ones.
    (B) respect is based on the individual, while fear is based on the organization as a whole.
    (C) respect for officers is generally easier to develop than fear of penalty.
    (D) officers who respect a supervisor are likely to give more than the minimum required performance.

82. A captain advised a new Corrections Officer not to permit inmates to address her by her first name. The captain's advice was
    (A) bad, because it creates a wider gap than necessary between officers and inmates.
    (B) bad, because no rule is applicable in every situation.
    (C) good, because familiarity between officers and inmates may lead to a breakdown of discipline.
    (D) good, because the more impersonally an inmate is treated, the easier he or she is to control.

83. A new officer asks you what to do if an inmate refuses to carry out an order. As captain, you should advise the officer to
    (A) reconsider if the order was a reasonable one.
    (B) avoid being drawn into a situation of this kind.
    (C) immediately summon a superior for assistance.
    (D) warn the inmate that he or she will be subject to disciplinary action.

84. A Corrections Officer is expected to report unusual situations to his superior and should use all of his senses. Which of the following statements regarding the use of sight by a Corrections Officer is correct?
    (A) The officer should constantly watch inmates in his charge, since observation is an effective medium for control and custody.
    (B) The officer should look just above inmates' heads (since this keeps them from becoming nervous) while his peripheral vision takes in that which is important.
    (C) The officer should not allow his eyes to rest on any one inmate, since this is certain to provoke hostility.
    (D) The officer should train himself to concentrate on the hands of inmates, since information gained from looking at inmates' faces is usually unreliable.

85. Which of the following guidelines is LEAST appropriate for a key control system in a correctional institution?
    (A) All keys should be issued from a central location such as the institution control room.
    (B) Officers should not be permitted to withdraw keys unless they give receipts for them.
    (C) The key control center should have at all times at least one duplicate set of each bunch of keys.
    (D) Only reliable prisoners, such as "trusties," should be permitted to handle keys.

86. The degree of security needed to confine an inmate depends upon the
    (A) caliber of personnel assigned to the institution.
    (B) personality and background of the inmate.
    (C) type of programs available in the institution.
    (D) type of security facilities within the institution.

87. The essential features of good organizational structure for an institution for adult prisoners should include all of the following EXCEPT

(A) a constructive system of communication with inmates.

(B) a program of personnel development for correctional staff, including the classification of positions and in-service training.

(C) separate administrative controls for the personnel, inmates, and programs of the institution.

(D) a system for developing constructive community relationships.

88. Where possible, the use of consolidated jails serving several jurisdictions has been recommended in lieu of individual local facilities. Of the following, the major advantage of consolidated jails is that

(A) a more effective correctional program can be offered when funds and other resources are pooled.

(B) the population of local jails is reduced to more manageable proportions.

(C) specialized institutions can develop their separate treatment methods.

(D) community acceptance is more easily obtained for one large facility than for several smaller ones.

89. A positive program of maintaining discipline is essential in preventing unrest or disturbances. A good disciplinary program is one that

(A) is based on the use of disciplinary committees to punish all infractions of the rules.

(B) does not include punishment for violations of the rules except in extreme cases.

(C) maintains order with minimal friction and uses punishment in a constructive manner.

(D) uses administrative segregation as the basic method for controlling inmates.

90. Which of the following statements concerning the relationship between custody and rehabilitative programs is *INCORRECT*?

(A) Services and facilities for rehabilitative treatment operate effectively only in a climate where control is constant.

(B) Positive programs of inmate activities generally weaken the effectiveness of security measures.

(C) Rehabilitative services must be correlated with a system of sound custody, security, and control of inmates.

(D) Security and control procedures produce maximum results when they are implemented in a manner that gains the cooperation of the majority of inmates.

91. Which one of the following has been a major obstacle to effective rehabilitation of prison inmates?

(A) Inmates have not been able to handle the permissiveness of the group approach to treatment.

(B) Most correctional staff members are not interested in assuming new roles or in communicating constructively with inmates.

(C) The inconclusive results of treatment programs have reinforced doubts that prison inmates are capable of behavioral change.

(D) The inmate culture itself raises barriers against genuine participation of prisoners in treatment programs.

92. While conducting a training session for Corrections Officers, the most valid of the following points you can make on the subject of suicide is that

(A) prisoners who are observed talking to themselves in a halting manner are suicidal and must be reported to the psychiatrist.

(B) those who try to commit suicide and fail often try again.

(C) the prisoner who tells a member of the staff that he is going to commit suicide should be ignored, as he is engaging in a manipulative device.

(D) minor attempts at suicide, such as injuring an arm with shallow cuts, should be reported to the captain for disciplinary action rather than to a psychiatrist.

93. The single most important factor when considering the problems involved in rehabilitating an offender is that the ultimate change sought

(A) depends upon the inmate's becoming a self-disciplined person, which, in turn, depends upon his or her accepting institutional discipline.

(B) is a harmonious adjustment to institutional life.

(C) is adjustment to freedom in the community.

(D) is making the offender aware that institutional life is not a penalty but an opportunity.

94. Decision making is a rational process calling for a suspended judgment by the supervisor until all the facts have been ascertained and analyzed and the consequences of alternative courses of action studied. Then the decision maker

(A) acts as both judge and jury and selects what he or she believes to be the best of the alternative plans.

(B) consults with those who will be most directly involved to obtain a recommendation as to the most appropriate course of action.

(C) reviews the facts already analyzed, reduces all thoughts to writing, and selects the course of action having the fewest negative consequences in case the thinking has contained an error.

(D) stops and considers the matter for at least 24 hours before referring it to a superior for evaluation.

95. The Corrections Officer must master certain proven principles and techniques if he or she is to successfully supervise incarcerated offenders. One of these principles states, "A Correction Officer should not be too anxious to reveal completely to inmates what he or she knows and thinks." Which of the following is a reason for applying this principle?

(A) A Corrections Officer should discipline him- or herself to think in terms of action rather than concepts.

(B) An inmate's action is often favorably influenced when the inmate fears the unknown.

(C) Inmate feelings of self-respect are enhanced if inmates believe they know something the Corrections Officer does not know.

(D) To the greatest extent possible, a Corrections Officer should speak to inmates only when spoken to.

96. Assume that you are a captain and that a Corrections Officer with a long and excellent record has recently begun to exhibit laziness and a lack of interest in her work. Of the following, the *best* course of action for you as her superior officer to follow is to

(A) call the attention of the other officers to this case in order to demonstrate that good work requires constant, diligent application.

(B) start disciplinary action immediately against this Corrections Officer as you would against any other.

(C) overlook the matter until the Corrections Officer again demonstrates her usual high quality of work.

(D) interview the Corrections Officer and attempt to determine the reason for her unusual behavior.

97. You observe that a Corrections Officer under your command is not carrying out a specific assignment in accordance with the instructions you gave. Of the following, the most important reason why you should have this officer repeat your instructions is that

(A) instructions can be misunderstood even by excellent Corrections Officers.

(B) it will indicate that incorrect instructions were given.

(C) inefficiency usually has serious consequences.

(D) oral instructions should be repeated when issued to ensure they are understood.

98. Since a Corrections Captain expects subordinates to carry out commands to the letter, it is most important for the captain to

(A) check on the execution of all commands immediately.

(B) issue commands clearly and make sure they are understood.

(C) issue only commands that would seem reasonable to anyone.

(D) make only one officer responsible for the execution of any one command.

99. Of the following, the one that is generally NOT a characteristic of individuals in a prison population is the

(A) lack of ability to articulate feelings and ideas.

(B) inability to postpone gratification.

(C) orientation of the individual as receiver and a tendency to view others as givers.

(D) preoccupation with concrete and immediate objects, wishes, and needs.

100. A Corrections Officer under your supervision comes to you to complain about a decision you have made in assigning the officers. You consider the matter to be unimportant, but it seems to be very important to him. He is excited and very angry. The *BEST* way to handle this case is to

- **(A)** tell the officer to take it up with the deputy warden.
- **(B)** refuse to talk to the officer until he has calmed down.
- **(C)** show the officer at once how unimportant the matter is and how absurd his argument is.
- **(D)** let the officer talk until he "gets it off his chest" and then explain the reasons for your decision.

ANSWER KEY

1. A	21. A	41. D	61. B	81. D
2. C	22. A	42. D	62. C	82. C
3. A	23. B	43. B	63. C	83. D
4. B	24. C	44. A	64. A	84. A
5. B	25. C	45. C	65. C	85. D
6. A	26. C	46. D	66. D	86. B
7. D	27. A	47. D	67. A	87. C
8. C	28. D	48. A	68. B	88. A
9. D	29. A	49. B	69. D	89. C
10. D	30. D	50. D	70. A	90. B
11. D	31. C	51. A	71. C	91. D
12. C	32. B	52. C	72. D	92. B
13. D	33. D	53. A	73. C	93. C
14. B	34. C	54. D	74. A	94. A
15. C	35. B	55. B	75. D	95. B
16. A	36. C	56. C	76. B	96. D
17. D	37. A	57. B	77. B	97. A
18. B	38. C	58. C	78. C	98. B
19. B	39. C	59. A	79. B	99. A
20. C	40. C	60. D	80. A	100. D

answers

APPENDIXES

Physical Fitness Course

In the law enforcement field, heavy emphasis is placed upon the candidate's physical status. Considering the demands made upon the law enforcement officer's body, the emphasis on physical fitness is entirely reasonable. From your own standpoint as a serious candidate, it makes sense to devote at least as much attention to preparing your body for the physical test as to preparing your mind for the written exam.

Obviously, if you are considering yourself as a law enforcement officer candidate, you consider yourself a healthy, physically fit person. Even so, it would be wise to consult your own doctor before proceeding. Tell your doctor about the type of work you have in mind, describe the physical demands, and ask for an assessment of your potential to withstand these rigors. If your doctor foresees any potential problems, either in passing the exams or in facing the demands of the job, discuss corrective measures and remedial programs right now. Follow the medical advice you receive concerning diet and general lifestyle. If the jurisdiction to which you are applying provides you with a description of the physical performance test you must take, describe it to your doctor. You may be able to pick up special tips to prepare yourself to do well on your exam. Your doctor may have a physical conditioning program to recommend. If not, design your own program. You may find the following suggestions prepared by the President's Council on Physical Fitness convenient to follow or design your own fitness program to fit your own needs and time requirements.

Physical fitness is to the human body what fine tuning is to an engine. It enables us to perform to our potential. Fitness can be described as a condition that helps us look, feel, and do our best. More specifically, it is:

> "The ability to perform daily tasks vigorously and alertly, with energy left over for enjoying leisure-time activities and meeting emergency demands. It is the ability to endure, to bear up, to withstand stress, and to carry on in circumstances where an unfit person could not continue and is a major basis for good health and well-being."

Physical fitness involves the performance of the heart, the lungs, and the muscles of the body. And, since what we do with our bodies also affects what we can do with our minds, fitness influences to some degree qualities such as mental alertness and emotional stability.

As you undertake your fitness program, it's important to remember that fitness is an individual quality that varies from person to person. It is influenced by age, sex, heredity, personal habits, exercise, and eating practices. You can't do anything about the first three factors. However, it is within your power to change and improve the others where needed.

KNOWING THE BASICS

Physical fitness is most easily understood by examining its components, or parts. There is widespread agreement that these five components are basic:

Cardiorespiratory Endurance—the ability to deliver oxygen and nutrients to tissues, and to remove wastes, over sustained periods of time. Long runs and swims are among the methods employed in measuring this component.

Muscular Strength—the ability of a muscle to exert force for a brief period of time. Upper-body strength, for example, can be measured by various weight-lifting exercises.

Muscular Endurance—the ability of a muscle, or a group of muscles, to sustain repeated contractions or to continue applying force against a fixed object. Push-ups are often used to test endurance of arm and shoulder muscles.

Flexibility—the ability to move joints and use muscles through their full range of motion. The sit-and-reach test is a good measure of flexibility of the lower back and the backs of the upper legs.

Body Composition—the makeup of the body in terms of lean mass (muscle, bone, vital tissue, and organs) and fat mass. An optimal ratio of fat to lean mass is an indication of fitness, and the right types of exercises will help you decrease body fat and increase or maintain muscle mass.

A WORKOUT SCHEDULE

How often, how long, and how hard you exercise, and what kinds of exercises you do, should be determined by what you are trying to accomplish. Your goals, present fitness level, age, health, skills, interests, and convenience are among the factors you should consider. For example, an athlete training for high-level competition would follow a different program from a person whose goals are good health and the ability to meet work and recreational needs.

Your exercise program should include something from each of the five basic fitness components described previously. Each workout should begin with a warm-up and end with a cool-down. As a general rule, space your workouts throughout the week and avoid consecutive days of hard exercise.

Here are the amounts of activity necessary for the average, healthy person to maintain a minimum level of overall fitness. Included are some of the popular exercises for each category.

Warm-up—5 to 10 minutes of exercises such as walking, slow jogging, knee lifts, arm circles, or trunk rotations. Low-intensity movements that simulate movements to be used in the activity can also be included in the warm-up.

Muscular Strength—a minimum of two 20-minute sessions per week that include exercises for all the major muscle groups. Lifting weights is the most effective way to increase strength.

Muscular Endurance—at least three 30-minute sessions each week that include exercises such as calisthenics, push-ups, sit-ups, pull-ups, and weight training for all the major muscle groups.

Cardiorespiratory Endurance—at least three 20-minute bouts of continuous aerobic (activity requiring oxygen) rhythmic exercise each week. Popular aerobic conditioning activities include brisk walking, jogging, swimming, cycling, rope-jumping, rowing, cross-country skiing, and some continuous-action games like racquetball and handball.

Flexibility—10 to 12 minutes of daily stretching exercises performed slowly, without a bouncing motion. This can be included after a warm-up or during a cool-down.

Cool-down—a minimum of 5 to 10 minutes of slow walking and low-level exercise, combined with stretching.

A Matter of Principle

The keys to selecting the right kinds of exercises for developing and maintaining each of the basic components of fitness are found in these principles:

Specify—Pick the right kind of activities to affect each component. Strength training results in specific strength changes. Also, train for the specific activity you're interested in. For example, optimal swimming performance is best achieved when the muscles involved in swimming are trained for the movements required. It does not necessarily follow that a good runner is a good swimmer.

Overload—Work hard enough, at levels that are vigorous and long enough to overload your body above its resting level, to bring about improvement.

Regularity—You can't hoard physical fitness. At least three balanced workouts a week are necessary to maintain a desirable level of fitness.

Progression—Increase the intensity, frequency, and/or duration of activity over periods of time in order to improve.

Some activities can be used to fulfill more than one of your basic exercise requirements.

For example, in addition to increasing cardiorespiratory endurance, running builds muscular endurance in the legs, and swimming develops the arm, shoulder, and chest muscles. If you select the proper activities, it is possible to fit parts of your muscular endurance workout into your cardiorespiratory workout and save time.

MEASURING YOUR HEART RATE

Heart rate is widely accepted as a good method for measuring intensity during running, swimming, cycling, and other aerobic activities. Exercise that doesn't raise your heart rate to a certain level and keep it there for 20 minutes won't contribute significantly to cardiovascular fitness.

The heart rate you should maintain is called your **target heart rate.** There are several ways of arriving at this figure. One of the simplest is: **maximum heart rate** (220 − age) × 70%. Thus, the target heart rate for a 40-year-old would be 126.

Some methods for figuring the target rate take individual differences into consideration. Here is one of them:

1 Subtract your age from 220 to find **maximum heart rate.**

2 Subtract your resting heart rate (see below) from maximum heart rate to determine **heart rate reserve.**

3 Take 70% of your heart rate reserve to determine **heart rate raise.**

4 Add your heart rate raise to your resting heart rate to find **target rate.**

Resting heart rate should be determined by taking your pulse after sitting quietly for 5 minutes. When checking heart rate during a workout, take your pulse within 5 seconds after interrupting exercise because it starts to go down once you stop moving. Count your pulse for 10 seconds and multiply by 6 to get the per-minute rate.

PROGRAM FOR WOMEN

The following program assumes that you have not been putting all of your muscles to any consistent use and that you are starting from close to "couch potato" status. If you are already in pretty good shape, you might be able to start more quickly. But don't overdo it. A gradual build-up makes sense.

The program starts with an orientation or "get-set" series of exercises that will allow you to bring all major muscles into use easily and painlessly. There are then five graded levels. As you move from one to the next, you will be building toward a practical and satisfying level of fitness. By building gradually, and progressively, you will be building soundly.

What the Exercises Are For

There are three general types: warm-up exercises, conditioning exercises, and circulatory activities.

The *warm-up exercises* stretch and limber up the muscles and speed up the action of the heart and lungs, thus preparing the body for greater exertion and reducing the possibility of unnecessary strain.

The *conditioning exercises* are systematically planned to tone up abdominal, back, leg, arm, and other major muscles.

The *circulatory activities* produce contractions of large muscle groups for longer periods than the conditioning exercises, to stimulate and strengthen the circulatory and respiratory systems.

The plan calls for doing ten mild exercises during the orientation period and, thereafter, the warm-up exercises and the seven conditioning exercises listed for each level. The first six exercises of the orientation program are used as warm-up exercises throughout the graded levels.

When it comes to the circulatory activities, you choose one for each workout. Possibilities include alternately running and walking, skipping rope, and running in place. All are effective. You can choose running and walking on a pleasant day and one of the others for use indoors when the weather is inclement. You can rotate activities for variety.

A sound physical conditioning program should take into account your individual tolerance—your ability to execute a series of activities without undue discomfort or fatigue. It should help develop your tolerance by increasing the work load so you gradually become able to achieve more and more with less and less fatigue and with increasingly rapid recovery.

As you move from level to level, some exercises will be modified so they call for increased effort. Others will remain the same, but you will build more strength and stamina by increasing the number of repetitions.

You will be increasing your fitness another way, as well.

At level 1, your objective will be to gradually reduce, from workout to workout, the "breathing spells" between exercises until you can do the seven conditioning exercises without resting. You will proceed in the same fashion with the more difficult exercises and increased repetitions at succeeding levels.

You will find the program designed—the progression carefully planned—to make this feasible. You will be able to proceed at your own pace, competing with yourself rather than with anyone else, and this is of great importance for sound conditioning.

Note: Gradually speeding up, from workout to workout, the rate at which you do each exercise will provide greater stimulation for the circulatory and respiratory systems and also help to keep your workouts short. However, the seven conditioning exercises should not be a race against time. Perform each exercise correctly to insure maximum benefit and avoid injury.

Duration

Your objective at each level will be to reach the point where you can do all the exercises called for, the number of times indicated, without resting between exercises.

Start slowly. It cannot be emphasized enough that by moving forward gradually you will be moving forward solidly, avoiding sudden strains and excesses that could cause injury and hold you back for several days.

If you find yourself at first unable to complete any exercises—to do continuously all the repetitions called for—stop when you encounter difficulty. Rest briefly, then take up where you left off and complete the count. If you have difficulty at first, keep in mind that there will be less and less with succeeding workouts.

Stay at each level for at least three weeks. If you have not passed the prove-out test at the end of that time, continue at the same level until you do. The prove-out test calls for performing, in three consecutive workouts, the seven conditioning exercises without resting and satisfactorily fulfilling the requirement for one circulatory activity.

Measuring Progress

You will, of course, be able to observe the increase in your strength and stamina from week to week in many ways—including the increasing ease with which you do the exercises at a given level. In addition, there is a 2-minute step test you can use to measure and keep a running record of the improvement in your circulatory efficiency, one of the most important of all aspects of fitness.

The immediate response of the cardiovascular system to exercise differs markedly between well-conditioned individuals and others. The step test measures the response in terms of pulse rate taken shortly after a series of steps up and down onto a bench or chair.

Although it does not take long, it is necessarily vigorous. Stop if you become overly fatigued while taking it. You should not try it until you have completed the orientation period.

The Step Test

Use any sturdy bench or chair 15 to 17 inches in height.

> Count 1—Place right foot on bench.
>
> Count 2—Bring left foot alongside of right and stand erect.
>
> Count 3—Lower right foot to floor.
>
> Count 4—Lower left foot to floor.
>
> REPEAT the 4-count movement 30 times a minute for 2 minutes.
>
> THEN sit down on bench or chair for 2 minutes.
>
> FOLLOWING the 2-minute rest, take your pulse for 30 seconds. Double the count to get the per-minute rate. (You can find the pulse by applying the middle and index fingers of one hand firmly to the inside of the wrist of the other hand, on the thumb side.)

Record your score for future comparisons. In succeeding tests—about once every two weeks—you probably will find your pulse rate becoming lower as your physical condition improves.

Three important points:

1 For best results, do not engage in physical activity for at least 10 minutes before taking the test. Take it at about the same time of day, and always use the same bench or chair.

2 Remember that pulse rates vary among individuals. This is an individual test. What is important is not a comparison of your pulse rate with that of anybody else, but rather a record of how your own rate is reduced as your fitness increases.

3 As you progress, the rate at which your pulse is lowered should gradually level off. This is an indication that you are approaching peak fitness.

Your Progress Records

Charts are provided for the orientation program and for each of the five levels. They list the exercises to be done and the goal for each exercise in terms of number of repetitions, distance, etc. They also provide space in which to record your progress: (1) in completing the recommended 15 workouts at each level, (2) in accomplishing the three prove-out workouts before moving on to the succeeding level, and (3) in the results as you take the step test from time to time. A sample chart and progress record for one of the five levels is shown below.

You do the warm-up exercises and the conditioning exercises, along with one circulatory activity, for each workout.

Check off each workout as you complete it. The last three numbers are for the prove-out workouts, in which the seven conditioning exercises should be done without resting. Check them off as you accomplish them.

You are now ready to proceed to the next level.

As you take the step test—at about two-week intervals—enter your pulse rate. When you move on to the next level, transfer the last pulse rate from the preceding level. Enter it in the margin to the left of the new progress record and circle it so it will be convenient for continuing reference.

Sample	Goal
Warm-up Exercises	Exercises 1–6 of Orientation Program
Conditioning Exercises:	**Uninterrupted Repetitions:**
1. Bend and stretch	10
2. Sprinter	6
3. Sitting stretch	15
4. Knee push-up	12
5. Sit-up (fingers laced)	10
6. Leg raiser	10 each leg
7. Flutter kick	30
Circulatory Activity (choose one for each workout):	
Jog-walk (jog 50, walk 50)	½ mile
Rope (skip 30 sec.; rest 60 sec.)	3 series
Run in place (run 100, hop 25—2 cycles)	3 minutes
Water Activities (see pages 291–292):	
Your progress record: 1 2 3 4 5 6 7 8 9 10 11 12 13 14 15	
Step test (pulse):	Prove-out workouts

Getting Set—Orientation Workouts

With the series of mild exercises listed in the chart that follows and is described on the next pages, you can get yourself ready—without severe aches or pains—for the progressive conditioning program.

Plan to spend a minimum of one week on preliminary conditioning. Don't hesitate to spend two weeks (or three), if necessary, for you to limber up enough to accomplish all the exercises easily and without undue fatigue or injury.

Note: The Corrections Officer physical performance test is identical for both men and women, because all Corrections Officers must be able to perform all tasks. The demands of corrections work do not cater to weakness of any form. The women who can meet the physical standards take their places as full-fledged Corrections Officers, sharing equally in duties, responsibilities, risks, and hard work.

There are, of course, real physiological differences between men and women. Some conditioning exercises are modified in recognition of these differences. Women with the potential to pass the correction officer physical performance test should find that the women's program described here, if followed faithfully, should prepare them well.

Women: Orientation Program	Goal
Conditioning Exercises:	**Repetitions:**
*1. Bend and stretch	10
*2. Knee lift	10 left, 10 right
*3. Wing stretcher	20
*4. Half knee bend	10
*5. Arm circles	15 each way
*6. Body bender	10 left, 10 right
7. Prone arch	10
8. Knee push-up	6
9. Head and shoulder curl	5
10. Ankle stretch	15
Circulatory Activity (choose one for each workout):	
Walking	½ mile
Rope (skip 15 sec.; rest 60 sec.)	3 series

* The first six exercises of the orientation program will be used as warm-up exercises throughout the graded levels.

Step Test Record—After completing the orientation program, take the 2-minute step test. Record your pulse rate here: _____. This will be the base rate with which you can make comparisons in the future.

1. Bend and Stretch

Starting Position: Stand erect, feet shoulder-width apart.

Action: Count 1. Bend trunk forward and down, flexing knees. Stretch gently in attempt to touch fingers to toes or floor. Count 2. Return to starting position.

Note: Do slowly; stretch and relax at intervals rather than in rhythm.

2. Knee Lift

Starting Position: Stand erect, feet together, arms at sides.

Action: Count 1. Raise left knee as high as possible, grasping leg with hands and pulling knee against body while keeping back straight. Count 2. Lower to starting position.

Counts 3 and 4. Repeat with right knee.

3. Wing Stretcher

Starting Position: Stand erect, elbows at shoulder height, fists clenched in front of chest.

Action: Count 1. Thrust elbows backward vigorously without arching back. Keep head erect, elbows at shoulder height. Count 2. Return to starting position.

4. Half Knee Bend

Starting Position: Stand erect, hands on hips.

Action: Count 1. Bend knees halfway while extending arms forward, palms down. Count

2. Return to starting position.

5. Arm Circles

Starting Position: Stand erect, arms extended sideward at shoulder height, palms up.

Action: Describe small circles backward with hands. Keep head erect. Do 15 backward circles. Reverse, turn palms down, and do 15 small circles forward.

6. Body Bender

Starting Position: Stand, feet shoulder-width apart, hands behind neck, fingers interlaced.

Action: Count 1. Bend trunk sideward to left as far as possible, keeping hands behind neck. Count 2. Return to starting position. Counts 3 and 4. Repeat to the right.

7. Prone Arch

Starting Position: Lie face down, hands tucked under thighs.

Action: Count 1. Raise head, shoulders, and legs from floor. Count 2. Return to starting position.

8. Knee Push-up

Starting Position: Lie on floor, face down, legs together, knees bent with feet raised off floor, hands on floor under shoulders, palms down.

Action: Count 1. Push upper body off floor until arms are fully extended and body is in straight line from head to knees. Count 2. Return to starting position.

9. Head and Shoulder Curl

Starting Position: Lie on back, hands tucked under small of back, palms down.

Action: Count 1. Tighten abdominal muscles, lift head and pull shoulders and elbows off floor. Hold for four seconds. Count 2. Return to starting position.

10. Ankle Stretch

Starting Position: Stand on a stair, large book, or block of wood, with weight on balls of feet and heels raised.

Action: Count 1. Lower heels. Count 2. Raise heels.

Circulatory Activities

WALKING—Step off at a lively pace, swing arms, and breathe deeply.

ROPE—Any form of skipping or jumping is acceptable. Gradually increase the tempo as your skill and condition improve.

Women: Level One	Goal
Warm-up Exercises	Exercises 1–6 of Orientation Program
Conditioning Exercises:	**Uninterrupted Repetitions:**
1. Toe Touch	5
2. Sprinter	8
3. Sitting Stretch	10
4. Knee Push-up	8
5. Sit-up (arms extended)	5
6. Leg Raiser	5 each leg
7. Flutter Kick	20
Circulatory Activity (choose one for each workout):	
Walking (120 steps a minute)	½ mile
Rope (skip 30 sec.; rest 60 sec.)	2 series
Run in place (run 50; straddle hop 10–2 cycles)	2 minutes
Water Activities (see pages 291–292):	
Your progress record: 1 2 3 4 5 6 7 8 9 10 11 12 13 14 15	
Step test (pulse):	Prove-out workouts

1. Toe Touch

Starting Position: Stand at attention.

Action: Count 1. Bend trunk forward and down, keeping knees straight, touching fingers to ankles. Count 2. Bounce and touch fingers to top of feet. Count 3. Bounce and touch fingers to toes. Count 4. Return to starting position.

2. Sprinter

Starting Position: Squat, hands on floor, fingers pointed forward, left leg fully extended to rear.

Action: Count 1. Reverse position of feet in bouncing movement, bringing left foot to hands, extending right leg backward—all in one motion. Count 2. Reverse feet again, returning to starting position.

3. Sitting Stretch

Starting Position: Sit, legs spread apart, hands on knees.

Action: Count 1. Bend forward at waist, extending arms as far forward as possible. Count 2. Return to starting position.

4. Knee Push-up

Starting Position: Lie on floor, face down, legs together, knees bent with feet raised off floor, hands on floor under shoulders, palms down.

Action: Count 1. Push upper body off floor until arms are fully extended and body is in straight line from head to knees. Count 2. Return to starting position.

5. Sit-up (Arms Extended)

Starting Position: Lie on back, legs straight and together, arms extended beyond head.

Action: Count 1. Bring arms forward over head and roll up to sitting position, sliding hands along legs, grasping ankles. Count 2. Roll back to starting position.

6. Leg Raiser

Starting Position: Right side of body on floor, head resting on right arm.

Action: Lift left leg about 24 inches off floor, then lower it. Do required number of repetitions. Repeat on other side.

7. Flutter Kick

Starting Position: Lie face down, hands tucked under thighs.

Action: Arch the back, bringing chest and head up, then flutter kick continuously, moving the legs 8 to 10 inches apart. Kick from hips and with knees slightly bent. Count each kick as 1.

Circulatory Activities

WALKING—Maintain a pace of 120 steps per minute for a distance of ½ mile. Swing arms and breathe deeply.

ROPE—Skip or jump rope continuously using any form for 30 seconds, then rest 60 seconds. Repeat two times.

RUN IN PLACE—Raise each foot at least 4 inches off the floor and while jogging in place. Count 1 each time left foot touches floor. Complete number of running steps called for in chart, then do specified number of straddle hops. Complete two cycles of alternate running and hopping for time specified on chart.

STRADDLE HOP—*Starting position:* At attention. *Action:* Count 1. Swing arms sideward and upward, touching hands above head (arms straight) while simultaneously moving feet sideward and apart in a single jumping motion. Count 2. Spring back to starting position. Two counts in one hop.

Women: Level Two	Goal
Warm-up Exercises	Exercises 1–6 of Orientation Program
Conditioning Exercises:	**Uninterrupted Repetitions:**
1. Toe Touch	15
2. Sprinter	12
3. Sitting Stretch	15
4. Knee Push-up	12
5. Sit-up (fingers laced)	10
6. Leg Raiser	10 each leg
7. Flutter Kick	30
Circulatory Activity (choose one for each workout):	
Jog-walk (jog 50, walk 50)	½ mile
Rope (skip 30 sec.; rest 60 sec.)	3 series
Run in place (run 80; hop 15—2 cycles)	3 minutes
Water Activities (see pages 291–292):	
Your progress record: 1 2 3 4 5 6 7 8 9 10 11 12 13 14 15	
Step test (pulse):	Prove-out workouts

1. Toe Touch

Starting Position: Stand at attention.

Action: Count 1. Bend trunk forward and down, keeping knees straight, touching fingers to ankles. Count 2. Bounce and touch fingers to top of feet. Count 3. Bounce and touch fingers to toes. Count 4. Return to starting position.

2. Sprinter

Starting Position: Squat, hands on floor, fingers pointed forward, left leg fully extended to rear.

Action: Count 1. Reverse position of feet in bouncing movement, bringing left foot to hands, extending right leg backward—all in one motion. Count 2. Reverse feet again, returning to starting position.

3. Sitting Stretch

Starting Position: Sit, legs spread apart, hands on knees.

Action: Count 1. Bend forward at waist, extending arms as far forward as possible. Count 2. Return to starting position.

4. Knee Push-up

Starting Position: Lie on floor, face down, legs together, knees bent with feet raised off floor, hands on floor under shoulders, palms down.

Action: Count 1. Push upper body off floor until arms are fully extended and body is in straight line from head to knees. Count 2. Return to starting position.

5. Sit-up (Fingers Laced)

Starting Position: Lie on back, legs straight and feet spread approximately 1 foot apart, fingers laced behind neck.

Action: Count 1. Curl up to sitting position and turn trunk to left. Touch right elbow to left knee. Count 2. Return to starting position. Count 3. Curl up to sitting position and turn trunk to right. Touch left elbow to right knee. Count 4. Return to starting position. Score one sit-up each time you return to starting position. Knees may be bent as necessary.

6. Leg Raiser

Starting Position: Right side of body on floor, head resting on right arm.

Action: Lift left leg about 24 inches off floor, then lower it. Do required number of repetitions. Repeat on other side.

7. Flutter Kick

Starting Position: Lie face down, hands tucked under thighs.

Action: Arch the back, bringing chest and head up, then flutter kick continuously, moving the legs 8 to 10 inches apart. Kick from hips with knees slightly bent. Count each kick as one.

Circulatory Activities

JOG-WALK—Jog and walk alternately for number of paces indicated on chart for distance specified.

ROPE—Skip or jump rope continuously using any form for 30 seconds, then rest 60 seconds. Repeat three times.

RUN IN PLACE—Raise each foot at least 4 inches off floor while jogging in place. Count 1 each time left foot touches floor. Complete the number of running steps called for in chart, then do specified number of straddle hops. Complete two cycles of alternate running and hopping for time specified on chart.

STRADDLE HOP—*Starting position:* At attention. *Action:* Count 1. Swing arms sideward and upward, touching hands above head (arms straight) while simultaneously moving feet sideward and apart in a single jumping motion. Count 2. Spring back to starting position. Two counts in one hop.

Women: Level Three	Goal
Warm-up Exercises	Exercises 1–6 of Orientation Program
Conditioning Exercises:	**Uninterrupted Repetitions:**
1. Toe Touch	20
2. Sprinter	16
3. Sitting Stretch (fingers laced)	15
4. Knee Push-up	20
5. Sit-up (arms extended, knees up)	15
6. Leg Raiser	16 each leg
7. Flutter Kick	40
Circulatory Activity (choose one for each workout): Jog–walk (jog 50, walk 50)	½ mile
Rope (skip 45 sec.; rest 30 sec.)	3 series
Run in place (run 110, hop 20–2 cycles)	4 minutes
Water Activities (see pages 291–292):	
Your progress record: 1 2 3 4 5 6 7 8 9 10 11 12 13 14 15	
Step test (pulse):	Prove-out workouts

1. Toe Touch

Starting Position: Stand at attention.

Action: Count 1. Bend trunk forward and down, keeping knees straight, touching fingers to ankles. Count 2. Bounce and touch fingers to top of feet. Count 3. Bounce and touch fingers to toes. Count 4. Return to starting position.

2. Sprinter

Starting Position: Squat, hands on floor, fingers pointed forward, left leg fully extended to rear.

Action: Count 1. Reverse position of feet in bouncing movement, bringing left foot to hands, extending right leg backward, all in one motion. Count 2. Reverse feet again, returning to starting position.

3. Sitting Stretch (Fingers Laced)

Starting Position: Sit, legs spread apart, fingers laced behind neck.

Action: Count 1. Bend forward at waist, reaching elbows as close to floor as possible. Count 2. Return to starting position.

4. Knee Push-up

Starting Position: Lie on floor, face down, legs together, knees bent with feet raised off floor, hands on floor under shoulders, palms down.

Action: Count 1. Push upper body off floor until arms are fully flexed and body is in a straight line from head to knees. Count 2. Return to starting position.

5. Sit-up (Arms Extended, Knees Up)

Starting Position: Lie on back, legs straight, arms extended overhead.

Action: Count 1. Sit up, reaching forward with arms encircling knees while pulling them tightly to chest. Count 2. Return to starting position. Do this exercise rhythmically, without breaks in the movement.

6. Leg Raiser

Starting Position: Right side of body on floor, head resting on right arm.

Action: Lift left leg about 24 inches off floor, then lower it. Do required number of repetitions. Repeat on other side.

7. Flutter Kick

Starting Position: Lie face down, hands tucked under thighs.

Action: Arch the back, bringing chest and head up. Then flutter kick continuously, moving the legs 8 to 10 inches apart. Kick from hips with knees slightly bent. Count each kick as 1.

Circulatory Activities

JOG-WALK—Jog and walk alternately for the number of paces indicated on the chart for distance specified.

ROPE—Skip or jump rope continuously using any form for 45 seconds, then rest 30 seconds. Repeat three times.

RUN IN PLACE—Raise each foot at least 4 inches off floor while jogging in place. Count 1 each time left foot touches floor. Complete number of running steps called for in chart, then do specified number of straddle hops. Complete two cycles of alternate running and hopping for time specified on chart.

STRADDLE HOP—*Starting position:* At attention.

Action: Count 1. Swing arms sideward and upward, touching hands above head (arms straight) while simultaneously moving feet sideward and apart in a single jumping motion. Count 2. Spring back to starting position. Two counts in one hop.

Women: Level Four	Goal
Warm-up Exercises	Exercises 1–6 of Orientation Program
Conditioning Exercises:	**Uninterrupted Repetitions:**
1. Toe Touch (twist and bend)	15 each side
2. Sprinter	20
3. Sitting Stretch (alternate)	20
4. Push-up	8
5. Sit-up (arms crossed, knees bent)	20
6. Leg Raiser (whip)	10 each leg
7. Prone Arch (arms extended)	15
Circulatory Activity (choose one for each workout):	
Jog-walk (jog 100, walk 50)	1 mile
Rope (skip 60 sec.; rest 30 sec.)	3 series
Run in place (run 145, hop 25—2 cycles)	5 minutes
Water Activities (see pages 291–292):	
Your progress record: 1 2 3 4 5 6 7 8 9 10 11 12 13 14 15	
Step test (pulse):	Prove-out workouts

1. Toe Touch (Twist and Bend)

Starting Position: Stand, feet shoulder-width apart, arms extended over head, thumbs interlocked.

Action: Count 1. Twist trunk to right and touch floor inside right foot with fingers of both hands. Count 2. Touch floor outside toes of right foot. Count 3. Touch floor outside heel of right foot. Count 4. Return to starting position, sweeping trunk and arms upward in a wide arc. On the next four counts, repeat action to left side.

2. Sprinter

Starting Position: Squat, hands on floor, fingers pointed forward, left leg fully extended to rear.

Action: Count 1. Reverse position of feet in bouncing movement, bringing left foot to hands, extending right leg backward—all in one motion. Count 2. Reverse feet again, returning to starting position.

3. Sitting Stretch (Alternate)

Starting Position: Sit, legs spread apart, fingers laced behind neck, elbows back.

Action: Count 1. Bend forward to left, touching forehead to left knee. Count 2. Return to starting position. Counts 3 and 4. Repeat to right. Score one repetition each time you return to starting position. Knees may be bent if necessary.

4. Push-up

Starting Position: Lie on floor, face down, legs together, hands on floor under shoulders with fingers pointing straight ahead.

Action: Count 1. Push body off floor by extending arms so that weight rests on hands and toes. Count 2. Lower the body until chest touches floor.

Note: Body should be kept straight, buttocks should not be raised; abdomen should not sag.

5. Sit-up (Arms Crossed, Knees Bent)

Starting Position: Lie on back, arms crossed on chest, hands grasping opposite shoulders, knees bent to right angle, feet flat on floor.

Action: Count 1. Curl up to sitting position. Count 2. Return to starting position.

6. Leg Raiser (Whip)

Starting Position: Right side of body on floor, right arm supporting head.

Action: Whip left leg up and down rapidly lifting as high as possible off the floor. Count each whip as 1. Reverse position and whip right leg up and down.

7. Prone Arch (Arms Extended)

Starting Position: Lie face down, legs straight and together, arms extended to sides at shoulder level.

Action: Count 1. Arch the back, bringing arms, chest, and head up, and raising legs as high as possible. Count 2. Return to starting position.

Circulatory Activities

JOG-WALK—Jog and walk alternately for number of paces indicated on the chart for the distance specified.

ROPE—Skip or jump rope continuously using any form for 60 seconds, then rest 30 seconds. Repeat three times.

RUN IN PLACE—Raise each foot at least 4 inches off floor while jogging in place. Count 1 each time left foot touches floor. Complete number of running steps called for in chart, then do specified number of straddle hops. Complete two cycles of alternate running and hopping for time specified on chart.

STRADDLE HOP—*Starting position:* At attention. *Action:* Count 1. Swing arms sideward and upward, touching hands above head (arms straight), while simultaneously moving feet sideward and apart in a single jumping motion. Count 2. Spring back to starting position. Two counts in one hop.

Women: Level Five	Goal
Warm-up Exercises	Exercises 1–6 of Orientation Program
Conditioning Exercises:	**Uninterrupted Repetitions:**
1. Toe Touch (twist and bend)	25 each side
2. Sprinter	24
3. Sitting Stretch (alternate)	26
4. Push-up	15
5. Sit-up (fingers laced, knees bent)	25
6. Leg Raiser (on extended arm)	10 each side
7. Prone Arch (fingers laced)	25
Circulatory Activity (choose one for each workout):	
Jog-run	1 mile
Rope (skip 2 mins.; rest 45 sec.)	2 series
Run in place (run 180, hop 30—2 cycles)	6 minutes
Water Activities (see pages 291–292):	
Your progress record: 1 2 3 4 5 6 7 8 9 10 11 12 13 14 15	
Step test (pulse):	Prove-out workouts

1. Toe Touch (Twist and Bend)

Starting Position: Stand, feet shoulder-width apart, arms extended over head, thumbs interlocked.

Action: Count 1. Twist trunk to right and touch floor inside right foot with fingers of both hands. Count 2. Touch floor outside toes of right foot. Count 3. Touch floor outside heel of right foot. Count 4. Return to starting position, sweeping trunk and arms upward in a wide arc. On the next four counts, repeat action to left side.

2. Sprinter

Starting Position: Squat, hands on floor, fingers pointed forward, left leg fully extended to rear.

Action: Count 1. Reverse position of feet in bouncing movement, bringing left foot to hands, extending right leg backward—all in one motion. Count 2. Reverse feet again, returning to starting position.

3. Sitting Stretch (Alternate)

Starting Position: Sit, legs spread apart, fingers behind neck, elbows back.

Action: Count 1. Bend forward to left, touching forehead to left knee. Count 2. Return to starting position. Counts 3 and 4. Repeat to right. Score 1 each time you return to starting position. Knees may be bent if necessary.

4. Push-up

Starting Position: Lie on floor, face down, legs together, hands on floor under shoulders with fingers pointing straight ahead.

Action: Count 1. Push body off floor by extending arms so that weight rests on hands and toes. Count 2. Lower the body until chest touches floor. Note: Body should be kept straight, buttocks should not be raised, abdomen should not sag.

5. Sit-up (Fingers Laced, Knees Bent)

Starting Position: Lie on back, fingers laced behind neck, knees bent, feet flat on floor.

Action: Count 1. Sit up, turn trunk to right, touch left elbow to right knee. Count 2. Return to starting position. Count 3. Sit up, turn trunk to left, touch right elbow to left knee. Count 4. Return to starting position. Score 1 each time you return to starting position.

6. Leg Raiser (On Extended Arm)

Starting Position: Lie on back, body rigidly supported by extended right arm and foot. Left arm is held behind head.

Action: Count 1. Raise left leg high. Count 2. Return to starting position slowly. Repeat on other side. Do required number of repetitions.

7. Prone Arch (Fingers Laced)

Starting Position: Lie face down, fingers laced behind neck.

Action: Count 1. Arch the back, legs and chest off floor. Count 2. Extend arms fully forward. Count 3. Return hands to behind neck. Count 4. Flatten body to floor.

Circulatory Activities

JOG-RUN—Jog and run alternately for distance specified on chart.

ROPE—Skip or jump rope continuously using any form for 2 minutes, then rest 45 seconds. Repeat two times.

RUN IN PLACE—Raise each foot at least 4 inches off floor while jogging in place. Count 1 each time left foot touches floor. Complete number of running steps called for in chart, then do specified number of straddle hops. Complete two cycles of alternate running and hopping in the time specified on the chart.

STRADDLE HOP—*Starting position:* At attention. *Action:* Count 1. Swing arms sideward and upward, touching hands above head (arms straight) while simultaneously moving feet sideward and apart in a single jumping motion. Count 2. Spring back to starting position. Two counts in one hop.

PROGRAM FOR MEN

The program assumes you have not—recently and consistently—been exposed to vigorous, all-around physical activity. This could be true even if you play golf once or twice a week or engage in some other sport; no one sport provides for balanced development of all parts of the body.

The plan starts with an orientation—"get-set"—series of mild exercises to limber up all major muscle groups and help assure a painless transition. There are then five graded levels.

As you move up from one level to the next, you will be building toward a practical and satisfactory level of fitness. By building gradually—progressively—you will be building soundly.

There are three general types: warm-up exercises, conditioning exercises, and circulatory activities.

The *warm-up exercises* stretch and limber up the muscles and speed up the action of the heart and lungs, thus preparing the body for greater exertion and reducing the possibility of unnecessary strain.

The *conditioning exercises* are systematically planned to tone up abdominal, back, leg, arm, and other major muscles.

The *circulatory activities* produce contractions of large muscle groups for relatively longer periods than the conditioning exercises, to stimulate and strengthen the circulatory and respiratory systems.

The plan calls for doing ten mild exercises during the orientation period and, thereafter, the warm-up exercises and the seven conditioning exercises listed for each level. The first six exercises of the orientation program are used as warm-up exercises throughout the graded levels.

When it comes to the circulatory activities, you select one for each workout. Alternately running and walking, skipping rope, and running in place are all effective. You can rotate these activities for variety.

How You Progress

Right now, you have limited tolerance for exercise; you can do just so much without discomfort and fatigue.

A sound conditioning program should gradually stretch your tolerance. It should give unused or little-used muscles moderate tasks at first, then make the tasks increasingly demanding so you become able to achieve more and more with less and less fatigue and with increasingly rapid recovery.

As you move from level to level, some exercises will be modified so they call for more effort. Others will remain the same, but you will build strength and stamina by increasing the number of repetitions.

At level one, your objective will be to gradually reduce, from workout to workout, the "breathing spells" between exercises until you can do the seven conditioning exercises without resting. You will proceed in the same fashion with the more difficult exercises and increased repetitions at succeeding levels.

You will find the program designed—the progression carefully planned—to make this feasible. You will be able to proceed at your own pace, competing with yourself rather than with anyone else—and this is of great importance for sound conditioning.

Note: Gradually speeding up, from workout to workout, the rate at which you do each exercise will provide greater stimulation for the circulatory and respiratory systems and also help to keep your workouts short. However, the seven conditioning exercises should not be a race against time. Perform each exercise completely to insure maximum benefit.

When And How Often To Work Out

To be most beneficial, exercise should become part of your regular daily routine—as much as bathing, shaving, and dressing. Five workouts a week are called for throughout the program.

You can choose any time that is convenient. Preferably, it should be the same time every day—but it does not matter whether it's first thing in the morning, before dinner in the evening, just before going to bed, or any other time.

The hour just before the evening meal is a popular time for exercise. The later afternoon workout provides a welcome change of pace at the end of the work day and helps dissolve the day's worries and tensions. Another popular time to work out is early morning, before the work day begins. Advocates of the early start say it makes them more alert and energetic on the job.

Among the factors you should consider in developing your workout schedule are personal preference, job and family responsibilities, availability of exercise facilities, and weather. It's important to schedule your workouts for a time when there is little chance that you will have to cancel or interrupt them because of other demands on your time.

You should not exercise strenuously during extremely hot, humid weather or within two hours after eating. Heat and digestion both make heavy demands on the circulatory system, and in combination with exercise can be an overtaxing double load.

Your Progress Records

Charts are provided for the orientation program and for each of the five levels. They list the exercises to be done and the goal for each exercise in terms of number of repetitions, distance, etc. They also provide space in which to record your progress: (1) in completing the recommended fifteen workouts at each level, (2) in accomplishing the three prove-out workouts before moving on to a succeeding level, and (3) in the results as you take the step test from time to time. A sample chart and progress record for one of the five levels is shown below.

You do the warm-up exercises and the conditioning exercises along with one circulatory activity for each workout.

Check off each workout as you complete it. The last three numbers are for the prove-out workouts, in which the seven conditioning exercises should be done without resting. Check them off as you accomplish them.

You are now ready to proceed to the next level.

As you take the step test—at about two-week intervals—enter your pulse rate. When you move on to the next level, transfer the last pulse rate from the preceding level. Enter it in the margin to the left of the new progress record and circle it so it will be convenient for continuing reference.

Sample	Goal
Warm-up Exercises	Exercises 1–6 of Orientation Program
Conditioning Exercises:	**Uninterrupted Repetitions:**
1. Toe Touch	20
2. Sprinter	16
3. Sitting Stretch	18
4. Push-up	10
5. Sit-up (fingers laced)	15
6. Leg Raiser	16 each leg
7. Flutter Kick	40
Circulatory Activity (choose one for each workout):	
Jog-walk (jog 100, walk 100)	1 mile
Rope (skip 60 sec.; rest 60 sec.)	3 series
Run in place (run 95, hop 15—2 cycles)	3 minutes
Water Activities (see pages 291–292)	
Your progress record: 1 2 3 4 5 6 7 8 9 10 11 12 13 14 15	
Step test (pulse):	Prove-out workouts

Getting Set—Orientation Workouts

With the series of preliminary exercises listed in the chart that follows and described on the next pages, you can get yourself ready—without severe aches or pains—for the progressive conditioning program.

Even if these preliminary exercises seem easy—and they are meant to be mild—plan to spend a minimum of one week with them. Do not hesitate to spend two weeks, or even three if necessary, for you to limber up enough to accomplish all the exercises easily and without undue fatigue.

Men: Orientation Program	Goal
Conditioning Exercises:	**Repetitions:**
*1. Bend and Stretch	10
*2. Knee Lift	10 left, 10 right
*3. Wing Stretcher	20
*4. Half Knee Bend	10
*5. Arm Circles	15 each way
*6. Body Bender	10 left, 10 right
7. Prone Arch	10
8. Knee Push-up	6
9. Head and Shoulder Curl	5
10. Ankle Stretch	15
Circulatory Activity (choose one for each workout):	
Walking	½ mile
Rope (skip 15 sec.; rest 60 sec.)	3 series

* The first six exercises of the orientation program will be used as warm-up exercises throughout the graded levels.

Step Test Record—After completing the orientation program, take the 2-minute step test. Record your pulse rate here: _____. This will be the base rate with which you can make comparisons in the future.

1. Bend and Stretch

Starting Position: Stand erect, feet shoulder-width apart.

Action: Count 1. Bend trunk forward and down, flexing knees. Stretch gently in attempt to touch fingers to toes or floor. Count 2. Return to starting position. Note: Do slowly; stretch and relax at intervals rather than in rhythm.

2. Knee Lift

Starting Position: Stand erect, feet together, arms at sides.

Action: Count 1. Raise left knee as high as possible, grasping leg with hands and pulling knee against body while keeping back straight. Count 2. Lower to starting position. Counts 3 and 4. Repeat with right knee.

3. Wing Stretcher

Starting Position: Stand erect, elbows at shoulder height, fists clenched in front of chest.

Action: Count 1. Thrust elbows backward vigorously without arching back. Keep head erect, elbows at shoulder height. Count 2. Return to starting position.

4. Half Knee Bend

Starting Position: Stand erect, hands on hips.

Action: Count 1. Bend knees halfway while extending arms forward, palms down. Count 2. Return to starting position.

5. Arm Circles

Starting Position: Stand erect, arms extended sideward at shoulder height, palms up.

Action: Describe small circles backward with hands. Keep head erect. Do 15 backward circles. Reverse, turn palms down, and do 15 small circles forward.

6. Body Bender

Starting Position: Stand, feet shoulder-width apart, hands behind neck, fingers interlaced.

Action: Count 1. Bend trunk sideward to left as far as possible, keeping hands behind neck. Count 2. Return to starting position. Counts 3 and 4. Repeat to the right.

7. Prone Arch

Starting Position: Lie face down, hands tucked under thighs.

Action: Count 1. Raise head, shoulders, and legs from floor. Count 2. Return to starting position.

8. Knee Push-up

Starting Position: Lie on floor, face down, legs together, knees bent with feet raised off floor, hands on floor under shoulders, palms down.

Action: Count 1. Push upper body off floor until arms are fully extended and body is in straight line from head to knees. Count 2. Return to starting position.

9. Head and Shoulder Curl

Starting Position: Lie on back, hands tucked under small of back, palms down.

Action: Count 1. Tighten abdominal muscles, lift head, and pull shoulders and elbows up off floor. Hold for four seconds. Count 2. Return to starting position.

10. Ankle Stretch

Starting Position: Stand on a stair, large book, or block of wood, with weight on balls of feet and heels raised.

Action: Count 1. Lower heels. Count 2. Raise heels.

Circulatory Activities

WALKING—Step off at a lively pace, swing arms, and breathe deeply.

ROPE—Any form of skipping or jumping is acceptable. Gradually increase the tempo as your skill and condition improve.

Men: Level One	Goal
Warm-up Exercises	Exercises 1–6 of Orientation Program
Conditioning Exercises:	**Uninterrupted Repetitions:**
1. Toe Touch	10
2. Sprinter	12
3. Sitting Stretch	12
4. Push-up	4
5. Sit-up (arms extended)	5
6. Leg Raiser	12 each leg
7. Flutter Kick	30
Circulatory Activity (choose one for each workout):	
Walking (120 steps a minute)	1 mile
Rope (skip 30 sec.; rest 30 sec.)	2 series
Run in place (run 60, hop 10–2 cycles)	2 minutes
Water Activities (see pages 291–292)	
Your progress record: 1 2 3 4 5 6 7 8 9 10 11 12 13 14 15	
Step test (pulse):	Prove-out workouts

1. Toe Touch

Starting Position: Stand at attention.

Action: Count 1. Bend trunk forward and down keeping knees straight, touching fingers to ankles. Count 2. Bounce and touch fingers to top of feet. Count 3. Bounce and touch fingers to toes. Count 4. Return to starting position.

2. Sprinter

Starting Position: Squat, hands on floor, fingers pointed forward, left leg fully extended to rear.

Action: Count 1. Reverse position of feet in bouncing movement, bringing left foot to hands and extending right leg backward—all in one motion. Count 2. Reverse feet again, returning to starting position.

3. Sitting Stretch

Starting Position: Sit, legs spread apart, hands on knees.

Action: Count 1. Bend forward at waist, extending arms as far forward as possible. Count 2. Return to starting position.

4. Push-up

Starting Position: Lie on floor, face down, legs together, hands on floor under shoulders with fingers pointing straight ahead.

Action: Count 1. Push body off floor by extending arms, so that weight rests on hands and toes. Count 2. Lower the body until chest touches floor. Note: Body should be kept straight; buttocks should not be raised; abdomen should not sag.

5. Sit-up (Arms Extended)

Starting Position: Lie on back, legs straight and together, arms extended beyond head.

Action: Count 1. Bring arms forward over head; roll up to sitting position, sliding hands along legs, grasping ankles. Count 2. Roll back to starting position.

6. Leg Raiser

Starting Position: Right side of body on floor, head resting on right arm.

Action: Lift left leg about 24 inches off floor, then lower it. Do required number of repetitions. Repeat on other side.

7. Flutter Kick

Starting Position: Lie face down, hands tucked under thighs.

Action: Arch the back, bringing chest and head up, then flutter kick continuously, moving the legs 8 to 10 inches apart. Kick from hips with knees slightly bent. Count each kick as 1.

Circulatory Activities

WALKING—Maintain a pace of 120 steps per minute for a distance of 1 mile. Swing arms and breathe deeply.

ROPE—Skip or jump rope continuously using any form for 30 seconds, then rest 30 seconds. Repeat two times.

RUN IN PLACE—Raise each foot at least 4 inches off floor and while jogging in place. Count 1 each time left foot touches floor. Complete the number of running steps called for in chart, then do specified number of straddle hops. Complete two cycles of alternate running and hopping for time specified on chart.

STRADDLE HOP—*Starting position:* At attention. *Action:* Count 1. Swing arms sideward and upward, touching hands above head (arms straight) while simultaneously moving feet sideward and apart in a single jumping motion. Count 2. Spring back to starting position. Two counts in one hop.

Men: Level Two	Goal
Warm-up Exercises	Exercises 1–6 of Orientation Program
Conditioning Exercises:	**Uninterrupted Repetitions:**
1. Toe Touch	20
2. Sprinter	16
3. Sitting Stretch	18
4. Push-up	10
5. Sit-up (fingers laced)	20
6. Leg Raiser	16 each leg
7. Flutter Kick	40
Circulatory Activity (choose one for each workout):	
Jog-walk (jog 100; walk 100)	1 mile
Rope (skip 1 min.; rest 1 min.)	3 series
Run in place (run 95, hop 15—2 cycles)	3 minutes
Water Activities (see pages 291–292)	
Your progress record: 1 2 3 4 5 6 7 8 9 10 11 12 13 14 15	
Step test (pulse):	Prove-out workouts

1. Toe Touch

Starting Position: Stand at attention.

Action: Count 1. Bend trunk forward and down keeping knees straight, touching fingers to ankles. Count 2. Bounce and touch fingers to top of feet. Count 3. Bounce and touch fingers to toes. Count 4. Return to starting position.

2. Sprinter

Starting Position: Squat, hands on floor, fingers pointed forward, left leg fully extended to rear.

Action: Count 1. Reverse position of feet in bouncing movement, bringing left foot to hands, extending right leg backward—all in one motion. Count 2. Reverse feet again, returning to starting position.

3. Sitting Stretch

Starting Position: Sit, legs apart, hands on knees.

Action: Count 1. Bend forward at waist, extending arms as far forward as possible. Count 2. Return to starting position.

4. Push-up

Starting Position: Lie on floor, face down, legs together, hands on floor under shoulders with fingers pointing straight ahead.

Action: Count 1. Push body off floor by extending arms, so that weight rests on hands and toes. Count 2. Lower the body until chest touches floor. Note: Body should be kept straight; buttocks should not be raised; abdomen should not sag.

5. Sit-up (Fingers Laced)

Starting Position: Lie on back, legs straight and feet spread approximately 1 foot apart, fingers laced behind neck.

Action: Count 1. Curl up to sitting position and turn trunk to left. Touch the right elbow to left knee. Count 2. Return to starting position. Count 3. Curl up to sitting position and turn trunk to right. Touch left elbow to right knee. Count 4. Return to starting position. Score one sit-up each time you return to starting position. Knees may be bent as necessary.

6. Leg Raiser

Starting Position: Right side of body on floor, head resting on right arm.

Action: Lift left leg about 24 inches off floor, then lower it. Do required number of repetitions. Repeat on other side.

7. Flutter Kick

Starting Position: Lie face down, hands tucked under thighs.

Action: Arch the back, bringing chest and head up, then flutter kick continuously, moving the legs 8 to 10 inches apart. Kick from hips with knees slightly bent. Count each kick as 1.

Circulatory Activities

JOG-WALK—Jog and walk alternately for number of paces indicated on chart for distance specified.

ROPE—Skip or jump rope continuously using any form for 60 seconds, then rest 60 seconds. Repeat five times.

RUN IN PLACE—Raise each foot at least 4 inches off floor while jogging in place. Count 1 each time left foot touches floor. Complete number of running steps called for in chart, then do specified number of straddle hops. Complete two cycles of alternate running and hopping for time specified on chart.

STRADDLE HOP—*Starting position:* At attention. *Action:* Count 1. Swing arms sideward and upward, touching hands above head (arms straight), while simultaneously moving feet sideward and apart in a single jumping motion. Count 2. Spring back to starting position. Two counts in one hop.

Men: Level Three	Goal
Warm-up Exercises	Exercises 1–6 of Orientation Program
Conditioning Exercises:	**Uninterrupted Repetitions:**
1. Toe Touch	30
2. Sprinter	20
3. Sitting Stretch (fingers laced)	18
4. Push-up	20
5. Sit-up (arms extended, knees up)	30
6. Leg Raiser	20 each leg
7. Flutter Kick	50
Circulatory Activity (choose one for each workout):	
Jog-walk (jog 200; walk 100)	½ mile
Rope (skip 1 min.; rest 1 min.)	5 series
Run in place (run 135, hop 20—2 cycles)	4 minutes
Water Activities (see pages 291–292)	
Your progress record: 1 2 3 4 5 6 7 8 9 10 11 12 13 14 15	
Step test (pulse):	Prove-out workouts

1. Toe Touch

Starting Position: Stand at attention.

Action: Count 1. Bend trunk forward and down keeping knees straight, touching fingers to ankles. Count 2. Bounce and touch fingers to top of feet. Count 3. Bounce and touch fingers to toes. Count 4. Return to starting position.

2. Sprinter

Starting Position: Squat, hands on floor, fingers pointed forward, left leg fully extended to rear.

Action: Count 1. Reverse position of feet in bouncing movement, bringing left foot to hands, extending right leg backward—all in one motion. Count 2. Reverse feet again, returning to starting position.

3. Sitting Stretch (Fingers Laced)

Starting Position: Sit, legs spread apart, fingers laced behind neck, elbows back.

Action: Count 1. Bend forward at waist, reaching elbows as close to floor as possible. Count 2. Return to starting position.

4. Push-up

Starting Position: Lie on floor, face down, legs together, hands on floor under shoulders with fingers pointing straight ahead.

Action: Count 1. Push body off floor by extending arms so that weight rests on hands and toes. Count 2. Lower the body until chest touches floor. Note: Body should be kept straight; buttocks should not be raised; abdomen should not sag.

5. Sit-up (Arms Extended, Knees Up)

Starting Position: Lie on back, legs straight, arms extended overhead.

Action: Count 1. Sit up, reaching forward with arms encircling knees while pulling them tightly to chest. Count 2. Return to starting position. Do this exercise rhythmically, without breaks in the movement.

6. Leg Raiser

Starting Position: Right side of body on floor, head resting on right arm.

Action: Lift left leg about 24 inches off floor, then lower it. Do required number of repetitions. Repeat on other side.

7. Flutter Kick

Starting Position: Lie face down, hands tucked under thighs.

Action: Arch the back, bringing chest and head up, then flutter kick continuously, moving the legs 8 to 10 inches apart. Kick from hips with knees slightly bent. Count each kick as one.

Circulatory Activities

JOG-WALK—Jog and walk alternately for number of paces indicated on chart for distance specified.

ROPE—Skip or jump rope continuously using any form for 60 seconds, then rest 60 seconds. Repeat five times.

RUN IN PLACE—Raise each foot at least 4 inches off floor while jogging in place. Count 1 each time left foot touches floor. Complete number of running steps called for in chart, then do specified number of straddle hops. Complete two cycles of alternate running and hopping for time specified on chart.

STRADDLE HOP—*Starting position:* At attention. *Action:* Count 1. Swing arms sideward and upward, touching hands above head (arms straight) while simultaneously moving feet sideward and apart in a single jumping motion. Count 2. Spring back to starting position. Two counts in one hop.

Men: Level Four	Goal
Warm-up Exercises	Exercises 1–6 of Orientation Program
Conditioning Exercises:	**Uninterrupted Repetitions:**
1. Toe Touch (twist and bend)	20 each side
2. Sprinter	28
3. Sitting Stretch (alternate)	24
4. Push-up	30
5. Sit-up (arms crossed, knees bent)	30
6 Leg Raiser (whip)	20 each leg
7. Prone Arch (arms extended)	20
Circulatory Activity (choose one for each workout):	
Jog	1 mile
Rope (skip 90 sec.; rest 30 sec.)	3 series
Run in place (run 180, hop 25—2 cycles)	5 minutes
Water Activities (see pages 291–292)	
Your progress record: 1 2 3 4 5 6 7 8 9 10 11 12 13 14 15	
Step test (pulse):	Prove-out workouts

1. Toe Touch (Twist and Bend)

Starting Position: Stand, feet shoulder-width apart, arms extended overhead, thumbs interlocked.

Action: Count 1. Twist trunk to right and touch floor inside right foot with fingers of both hands. Count 2. Touch floor outside toes of right foot. Count 3. Touch floor outside heel of right foot. Count 4. Return to starting position, sweeping trunk and arms upward in a wide arc. On the next four counts, repeat action to left side.

2. Sprinter

Starting Position: Squat, hands on floor, fingers pointed forward, left leg fully extended to rear.

Action: Count 1. Reverse position of feet in bouncing movement, bringing left foot to hands, extending right leg backward—all in one motion. Count 2. Reverse feet again, returning to starting position.

3. Sitting Stretch (Alternate)

Starting Position: Sit, legs spread apart, fingers laced behind neck, elbows back.

Action: Count 1. Bend forward to left, touching forehead to left knee. Count 2. Return to starting position. Counts 3 and 4. Repeat to right. Score 1 each time you return to starting position. Knees may be bent if necessary.

4. Push-up

Starting Position: Lie on floor, face down, legs together, hands on floor under shoulders with fingers pointing straight ahead.

Action: Count 1. Push body off floor by extending arms, so that weight rests on hands and toes. Count 2. Lower the body until chest touches floor. Note: Body should be kept straight; buttocks should not be raised; abdomen should not sag.

5. Sit-up (Arms Crossed, Knees Bent)

Starting Position: Lie on back, arms crossed on chest, hands grasping opposite shoulders, knees bent to right angle, feel flat on floor.

Action: Count 1. Curl up to sitting position. Count 2. Return to starting position.

6. Leg Raiser (Whip)

Starting Position: Right side of body on floor, right arm supporting head.

Action: Whip left leg up and down rapidly, lifting as high as possible off the floor. Count each whip as 1. Reverse position and whip right leg up and down.

7. Prone Arch (Arms Extended)

Starting Position: Lie face down, legs straight and together, arms extended to sides at shoulder level.

Action: Count 1. Arch the back, bringing arms, chest, and head up, and raising legs as high as possible. Count 2. Return to starting position.

Circulatory Activities

JOG—Jog continuously for 1 mile.

ROPE—Skip or jump rope continuously using any form for 90 seconds, then rest for 30 seconds. Repeat three times.

RUN IN PLACE—Raise each foot at least 4 inches off the floor while jogging in place. Count 1 each time left foot touches floor. Complete number of running steps called for in chart, then do specified number of straddle hops. Complete two cycles of alternate running and hopping in time specified on chart.

STRADDLE HOP—*Starting position:* At attention. *Action:* Count 1. Swing arms sideward and upward, touching hands above head (arms straight) while simultaneously moving feet sideward and apart in a single jumping motion. Count 2. Spring back to starting position. Two counts in one hop.

Men: Level Five	Goal
Warm–up Exercises	Exercises 1–6 of Orientation Program
Conditioning Exercises:	**Uninterrupted Repetitions:**
1. Toe Touch (twist and bend)	30 each side
2. Sprinter	36
3. Sitting Stretch (alternate)	30
4. Push-up	50
5. Sit-up (fingers laced, knees bent)	40
6. Leg Raiser (on extended arm)	20 each side
7. Prone Arch (fingers laced)	30
Circulatory Activity (choose one for each workout):	
Jog-run	3 mile
Rope (skip 2 mins.; rest 30 sec.)	3 series
Run in place (run 216, hop 30–2 cycles)	6 minutes
Water Activities (see pages 291–292)	
Your progress record: 1 2 3 4 5 6 7 8 9 10 11 12 13 14 15	
Step test (pulse):	Prove-out workouts

1. Toe Touch (Twist and Bend)

Starting Position: Stand, feet shoulder-width apart, arms extended overhead, thumbs interlocked.

Action: Count 1. Twist trunk to right and touch floor inside right foot with fingers of both hands. Count 2. Touch floor outside toes of right foot. Count 3. Touch floor outside heel of right foot. Count 4. Return to starting position, sweeping trunk and arms upward in a wide arc. On the next four counts, repeat action to left side.

2. Sprinter

Starting Position: Squat, hands on floor, fingers pointed forward, left leg fully extended to rear.

Action: Count 1. Reverse position of feet in bouncing movement, bringing left foot to hands and extending right leg backward—all in one motion. Count 2. Reverse feet again, returning to starting position.

3. Sitting Stretch (Alternate)

Starting Position: Sit, legs spread apart, fingers laced behind neck, elbows back.

Action: Count 1. Bend forward to left, touching forehead to left knee. Count 2. Return to starting position. Counts 3 and 4. Repeat to right. Score 1 each time you return to starting position. Knees may be bent if necessary.

4. Push-up

Starting Position: Lie on floor, face down, legs together, hands on floor under shoulders with fingers pointing straight ahead.

Action: Count 1. Push body off floor by extending arms so that weight rests on hands and toes. Count 2. Lower body until chest touches floor. Note: Body should be kept straight; buttocks should not be raised; abdomen should not sag.

5. Sit-up (Fingers Laced, Knees Bent)

Starting Position: Lie on back, fingers laced behind neck, knees bent, feet flat on floor.

Action: Count 1. Sit up, turn trunk to right, touch left elbow to right knee. Count 2. Return to starting position. Count 3. Sit up, turn trunk to left, touch right elbow to left knee. Count 4. Return to starting position. Score 1 each time you return to starting position.

6. Leg Raiser (on Extended Arm)

Starting Position: Body rigidly supported by extended right arm and foot. Left arm is held behind head.

Action: Count 1. Raise left leg high. Count 2. Return to starting position slowly. Do required number of repetitions. Repeat on other side.

7. Prone Arch (Fingers Laced)

Starting Position: Lie face down, fingers laced behind neck.

Action: Count 1. Arch back, legs, and chest off floor. Count 2. Extend arms forward. Count 3. Return hands to behind neck. Count 4. Flatten body to floor.

Circulatory Activities

JOG RUN—Alternately jog and run the specified distance. Attempt to increase the proportion of time spent running in each succeeding workout.

ROPE—Skip or jump rope continuously using any form for 2 minutes, then rest 30 seconds. Repeat three times.

RUN IN PLACE—Raise each foot at least 4 inches off floor while jogging in place. Count 1 each time left foot touches floor. Complete number of running steps called for in chart, then do specified number of straddle hops. Complete two cycles of alternate running and hopping for time specified on the chart.

STRADDLE HOP—*Starting position:* At attention. *Action:* Count 1. Swing arms sideward and upward, touching hands above head (arms straight) while simultaneously moving feet sideward and apart in a single jumping motion. Count 2. Spring back to starting position. Two counts in one hop.

STAYING FIT

Once you have reached the level of conditioning you have chosen for yourself, you will wish to maintain your fitness. To do so, continue the workouts at that level.

While it has been found possible to maintain fitness with three workouts a week, ideally, exercise should be a daily habit. If you can, by all means continue your workouts on a five-times-a-week basis.

If at any point—either after reaching your goal or in the process of doing so—your workouts are interrupted because of illness or other reason for more than a week, it will be best to begin again at a lower level. If you have had a serious illness or surgery, proceed under your physician's guidance.

BROADENING YOUR PROGRAM

The exercises and activities you have engaged in are basic. They are designed to take you soundly and progressively up the ladder to physical fitness without need for special equipment or facilities.

There are many other activities and forms of exercise that, if you wish, you may use to supplement the basic program. They include a variety of water activities you can use if you have access to a pool; isometrics—sometimes called exercises without movement—that take little time (6 to 8 seconds each); and sports.

Isometrics

Isometric contraction exercises take very little time and require no special equipment. They're excellent muscle strengtheners and, as such, valuable supplements.

The idea of isometrics is to work out a muscle by pushing or pulling against an immovable object, such as a wall, or by pitting it against the opposition of another muscle.

The basis is the "overload" principle of exercise physiology, which holds that a muscle required to perform work beyond the usual intensity will grow in strength. Research has indicated that one hard, 6- to 8-second isometric contraction per workout can, over a period of six months, produce a significant strength increase in a muscle.

The exercises described in the following pages cover major large muscle groups of the body. They can be performed almost anywhere and at almost any time.

There is no set order for doing these exercises, nor do all have to be completed at one time. You can, if you like, do one or two in the morning, and the others at various times during the day whenever you have half a minute or even less to spare.

For each contraction, maintain tension no more than 8 seconds. Do little breathing during a contraction; breathe deeply between contractions.

Start easily. Do not apply maximum effort in the beginning. For the first three or four weeks, you should exert only about one half of what you think is your maximum force. Use the first 3 or 4 seconds to build up to this degree of force, and the remaining 4 or 5 seconds to hold it.

For the next two weeks, gradually increase force to more nearly approach maximum. After about six weeks, it will be safe to exert maximum effort.

Pain indicates you're applying too much force; reduce the amount immediately. If pain continues to accompany any exercise, discontinue doing that exercise for a week or two. Then try it again with about 50 percent of maximum effort; if no pain occurs, you can go on to gradually build up toward maximum.

NECK

Starting Position: Sit or stand, with interlaced fingers of hands on forehead.
Action: Forcibly exert a forward push of head while resisting equally hard with hands.

Starting Position: Sit or stand, with interlaced fingers of hands behind head.
Action: Push head backward while exerting a forward pull with hands.

Starting Position: Sit or stand, with palm of left hand on left side of head.
Action: Push with left hand while resisting with head and neck. Reverse using right hand on right side of head.

UPPER BODY

Starting Position: Stand, back to wall, hands at sides, palms toward wall.
Action: Press hands backward against wall, keeping arms straight.

Starting Position: Stand, facing wall, hands at sides, palms toward wall.
Action: Press hands forward against wall, keeping arms straight.

Starting Position: Stand in doorway or with side against wall, arms at sides, palms toward legs.
Action: Press hand(s) outward against wall or doorframe, keeping arms straight.

ARMS

Starting Position: Stand with feet slightly apart. Flex right elbow, close to body, palm up. Place left hand over right.

Action: Forcibly attempt to curl right arm upward, while giving equally strong resistance with the left hand. Repeat with left arm.

ARMS AND CHEST

Starting Position: Stand with feet comfortably spaced, knees slightly bent. Clasp hands, palms together, close to chest.

Action: Press hands together and hold.

Starting Position: Stand with feet slightly apart, knees slightly bent. Grip fingers, arms close to chest.

Action: Pull hard and hold.

ABDOMINAL

Starting Position: Stand, knees slightly flexed, hands resting on knees.

Action: Contract abdominal muscles.

LOWER BACK, BUTTOCKS, AND BACK OF THIGHS

Starting Position: Lie face down, arms at sides, palms up, legs placed under bed or other heavy object.

Action: With both hips flat on floor, raise one leg, keeping knee straight so that heel pushes hard against the resistance above. Repeat with opposite leg.

LEGS

Starting Position: Sit in chair with left ankle crossed over right, feet resting on floor, legs bent at 90-degree angle.

Action: Forcibly attempt to straighten right leg while resisting with the left. Repeat with opposite leg.

INNER AND OUTER THIGHS

Starting Position: Sit, legs extended with each ankle pressed against the outside of sturdy chair legs.

Action: Keep legs straight and pull toward one another firmly. For outer thigh muscles, place ankles inside chair legs and exert pressure outward.

Water Activities

Swimming is one of the best physical activities for people of all ages, including many people with disabilities.

With the body submerged in water, blood circulation automatically increases to some extent. Pressure of water on the body also helps promote deeper ventilation of the lungs; and with well-planned activity, both circulation and ventilation increase still more.

The water exercises described below can be used either as supplements to, or replacements for, the Circulatory Activities of the basic program. The goals for each of the five levels are shown in the chart below.

Women					
Level	**1**	**2**	**3**	**4**	**5**
Bobbing	10	15	20	50	100
Swimming	5 min.	10 min.	15 min.	—	—
Interval swimming	—	—	—	25 yds. (Repeat 10 times)	25 yds. (Repeat 20 times)

Men					
Level	**1**	**2**	**3**	**4**	**5**
Bobbing	10	15	25	75	125
Swimming	5 min.	10 min.	15 min.	—	—
Interval swimming	—	—	—	25 yds. (Repeat 20 times)	50 yds. (Repeat 20 times)

BOBBING

Starting Position: Face out of water.

Action: Count 1. Take a breath. Count 2. Submerge while exhaling until feet touch bottom. Count 3. Push up from the bottom to the surface while continuing to exhale. Three counts to one bob.

SWIMMING

Use any type of stroke. Swim continuously for the time specified.

INTERVAL SWIMMING

Use any type of stroke. Swim moderately fast for distance specified. You can then either swim back slowly to starting point or get out of pool and walk back. Repeat specified number of times.

Weight Training

Weight training also is an excellent method of developing muscular strength and muscular endurance. Where equipment is available, it may be used as a supplement to the seven conditioning exercises.

Because of the great variety of weight-training exercises, there will be no attempt to describe them here. There are numerous gyms and fitness centers in most cities with qualified trainers. A good rule to follow in deciding the maximum weight you should lift is to select a weight you can lift six times without strain.

Sports

Soccer, basketball, handball, squash, ice hockey, and other sports that require sustained effort can be valuable aids to building circulatory endurance. But if you have been sedentary, it's important to pace yourself carefully in such sports, and it may even be advisable to avoid them until you are well along in your physical conditioning program. That doesn't mean you should avoid all sports.

There are many excellent conditioning and circulatory activities in which the amount of exertion is easily controlled and in which you can progress at your own rate. Bicycling is one example. Others include hiking, skating, tennis, running, cross-country skiing, rowing, canoeing, water skiing, and skin diving.

You can engage in these sports at any point in the program, if you start slowly. Games should be played with full speed and vigor only when your conditioning permits doing so without undue fatigue.

On days when you get a good workout in sports, you can skip part or all of your exercise program. Use your own judgment.

If you have engaged in a sport that exercises the legs and stimulates the heart and lungs—such as skating—you could skip the circulatory activity for that day, but you still should do some of the conditioning and stretching exercises for the upper body. On the other hand, weight lifting is an excellent conditioning activity, but it should be supplemented with running or one of the other circulatory exercises.

Whatever your favorite sport, you will find your enjoyment enhanced by improved fitness. Every weekend athlete should invest in frequent workouts.

Training

Being a Corrections Officer is a difficult, yet very rewarding, career. It is a profession that demands not only the right people, but intensive training before contact with inmates, and continued training throughout your career.

Your training program may be different from the examples given in this section, but there is little variation in the training subjects that are necessary before a Corrections Officer begins to work in any facility. Almost all prisons and jails have a preservice training program that is required after being hired. The American Correctional Association (ACA) published training standards that are quickly being adopted by Federal, state, and private prisons and local jails.

The length of training will vary among prison systems, but a standard has been set at 160 hours of preservice training for Corrections Officers, to include federal, state, and private prisons. Larger jails typically require the same formal pre-service training, but the smaller jails have developed very good in-service and on-the-job training to supplement the shortened preservice.

Most prisons have a preservice training period of 160 hours, or approximately four months, followed by an additional 80 hours each year after the first. The ACA standards require the 160 hours and 80 hours thereafter.

Time and experiences have shaped the preservice and in-service training of Corrections Officers. Prison administrators now have a very good understanding of what each Corrections Officer needs to know before supervising inmates. Corrections Officer training covers basic security, relationships with inmates, emergency plans, and key control. Also important are the rules and regulations of the prison or jail and employee grievance procedures. All training curriculum at any prison or jail will cover these subjects.

STATE PRISON

Here is an example of a state's Basic Training Program for County Corrections Officers. The format and methodology of your own training may be quite different, but the topics covered will be similar.

The Corrections Officer's Role and Stress—4 Hours

This presentation examines correctional stress and the correctional stressors associated with its existence. Observable signs of stress are discussed, as well as possible methods of dealing with and/or reducing stress.

Essential Services—7 Hours

The U.S. Constitution guarantees certain fundamental rights to all citizens of the United States. In the discussion of Essential Services in corrections, correctional requirements will be examined to illustrate how they translate into a minimum standard of service that a jail must provide for inmates to insure a safe, secure, and humane environment. The following Essential Services will be discussed in detail: Food Service, Medical Care, Personal Hygiene, Inmate Mail, Telephone Calls, Commissary, Visitation, Recreation, Access to Courts, Inmate Packages, Published and Printed Materials, Access to Media, Library, and Religious Practices.

Interpersonal Communications—7½ Hours

The most effective tool Corrections Officers have at their disposal is their communication skill. This course will acquaint officers with various issues relative to nonverbal and verbal communications. Also, different communication climates will be explored and related to different correction situations.

Officers will also be instructed in ways in which they can influence the behavior of inmates; that is, how they can get an inmate to move from point "A" to point "B." Issues such as motivation, attitudes, and the environment of a correctional facility will be examined to see how they affect officer–inmate interaction.

Special Inmates—4 Hours

This segment will deal with the detection and proper handling of special prisoners who require medication, close scrutiny, and strict supervision. Such types include the alcoholic, mentally ill, drug addict, suicidal, diabetic, epileptic, and homosexual. Alcoholics Anonymous, suicide prevention, and counseling are discussed, among other intervention techniques, for reducing anxiety among individuals who experience mental or emotional stress while incarcerated.

This segment will also deal with inmates in the 16- to 20-year age bracket. Trainees will become familiar with the characteristics of young offenders and what motivates them. Personality traits and characteristics will be explored in order to give the line officer insight into how to respond to these individuals.

Security Skills—7½ Hours

Trainees will discuss the following topics: population counts, inmate movement and control, searches, firearms, key control, dangerous material control, inmate supervision, tool control, administrative segregation, discipline, and grievance procedures.

Trainees will be acquainted with generally accepted codes of inmate conduct. Inmates' responsibility in adherence to a code of conduct will be explored, and the privileges available to inmates who act responsibly will be discussed.

Trainees will also be introduced to the nature of discipline and the objectives that effective discipline can obtain, the handling of serious and minor infractions of facility rules, and how to reprimand an inmate properly. Also, introduction will be made to the informal and formal resolution of complaints. Procedures for the filing and keeping of records and appeals procedures will be explored. There will also be a discussion of how proper use of a grievance procedure will minimize conflict.

Fire Prevention—3½ Hours

This will not be a hands-on or how-to-prevent-fire presentation. It will, however, familiarize trainees with first-aid and fire-protection equipment and, most important, spell out the hidden, dangerous shortcomings of the basic instruments. Through a video presentation and visual transparencies, trainees will also focus on the factors of rapid fire spread, heat flow, the major problems in dealing with fire situations in jails today, developing good professional role attitudes between county jail administrations and the county fire personnel, and, most important, the need for good fire-prevention practices.

Hostage Survival—4 Hours

Trainees will be given an overview of hostage survival techniques. Emphasis will be placed on the dynamics that take place while an officer is held hostage and what officers can do to prepare for and survive a hostage situation.

Objective Observation and Report Writing—7 Hours

This class acquaints the trainees with the ease with which preconceived assumptions and prejudices can negatively affect their performance on the job. The trainees will receive instruction relating to problems in perception that will enable them to safeguard their own objectivity while performing their duties. Trainees will have the opportunity to relate these concepts to the technical areas of report writing.

The balance of this class will deal with the actual writing of a report. Problems often encountered by officers, as well as certain report-writing pitfalls, will be discussed. Participants will be asked to write a report based on a video presentation of a jail incident, and the reports will be critiqued in class.

Legal Issues—7½ Hours

Topics that will be discussed are Corrections and the U.S. Constitution, Courts, Corrections Law, Corrections Standards, and Rights and Liabilities of Corrections Personnel.

Transportation of Inmates—2 Hours

Trainees will receive instruction in generally accepted methods of transporting prisoners. Special problems that may arise during transport procedures are spelled out. Equipment and tactics for accomplishing prisoner transport are displayed and explained.

Crime Scene Preservation—1½ Hours

Participants will be given instruction in how to secure a crime scene and preserve and collect evidence. Proper handling and recording of evidence will be stressed.

Standard First-Aid (Modular System)—3½ Hours

Trainees will receive instruction in the following topics: Emergency Action Principles, Respiratory Emergencies, First-Aid for Wounds, First-Aid for Burns, First-Aid for Sudden Illness, and Emergency Rescue and Transfer. Trainees successfully completing the requirements of this segment, including satisfactory testing, will receive American Red Cross certification.

Trainees not presenting proof of current accredited Standard First-Aid (or better) certification will be required to attend this training segment. Trainees will be provided with approved American Red Cross Modular Books, which must be returned at the completion of this training segment, and a Workbook, which they may retain. Trainees will be required to spend a minimum of 4 hours in independent study outside of the formal classroom, reading the Modular text material and completing the Workbook, prior to this formal lecture segment.

NOTES

NOTES

NOTES

NOTES

NOTES

NOTES

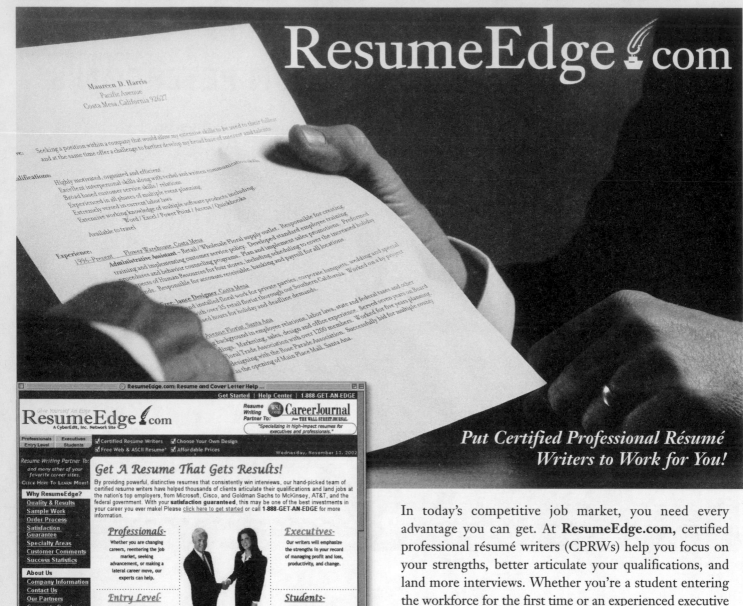